MATCH WITS
WITH THE KIDS

MATCH WITS
WITH THE KIDS

A Little Learning for all the Family

ICON BOOKS

Published in the UK in 2008 by
Icon Books Ltd, The Old Dairy, Brook Road,
Thriplow, Cambridge SG8 7RG
email: info@iconbooks.co.uk
www.iconbooks.co.uk

Sold in the UK, Europe, South Africa and Asia
by Faber & Faber Ltd, 3 Queen Square,
London WC1N 3AU or their agents

Distributed in the UK, Europe, South Africa and Asia
by TBS Ltd, TBS Distribution Centre, Colchester Road
Frating Green, Colchester CO7 7DW

This edition published in Australia in 2008
by Allen & Unwin Pty Ltd, PO Box 8500,
83 Alexander Street, Crows Nest, NSW 2065

Distributed in Canada by Penguin Books Canada
90 Eglinton Avenue East, Suite 700
Toronto, Ontario M4P 2YE

ISBN: 978-184831-000-1

Typeset in 10.5 on 15pt Palatino by Marie Doherty

Printed and bound in the UK by
CPI Bookmarque, Croydon, CR0 4TD

For the Longfield family
(and for Jake and Mattie, one day)

Jonathan Green has worked as a teacher for the last fourteen years, four of those as a Deputy Head. In that time he has also written numerous popular books for children – everything from *Sonic the Hedgehog* to *Doctor Who* – as well as science fiction and fantasy novels for adults. He lives in West London with his wife and two young children.

There are a number of people, without whom this book would not have been what it is, who deserve a special mention. So thanks to Simon Flynn and Nick Sidwell, for their hard work and wise counsel; Simon Bird and Emma Brown, *merci* and *danke* respectively; and to my family – my wife Clare in particular – for all the really important stuff.

CONTENTS

Introduction 1

1 English: The Story of English 5
*Standard English and Received Pronunciation; English
Grammar; Spelling; English Idioms; Literary Terms;
English Literature*

2 Mathematics: Think of a Number 55
*As Easy As 1, 2, 3; As Easy As A, B, C; Keeping in Shape;
Lies, Damned Lies and Statistics; The Law of Averages;
Probability*

3 Biology: That's Life! 105
Life and Living Processes

4 Chemistry: Elementary, My Dear Watson 135
*Materials and their Properties; Geological Changes;
Chemical Reactions*

5 Physics: Ye Cannae Change the Laws of Physics! 157
Physical Processes; Light; Sound; Spaceship Earth

70 Scientists Who Changed The World 190

6 History: History Today 201
*History is Written by the Winners; The Passage of Time;
Kings and Queens of England; Prime Ministers; Famous
Battles; A Brief History of Britain (from 1066–1945)*

7   **Geography: Around the World in a Day**   **249**
X Marks the Spot; The World Map; The Restless Planet;
Water World; Weather

8   **Modern Foreign Languages:**   **297**
     Mind Your Language!
French; German; Spanish

9   **Classics: Latin is a language as dead as dead**   **329**
     can be ...
The Latin Alphabet; Latin Grammar; Classical Civilisation;
Famous Classical Faces

10   **Match Wits With The Kids**   **367**
Tests; Answers; How Did You Do?

Index   **389**

INTRODUCTION

'An education isn't how much you have committed to memory, or even how much you know. It's being able to differentiate between what you know and what you don't.'

Now, of course being able to tell the difference between what you know and what you don't isn't the same as admitting it. We've all had an education of one kind or another, and much of what we've learnt will have been taught by those much vaunted academic establishments the School of Hard Knocks and the University of Life. But it all began when, as a small child, you first went to infant school …

School days; best days of your life, apparently. And if you still happen to be at school yourself, make the most of it; the need to provide a living for yourself, put a roof over your head and pay taxes are – comparatively – just around the corner.

But if your school days are now more a case of Ancient History than Current Affairs, how much do you remember of what you learnt at school? And I don't mean what you learnt behind the bike sheds. Do you remember how to calculate the area of a circle? Can you recall who won the Battle of Naseby? Do you still know how to conjugate the Latin verb *amare*? If the answer to any of these questions is 'No' and your school days now seem more like something of a school daze, then you've come to the right place! *Match Wits With The Kids* is for you.

There is a rebellious saying that has probably been repeated any number of times over the years, which I first came across, printed on a postcard, when I was a secondary school student. This postcard took pride of place on the noticeboard above the desk where I was religiously made to do my homework every night by my mother, who just happened to be a lecturer. It obviously struck a chord with me at the time. It went something like this:

The more I study, the more I learn;
The more I learn, the more I forget;
The more I forget, the less I know;
So why study?

As someone who has just picked up *Match Wits With The Kids: A Little Learning for all the Family*, you can probably answer that question for yourself. I suspect that it has been some time since you were last a student yourself and although you rigorously completed your homework and no matter how thorough you were when it came to revising for exams, over the years the pressures of modern living have slowly but surely corroded your memory. In my case, I put this down to having children of my own.

If you are a parent yourself, you have probably picked up this book because somewhere down the line a child of yours is going to come up to you, crumpled exercise book in hand, and ask some dread question such as, 'Dad, what is Pythagoras' Theorem?' or 'Mum, who was the fifth wife of Henry VIII?' or even, 'What does VIII mean?'

It may be that you are a student yourself and despite having the word 'learning' in the subtitle you have not been put off, so here you are reading this introduction. Well you *need* this book because, whether you like it or not, if you are going to get on in life, a few letters after your name along the lines of BA, MSc or PhD are going to make the world of difference. To acquire those letters you are going to need some other letters first, namely G, C, S and E. If you're lucky, there might be an AS or an A thrown into the mix a couple of years after that.

And there's always the possibility that you are a teacher yourself. In my experience, if you are going to be a good teacher you need to do your homework, just as much as your pupils do. If all the kerfuffle surrounding selling a house boils down to location, location, location, then for a lesson to be a success – any lesson in which you wish to impart your hard-won knowledge – then preparation, preparation, preparation is the key. Failing that, blag it. As long as you know more than your students on the day, you'll be okay. And that's where this handy little revision guide comes in.

This is not an exhaustive textbook; it couldn't hope to be. It's a prompt, to remind you of the important facts that you may have forgotten. If you want to know more than just the bare bones, I would suggest you then turn to an encyclopaedia or one of any number of helpful, considerably more detailed and longer textbooks on whatever subject it is you need to gen-up on most. However, hopefully by dipping your toes into the warm paddling pool that is *Match Wits With The Kids*, you will gain a better idea of what it is that you want to glean from the depthless oceans of knowledge.

So sit back, relax, and turn the page, because class is in session!

Jonathan Green
London 2008

Chapter One

ENGLISH
The Story of English

The English spoken today is not the same as that spoken 50 years ago, let alone 100 or 1,000 years ago, and it will continue to change throughout the 21st century. That is because it is a living spoken language by which millions of people all over the world, from widely varying cultures, communicate.

However, much of the English you will have learnt at school still applies, even if in some cases it is not with quite the same vigour or emphasis on grammatical correctness. Whether students of English realise it or not, others (notably examiners) will appreciate it if they use what is referred to as Standard English, in other words, the form of English as taught in schools in the good old days.

So, if you can't tell the difference between a preposition and a pronoun, if you've forgotten what a simile is, and if you've never understood how to use apostrophes correctly, have no fear; this chapter's[1] for you.

---

[1] Note that the apostrophe comes after the word 'chapter' but before the 's', denoting that in this case the apostrophe is standing in for a missing letter – the 'i' of 'is' – and hence represents a contraction and has nothing to do with possession, which is the other area in which the apostrophe is used. Got it?

Standard English and ✍ Received Pronunciation ✍

These days **Standard English** effectively means formal English. It is considered to be that form of the English language used by educated speakers, people just like you and me. In other words, when you are using Standard English, whether spoken or written, you are not using slang, colloquialisms (informal expressions) or dialect.

English has become the second most widely used language in the world[2] and is the first language of over 300 million people across the globe. It is the second language of many millions more, to the extent where one in five people in the world speaks English to a competent degree or better. In fact, within the next few years there will be more people speaking English as a second language than there are native speakers of English. As a result, English is subject to alteration by non-native speakers, which will inevitably have a profound effect on the evolution of the language.

The main regional standards of English are British, US and Canadian, Australian and New Zealand, South African, Indian, and West Indian. Although each of these regional varieties houses a staggeringly wide array of differing local dialects, standardised English is continually being spread around the world by the media and the internet.

Received Pronunciation[3] is a form of pronunciation of the English language which is still considered by many to be the correct way of delivering words in an accent that is also considered to be from the top echelons of British society.

---

[2] The most widely used language in the world is Chinese Mandarin.

[3] Referred to as RP on an actor's CV, luvvie!

It is more often than not referred to as the Queen's English because it is spoken by the monarch. It is also sometimes called BBC English because for a long time it was used by the BBC, although things have changed dramatically in that area in the last decade or more. BBC presenters and staff are no longer restricted to using one type of accent, and many regional accents are now heard on the network.

The use of Received Pronunciation still carries with it a great deal of assumptions about the social and educational background of the person using it. If an individual uses Received Pronunciation, they will normally speak Standard English. Its common root is with the dialects of Northamptonshire, Bedfordshire and Huntingdonshire, via a move to London 500 years ago.[4]

---

[4] By the end of the 15th century, Standard English was established in the City of London.

✍ English Grammar ✎

Inevitably, a section on English grammar is going to regularly use expressions which themselves need explaining elsewhere, probably in the same section. As a result, while going through the next few pages you are going to need to be prepared to flick back and forth to check the definitions of anything you are not sure of. But then who ever said this was going to be easy?

Sentences, Clauses and Paragraphs

Sentences

A **sentence** is a set of words that make sense of a thought or idea and together convey a statement, a question, an exclamation or a command. These four categories of sentence are described as follows:

Declarative (statements)	The girl sulked.
Interrogative (questions)	Why are you sulking?
Imperative (commands)	Go and tidy your room.
Exclamatory (exclamations)	Stop sulking!

A sentence usually contains a **subject** and a **verb**. Consider the following sentence:

The cat sat on the mat.

The subject of the sentence is 'the cat', the verb is 'sat', and there is also a phrase in there 'on the mat', which tells us where the action took place. There are three types of sentence: simple, compound and complex.

Simple sentences are ones that give you one main piece of information.

I read the book. I understood everything. I finished my homework.

Compound sentences are made by combining simple sentences or clauses using conjunctions (and, but, or).

I read the book and understood everything. I finished my homework but forgot to hand it in the next day.

Complex sentences are ones that are made up of two or more clauses, one of which will be a subordinate clause.

I finished my homework and, despite reading the book and understanding everything, still forgot to hand it in the next day.

Clauses

A **clause** always has to contain a subject and a verb.

A **main clause** is one that makes sense by itself and so could be written as a simple sentence in its own right. An example of a main clause would be:

I was hungry.

However, a **subordinate clause** is one that does not make sense by itself; it needs a main clause to give it context and so clarify its meaning. The following is a subordinate clause:

because I overslept and missed breakfast

When you combine this subordinate clause with the main clause above, suddenly everything becomes clear.

I was hungry because I overslept and missed breakfast.

Subordinate clauses are introduced by either a subordinating conjunction (such as however, because, although), a relative pronoun (such as who, whose, which, that), which turns it into a relative clause, or a non-finite verb.[5] In this last case, the verb can be placed before or after the noun which allows you to move the subordinate clause around within the sentence, making for more interesting writing.

With a subordinating conjunction	The soldier kept on fighting, **although** he knew the battle was lost.
With a relative pronoun	The war, **which** was long and bloody, cost many lives.
With a non-finite verb	**Consumed** by rage, the weary soldier fought on regardless.

In the last example above, we could place the subordinate clause in the middle of the sentence.

The weary soldier, **consumed by rage**, fought on regardless.

In this case, the subordinate clause has now become an embedded clause, because it has been placed in the middle of the main clause 'The weary soldier fought on regardless'.

Paragraphs

Paragraphs are tools which help you to organise your writing. A paragraph is a group of sentences that are all connected to the same topic, although it is possible to have a paragraph made up of just one sentence. You should always start a new paragraph when somebody new starts speaking.

📖📖📖

---

[5] See the section entitled 'Parts of Speech' on page 11.

Parts of Speech

There are eight different **parts of speech**. These are **nouns**, **pronouns**, **verbs**, **adjectives**, **adverbs**, **prepositions**, **conjunctions** and **interjections**. A part of speech explains how a word is used, rather than what it is, whether it names something, describes something, or is just used to join clauses together. As a result, the same word can often be employed in a number of different ways – as a noun in one sentence, a verb in another or even as an adjective.

Nouns

These are naming words. Common nouns are things that you can see or touch, such as a book, a tree, a cat or a computer.

Proper nouns are the specific names of people, places or even certain objects. Wales, Nottingham, Mary and Tower Bridge are all examples of proper nouns.

Abstract nouns are the names given to intangible things such as thoughts, emotions, qualities and ideas. Examples of abstract nouns would be envy, love, truth and peace.

Collective nouns are those names that are given to groups of things, people or animals, such as crowd, flock or herd. There are some marvellous collective nouns for particular bunches[6] of animals, from the classic murder of crows, to the fantastic crash of rhinoceroses and the downright strange smack of jellyfish.

---

[6] 'Bunches' is a collective noun, as it happens, as is 'groups' in the first line of this paragraph.

Did you know...?
One of the recognised names for a group of baboons is a flange. This was first used in a comedy sketch show on television as a joke. However, since then the word, in reference to a 'flange of baboons', has migrated via the internet into academic usage.

Pronouns

A **pronoun** is a word which takes the place of a noun that has already been used in a sentence. Actual examples of pronouns are he, she, it, you, me and they. A possessive pronoun is used in place of a noun and demonstrates ownership at the same time. Examples of possessive pronouns are yours, mine, his, hers, its, ours and theirs. The use of pronouns stops your writing becoming repetitious.

Without pronouns	**Samir** finished **the book** and gave **the book** to **Samir's** teacher.
With pronouns	**Samir** finished **the book** and gave **it** to **his** teacher.

Verbs

If nouns are naming words, then **verbs** are doing words. Every verb will refer to some action or other. They are used with nouns and pronouns to make the most basic of sentences.

Main verbs (or **full verbs**) are the ones that, on the whole, you can put the word 'to' in front of to describe[7] an action. To sing, to run, to eat, to sleep are all main verbs. When a verb has the word 'to' in front of it, it can also be referred to as the infinitive. The once-loathed split infinitive, as in 'to boldly go', is actually perfectly acceptable in English grammar.

---

[7] To describe – that's a main verb for you right there!

Auxiliary verbs help the main verb, changing the emphasis of its meaning in some way. Should, would, could and might are all examples of auxiliary verbs. So, to use the main verbs listed above, we could say: we should sing, he would run, I could eat, she might sleep.

Primary verbs is the term given to those verbs which can either be used as main verbs or auxiliary verbs. They are be, have and do.

As a main verb   She **is** beautiful.
As an auxiliary verb She **is** shopping.

Verbs can also be described as either finite or non-finite. The finite form of the verb changes depending on who it is referring to, how many things it is referring to, and the tense it is in.

Affected by person   I **am**/We **are**
Affected by number He **swims**/They **swim**
Affected by tense   I **dance** well/I **danced** well

These contrasts are not shown by the non-finite form of a verb. There are three of them to remember.

The **present participle** is created when –ing is added to the verb. It is not affected by either person, number or tense.

Person   I am **working** late at the office, dear.
Number   But darling, we're all **working** late tonight.
Tense   He was **working** late at the office. Honestly.

The **past participle** is created by adding –ed to the end of the verb. Once again, it is not affected by person, number or tense.

Person   I **painted** the living room.
Number   They **painted** the whole house.
Tense   The cat was **painted** by accident.

The last form of non-finite verb is when the base form of the verb is used as an infinitive.

Person	I'll **cry**.
Number	We all might **cry**.
Tense	She wanted to **cry**.

Adjectives

Adjectives are, to put it simply, describing words; they tell us what something is like. So our nouns from before – book, tree, cat, computer – become a wonderful book, a tall tree, a smelly cat and a broken computer when we use adjectives to give them a little more character.

Adverbs

Adverbs are to verbs what adjectives are to nouns, in other words, they describe them, telling you how something is or was done. He sings loudly, they run quickly, she ate noisily, I slept badly. This most basic form of adverb is created by simply adding –ly to the end of an adjective.

Adverbs can also be used as the adverbial element of a clause. This may sound rather academic but, to put it simply, an adverbial can either be:

- A phrase which contains single adverbs.

  He painted the house **carelessly**.

- A phrase beginning with a preposition.[8]

  The bride ran **to the church**.

---

[8] Also known as a 'prepositional phrase', funnily enough.

- Some subordinate clauses.

  She challenged him **when he walked into the kitchen**.

It is worth remembering that adverbials usually provide an answer to the questions how, where or when.

Prepositions

Prepositions are those words that tell you where something is in relation to something else. They are used within sentences to link nouns, pronouns and phrases to other parts of a sentence. The following words are all prepositions: on, under, between, above, beside, along, in, during. Here are some examples of prepositions in action:

  The book is **on** the bookshelf.
  We went **to** Wales.
  The cat is stuck **in** the tree.
  The River Thames flows **under** Tower Bridge.
  I tackled my chores **without** enthusiasm.

Conjunctions

A **conjunction** is simply a word that is used to join other words and phrases together. (You may have heard of **connectives** as well. These are words which have a similar function to conjunctions.) Common conjunctions are: and, but, because, or, when, unless.

  You should finish your homework **and** do your chores.
  I will never eat another Turkish delight **because** they make me fat.
  They are going to call back either later today **or** tomorrow.

Interjections

An **interjection** is a word – sometimes just one syllable – which is added to a sentence to convey a sense of emotion. An interjection is often used as part of an exclamation. The following words can all be used as interjections: psst, ugh, excellent, oh no, hey, eh, ouch, good lord.

> **Oh no**, I've left the oven on!
> **Ouch**! What did you do that for?
> **Psst**, over here!
> **Ugh**, that looks disgusting!

ꕔꕔꕔ

Punctuation

No matter how much you might not like it, **punctuation** matters. When we speak to one another, tone of voice and emphasis of particular words allow others to grasp the meaning of what we are saying. When we write, we have to use punctuation to make our meaning clear instead, otherwise it could all too easily be misinterpreted. Consider this well-known example.

> Caesar entered on his head
> a helmet on each foot
> a sandal in his hand he held
> his trusty sword to boot

Very funny, but of course it makes sense only once it is properly punctuated.[9]

> Caesar entered, on his head
> a helmet, on each foot
> a sandal, in his hand he held
> his trusty sword to boot.

---

[9] But then it isn't half as amusing.

Let's face it, proper punctuation can be a bit of a nightmare for the uninitiated, so let's start at the beginning with the basics.

Capital letters and full stops

The most basic elements of punctuation must surely be **capital letters** and **full stops**. When used correctly, these tell us where a sentence begins and ends.

> the trees shed their leaves winter was on the way
> The trees shed their leaves. Winter was on the way.

Capital letters are also used for the pronoun 'I', for initials (such as OAP and VAT), and for the names of people, places and products (for example, Fred, London, Windows Vista).

Commas

Commas help to make sense of the meaning within a sentence. This usually means that they are used to separate parts of a sentence.

- They can separate items on a list.

  To boil an egg you will need a source of heat, a saucepan, some water and one egg.

- They can separate additional information, usually in the form of an embedded clause, from the rest of a sentence.

  Keith, who had never cooked anything before in his life, struggled to boil an egg.

- They separate subordinate clauses from main clauses.

  When he couldn't even manage to boil an egg, Keith phoned for a takeaway.

- They come after the following words: therefore, however, nevertheless, of course.

Colons and semicolons

Now that you have mastered the basics of the capital letter, the full stop and the comma, you are ready to move on to the advanced punctuation marks. **Colons** indicate something which is to follow, such as a list (as in the last bullet point about commas), or possibly a quotation, if you are using one in an essay.

The following are all examples of punctuation marks: full stops, commas, colons, semicolons, apostrophes, speech marks.

Semicolons, on the other hand, are used to join two sentences which are very closely linked where a full stop would seem too strong and a comma too weak. Quite often, the information which follows a semicolon provides extra detail for the sentence which came before it.

On the fifth day of Christmas my true love gave to me five gold rings; my husband gave me some soap.

Semicolons are also used to separate items on a list when, rather than single words, the list is made up of a collection of phrases.

When attempting comprehension questions you should: read the passage through carefully; read all of the questions carefully; answer in full sentences, unless told otherwise.

Apostrophes

Apostrophes are either used to show that a letter or letters have been omitted from a word or words, or they are used to indicate that something belongs to someone.

When a word or words are contracted – for example, when is not becomes isn't – an apostrophe is used to replace the missing letter or letters, in this case the 'o' of 'not'. The apostrophe does not fill the gap between the two words that are being joined. It is being used here to indicate an omission.

isn't = is not
haven't = have not
wouldn't = would not

Nor should an apostrophe be used to join the letter 's' to numbers or acronyms[10] to make the plural, just as the ordinary plural of a noun does not require an apostrophe. Hence, none of the following need an apostrophe when used in the plural: CDs, 6s and the 1990s.

So, if you walk into a High Street store and see a sign that reads:

… you can confidently tell the manager that he is informing his customers that the £5.99 belongs to the CD – and then walk out.

Of course apostrophes are also used to demonstrate possession, to show that something belongs to someone or something.

An apostrophe followed by the letter 's' shows us when single nouns are used in the possessive case. For example, Jack's house

---

[10] Acronym – a word made from the initial letters of a group of other words. E.g. NATO = North Atlantic Treaty Organisation.

(the house that belongs to Jack), or the cat's whiskers (the whiskers belonging to the cat).

This also applies to nouns which already end in 's' unless this might produce an awkward sequence of letters. So we have Dickens's novels but not Jesus's teachings. In such cases, these special single nouns are treated like plural nouns. Hence, Jesus' teachings.

The possessive case of plural nouns, indicating that something belongs to more than one person or thing, is shown by putting an apostrophe after the final 's'. For example, the ladies' gym, the boys' football team or the hens' coop.

If the plural form of a word does not end with the letter 's' already[11] then the apostrophe comes before the 's', as with a single noun. So we have the children's school and the fish's aquarium.

The exception that proves the rule with the possessive case and apostrophes is the possessive of it; in other words you are saying that something 'belongs to it'. In this case, and this case only, it becomes its, without the addition of an apostrophe. It's (with an apostrophe) is the shortened form of **it is** and does not signify possession.

Question marks and exclamation marks

Of course, it really goes without saying that a **question mark** is used to indicate a question, and an **exclamation mark** is used to denote that something has been exclaimed.

---

[11] What we call a 'singular plural'.

Did you know...?

In 1905, Bolshevik printers in St Petersburg went on strike because they wanted to be paid the same rate for punctuation marks as they were for letters. Through their actions they directly hastened the beginning of the first Russian Revolution.

Direct speech

When writing, you use speech marks to show that someone has said something. To correctly punctuate speech you need to use more than just the speech marks themselves, but you do need them, so that's where we'll start.

Speech marks are either written as "..." or '...' and are placed around the words someone actually says. The first word inside the speech marks must begin with a capital letter, and some form of punctuation mark – whether it be a comma, full stop, question mark or exclamation mark – must follow the last word spoken.

'No, the punctuation mark goes inside the speech marks,' the teacher sighed.

You put a comma at the end of the spoken words if the sentence is to continue after the speech marks are closed. The first word following the speech marks then begins with a lower case letter.

'You write it like this,' explained Mr Lucas.

You can also use a question mark or an exclamation mark in this way.

'Like this?' asked the boy, who hadn't really been paying attention.
'How many times do I have to tell you?' roared the master.

However, if you end the words spoken between the speech marks with a full stop, that then becomes the end of the sentence.

'Obviously more times than you would like, sir.'

If the sentence begins by explaining who's speaking, a comma must follow this before speech marks are opened.

Mr Lucas peered down his nose at the boy and hissed, 'Get it right, Anderson, or you will be spending the afternoon in detention.'

When a new person starts speaking, you must always start a new paragraph as well.

'I am trying,' whined the boy.
'Yes,' agreed his teacher, 'very.'

📖📖📖

Tenses

The **tense** of a verb helps to express when something happened. There are many different tenses (some a lot more straightforward than others) and if used correctly they can add another level of clarity and complexity to written work. A commonly repeated error in written English is the failure to use the correct tense or to stick to one tense when that is what is required.

But before we look at the verb tenses, to aid you in using them correctly it helps if you know a little more about verbs themselves. For the purposes of verb tenses you need to understand that there are three groups of verbs: **normal verbs**, **non-continuous verbs**, and **mixed verbs**.

You will be pleased to learn that most verbs are **normal verbs**. These are the verbs which are physical actions which you could see somebody doing. These verbs can be used in all tenses and include such examples as: to walk, to jump, to go, to touch, to take, to say.

There are fewer **non-continuous verbs**, and these are things you cannot see somebody doing, even though they are still doing them. They include:

- **Abstract verbs**: to be, to seem, to need, to want, to care, to cost.
- **Possession verbs**: to possess, to belong, to own.
- **Emotion verbs**: to love, to hate, to fear, to desire.

Mixed verbs form the smallest group of all. These are the verbs which have more than one meaning. Some of these meanings will behave like normal verbs, while others will be just like non-continuous verbs. Some examples of mixed verbs are: to feel, to hear, to see, to appear, to have, to miss.

And so to the tenses themselves. As any scholar of a classical language such as Latin will tell you,[12] there are many, many tenses. However, as tenses are an expression of when things happened, in their most basic form they have either happened in the past, are happening in the present, or are going to happen in the future. As a result we have past, present and future tenses. If they are presented just as they are here, then they are also known as simple tenses.

We can also group tenses together in terms of whether something has finished (either in the past or even will be finished in the future), whether it is an ongoing activity, and so on. So we gain perfect, continuous and perfect continuous tenses. A tense

---

[12] And if you've already jumped ahead and read the chapter on Classics, that goes for you too now.

can be a combination of more than one group as well. Here are some examples:

Simple Present	I **sing** in the shower every day.
Simple Past	I **sang** at my brother's wedding last year.
Simple Future	I **am going** to sing at the Karaoke bar tonight.
Present Continuous	I **am cleaning** now.
Past Continuous	I **was cleaning** the house when you called.
Future Continuous	I **will be cleaning** the house all day tomorrow for your mother's visit.
Present Perfect	I **have written** a poem for you.
Past Perfect	I **had written** a poem for you, but I threw it away by mistake.
Future Perfect	I **will have written** a poem for you, in time for Valentine's Day.
Present Perfect Continuous	I **have been learning** French for four years now.
Past Perfect Continuous	I **had been learning** French for four years, before I moved to Spain.
Future Perfect Continuous	I **am going to have been learning** French for two weeks by the time I go on holiday to Paris.

✍ Spelling ✎

Spelling – mere mention of the word is enough to turn children into gibbering wrecks and send a shiver down the spine of many an adult. But then, that seems hardly surprising when you consider the following:

I take it you already know
Of *tough* and *bough* and *cough* and *dough*?
Others may stumble, but not you,
On *hiccough*, *thorough*, *slough* and *through*?
Well done! And now you wish, perhaps,
To learn of less familiar traps?
Beware of *heard*, a dreadful word
That looks like *beard* and sounds like *bird*,
And *dead*: it's said like *bed*, not *bead* –
For goodness sake don't call it *deed*!
Watch out for *meat* and *great* and *threat*
(They rhyme with *suite* and *straight* and *debt*).
A *moth* is not a moth in *mother*,
Nor *both* in *bother*, *broth* in *brother*,
And *here* is not a match for *there*
Nor *dear* and *fear* for *bear* and *pear*,
And then there's *dose* and *rose* and *lose* –
Just look them up – and *goose* and *choose*,
And *cork* and *work* and *card* and *ward*,
And *font* and *front* and *word* and *sword*,
And *do* and *go* and *thwart* and *cart* –
Come, come, I've hardly made a start!
A dreadful language? Man alive!
I'd mastered it when I was five!

It seems that spelling is just one of those things that either you can do, or you can't – isn't it? Don't believe a word of it!

If spelling has never been your strong suit, or you are helping someone less experienced than yourself equip themselves with the strategies they need to spell effectively, consistently and correctly, then read on. Prepare to be initiated into secret art of spelling.

᠁᠁᠁

Look, Say, Cover, Write, Check

For anyone wanting to learn to spell a new word (or reacquaint themselves with a word they know they should be able to spell) still the best, most tried-and-tested method is the one often abbreviated to the letters **LSCWC**. But don't be put off by that less-than-clear acronym – there's nothing to it really. Whenever you need to learn a new word, follow these five simple steps:

1. **Look** at the word you are learning to spell and look at it closely, identifying patterns that will help you to grasp it. With a longer word, break it up into manageable segments that you *can* spell (e.g. *man-age-able*).

2. **Say** the word. Come on, don't be shy. You might feel a little stupid the first few times you do this, but if you can sound out the word, you're halfway to spelling it. It can help to sound out the silent letters in a word as well when you are learning it – so Wednesday becomes *Wed-nes-day*, emphasising the unspoken 'd'.

3. **Cover** the word up (with your hand or a piece of paper) and then …

4. **Write** it down for yourself.

5. **Check** your spelling of the word against the original. If you've made a mistake, look at the word again closely to see where you went wrong. Then go back to Step 1 and try again. If you've got it right, well done you! Now move on to the next word you want to learn.

Of course there are other ways to help you check your spelling. Don't forget, the humble dictionary is your friend and makes for fascinating reading,[13] giving you the origin of words as well as their meaning – and of course telling you how to spell them. And then there's the modern spellchecker. You are not a fraud if you use one, you are merely being thorough.

Some people find that mnemonics help them remember how to spell particularly tricky words.[14] A mnemonic is a phrase in which the initial letter of each of the words when put together spell another word or give a sequence of letters related to something else.

> **B**ig **E**lephants **C**an **A**lways **U**nderstand **S**mall **E**lephants – *the initial letters spell BECAUSE.*
> **R**ichard **O**f **Y**ork **G**ave **B**attle **I**n **V**ain – *reminds us of the order of colours in a rainbow: Red, Orange, Yellow, Green, Blue, Indigo, Violet.*

📖📖📖

Spelling Rules

The following rules will help you to learn and then recall all manner of spellings. However, you should take note that the English

---

[13] In small doses.

[14] Mnemonics are used as aide memoires in all subjects, as you will see later in this book.

language is notorious for having many exceptions to all of these. But then any rules are better than none, right?

Plurals

To turn a singular word into a plural add –s.

cat → cats   house → houses   pizza → pizzas

However, if the word ends in –ch, –ss, –sh, –x or –zz, add –es.

church → churches   tress → tresses   quiz → quizzes

Words ending in –y

If the word ends in a vowel followed by –y, you should add –s to make it plural.

boy → boys

If the word ends in a consonant followed by –y, rather than end the word –ys, turn the –y into an –i and add –es.

story → stories

Words ending in –f, –ff and –fe

If a word ends –ff, add –s to make it plural.

skiff → skiffs

If a word ends –f or –fe, the plural is formed one of two ways. For some –f and –fe words, the plural is made by simply adding –s.

waif → waifs

Others will need you to change the –f to a –v and then add –es.

knife → knives

However, just to confuse matters, some words that end in –f can be made plural by either method. So we have:

hoof → hoofs   as well as   hoof → hooves

Irregular plurals

There are certain words for which none of these rules apply. Instead the whole word changes. These are the words that you are just going to need to learn as and when you come across them. Some examples are:

child → children   mouse → mice   goose → geese

Words that end in –o or –oo don't follow set patterns for forming plurals either and will also have to be learnt individually.

And lastly there are some words which don't change in the plural at all, such as fish, sheep and deer.

Prefixes and suffixes

The group of two or three letters added to the beginning of a word to change its meaning is called a **prefix**. When you add a prefix to a word, you don't change the spelling of the original word. Some common prefixes are un–, in–, dis–, and mis–.

happy → unhappy
wanted → unwanted
capable → incapable
dependent → independent
appear → disappear
embark → disembark
fire → misfire
interpret → misinterpret

The opposite of a prefix is a **suffix**, a group of two or three letters that are added to the end of a word. Unlike a prefix, a suffix will sometimes alter the spelling of the original word. Common suffixes are –ed, –ing, –y, –ly , –able, –ful, –ment.

Adding –ed, –ing or –y

If the word has one syllable, a short vowel and ends with a single consonant, when you add the suffix, double the consonant.

drop → dropped
rot → rotting
bat → batty

For words with more than one syllable or vowel, add the suffix without changing the root word. This goes for words that end with a double consonant as well.

cover → covered
jump → jumping
speed → speedy

If a word already ends in –e, only add the –d of –ed, but if you are adding –ing (or –able),[15] remove the –e first.

bake → baked
recite → reciting

Adding –ful

When adding the suffix –ful to a word, you change the spelling of the original root word only if it ends in –y (and even then, not always).

boast → boastful
beauty → beautiful

---

[15] Naturally there are exceptions to this rule as well, such as 'manageable', which, if you've been paying attention, you will remember from the tip to spelling long words mentioned earlier.

N.B. You only ever add –ful as a suffix. There is no such suffix as –full!

Adding –ly

When you add –ly to a word, the spelling of that word doesn't change, unless that word ends in –le. In this case drop the –e and add –y.

decent → decently
final → finally
hopeful → hopefully
gentle → gently

Words ending in –y or –f

When adding a suffix to a word ending in –y or –f, you do the same as you would if you were turning them into plurals. For words ending in –y, you change the –y into an –i before adding the suffix. For words ending in –f, you swap the –f for a –v.

clarify → clarified
stroppy → stroppily
life → living

There are – it would seem, almost inevitably – exceptions to this rule as well. See, for example:

dry → drying
stray → strayed

📖📖📖

Commonly Misspelt Words

Many words in the English language sound the same although they may be spelt differently and have very different meanings. Because of these similarities it is very easy to use the wrong word in the wrong place and so, effectively, end up misspelling the word you are trying to use.

The problem lies really with the Three Hs. 'I've heard of the Three Rs,'[16] I hear you say, 'but what on Earth are the Three Hs?' Well, let me elaborate for you.

The Three Hs

The three Hs we're talking about here are **homophones**, **homographs** and **homonyms**; the technical terms given to words which are either written the same way, or sound the same, or both. The trouble is that many of the words we use every day fall into these tricky categories, so let's have a look at them more closely.

Homophones

A **homophone** is the name given to a word which sounds the same as another word, but which has a different spelling or meaning. Here are some classic homophones, along with examples that put the words in context:

allowed	You are **allowed** into the main pool if you are wearing a swimming hat.
aloud	She read **aloud** to the rest of the class.
are	Where **are** you going for your summer holidays?
our	We are going to stay at **our** grandmother's cottage on the coast.
bare	In the summer I always walk around with **bare** feet.
bear	With a growl, the grizzly **bear** went for the picnic basket. I couldn't **bear** it!
board	Dad nailed a wooden **board** over the broken window.
bored	I got **bored** waiting for the bus to turn up.

---

[16] A bad case of misspelling if ever there was one. After all, the Three Rs are in fact one R, one W and an A: Reading, Writing and Arithmetic.

caught	You don't want to get **caught** speeding by the police.
court	If you do, you may end up in the magistrates' **court**.
check	**Check** your spellings carefully before handing in your English homework.
cheque	The quiz master handed over a **cheque** for one million pounds.
flower	The lily is a beautiful **flower**.
flour	Wheat is turned into **flour**, which is then used to make bread.
grate	They toasted bread over the fire in the **grate**. They then decided to **grate** some cheese to go on top.
great	Everyone agreed it tasted **great**.
hear	I could **hear** you shouting from the other end of the street.
here	Come over **here** and say that!
higher	The mountaineer climbed **higher** and higher, heading for the summit.
hire	You can **hire** a suit from that shop on the High Street.
hole	He deftly tapped the golf ball into the **hole**.
whole	As a result he won the **whole** round.
knew	I **knew** giving him responsibility for that account was a mistake.
new	Well, you can hardly blame him; he is **new** here after all.
made	When his wife went back to work, John was **made** to do his fair share of the chores.
maid	The next day he hired a **maid** to clean the house for them.
pair	The student struggled to find a clean **pair** of socks to wear.
pear	For pudding she ate a nice crunchy **pear** and a juicy orange.
paw	After the dog returned from its walk in the park, there were muddy **paw** prints all over the kitchen floor.
poor	His **poor** mother had to mop the floor all over again.
pore	The zit formed where a **pore** had become clogged with dirt and grease.
pour	If you're opening another bottle, can you **pour** me a glass of wine as well?
right	Did he get all the answers **right**?
write	What do you think? He couldn't even **write** his name correctly.

saw	He **saw** quite clearly where she had left the **saw** next to the plank of wood.
sore	His feet were **sore** after walking for miles in his new shoes.
stair	She slipped on the last **stair** and fell flat on her bottom.
stare	Don't you know it's rude to **stare**?
their	Did you see **their** new car?
there	How could I miss it when they parked it right over **there**?
they're	I tell you, **they're** [they are] rolling in it if they can afford to buy a new Porsche.
threw	The girl **threw** the stick for the dog.
through	The dog ran right **through** the stream to fetch it.
to	We're going **to** the beach tomorrow.
too	Can I come **too**, or would that be too many people to fit in your car?
two	It's okay, there are only **two** of us going.
ware	They set out a stall at the market to sell their **wares**.
wear	Are you really going to **wear** that dress to the party?
where	**Where** do you think you're going looking like that?
weather	The **weather** forecast is good for tomorrow so we won't need waterproofs.
whether	I'm not sure **whether** going for a walk in a rainstorm was such a good idea.
who's	**Who's** [who is] that they've brought with them?
whose	**Whose** house is that?
yore	In days of **yore** Robin Hood and his Merry Men lived in Sherwood Forest.
your	Was it **your** idea to go to the fancy dress party dressed as Robin Hood?
you're	Oh, **you're** [you are] no fun anymore.

Homographs

A **homograph** differs from a homophone in that it is spelt in exactly the same way as another word but has a different meaning entirely. The English language is full of them; just take a look at the number of different meanings listed after a word in any dictionary. Sometimes it is as simple a thing as the word being both a noun and a verb, and thereby having a slightly different meaning in each case. What follows here is a list of just some of those homographs you should look out for:

absent	entrance	object	rose
address	field	overall	separate
axes	graduate	polish	sow
bow	house	pool	suspect
buffet	import	present	tear
close	knot	quarry	transport
console	lead	read	upset
content	live	rebel	use
desert	minute	record	voyage
dove	moped	refuse	wind
effect	number	root	wound

Homonyms (and heteronyms)

A **homonym** is the term given to any word that has the same spelling or sound as another word but a different meaning. In other words, it's a catch-all term for both homophones and homographs. (See above for examples of both.)

An alternative third H is the **heteronym**. This is a word that has the same spelling as another word but is pronounced differently, as well as having a different meaning. A good example of a heteronym is **arithmetic**. If you emphasise the second syllable (a-*rith*-me-tic) it means the science of numbers. If you place the emphasis on the third syllable (a-rith-*me*-tic) it means of or concerning arithmetic (a-*rith*-me-tic).

📖📖📖

Commonly Misused Words

Probably just as frequent an occurrence as the misspelling of words is the misuse of words. To save you from falling into that trap yourself, in the list of words below, as well as some commonly misspelt words there are also a number of words which are all too often used in the wrong way. (You will, of course, notice that some of these are homophones.)

adverse, averse	Where **adverse** means hazardous or dangerous (as in 'adverse driving conditions'), **averse** means you're not keen on something yourself. You might be averse to helping your children with their homework.
advice, advise	You take **advice** but you **advise** others on what they should do.
affect, effect	If you **affect** (a verb) something, you cause an **effect** (a noun). **Effect** as a verb means to bring something about.
amoral, immoral	If you are **amoral**, you have no moral principles at all and are not bothered about morality in any way. Something which is **immoral** is considered to be corrupt in some way or unethical.
biannual, biennial	If an event is **biannual**, it happens twice a year. However, if it is **biennial** it takes place only every two years.
classic, classical	**Classic** is usually used to refer to a fantastic work of art, the appeal of which has stood the test of time. **Classical** applies specifically to the civilisations of Ancient Greece and Rome, and by extension to the art and architecture of those civilisations.
complement, compliment	You might have a full **complement** of cabin crew on board a plane (in that 'complement' means to complete something) but they might give you a **compliment**, which is a kind remark.
continually, continuously	Something which happens **continually** does so repeatedly, but this doesn't mean it goes on and on without ceasing, which is the meaning of **continuously**.
council, counsel	A **council** is a group of people who you would hope would give good **counsel** (or, in other words, good advice).
dependant, dependent	A **dependant** (a noun) is someone who relies entirely on another for their living. Your children are good examples of dependants. **Dependent** (an adjective) means relying on something, or someone, else. E.g. you might be dependent on caffeine.

exhausting, exhaustive	If something is **exhausting**, it is tiring and drains you. If something is **exhaustive**, it is thorough, comprehensive and (you would hope) complete.
flammable, inflammable	Both these adjectives actually mean the same thing: easy to set on fire.
imply, infer	To **imply** something is to suggest it indirectly. To **infer** is to work out what something means from its context.
ingenious, ingenuous	Something that is **ingenious** is incredibly clever and/ or inventive. To describe something as **ingenuous**, however, is to say that it is overly simple or, in a person, gullible and naive.
naught, nought	**Naught** means nothing, whereas **nought** is the number zero which, coincidentally, could also be described as nothing.
prescribe, proscribe	Normally the word **prescribe** is used to mean something the doctor tells us to do, although it can be any authority figure. To **proscribe** something means to forbid it, declare it illegal or ban it.
principal, principle	The **principal** is the person in charge of a college or university (from the adjective principal, meaning 'first in importance'). A **principle** is a law, a rule or a personal code of conduct. You would hope, however, that principals also have principles.
stimulant, stimulus	**Stimulant** is the term applied to things like coffee, alcohol and drugs which might revitalise you in the short term. On the other hand, a **stimulus** is anything that inspires or stimulates you.
tortuous, torturous	If something is **tortuous**, it is twisting, winding or convoluted. Something that is **torturous** is painful to endure (as in 'torture').
trustful, trustworthy	If someone is **trustful**, they are full of trust (or you could say trusting). Someone who is **trustworthy** deserves the trust of others.

Comparison

When people talk about comparison in English, they are actually either talking about **degrees of comparison of adjectives** or **imagery**, when one thing is compared to being like something else. We will deal with each in turn.

Degrees of comparison of adjectives

There are three degrees of comparison, the **positive**, **comparative** and **superlative**. The positive describes a quality (e.g. bright), the comparative compares that quality to another of its kind (e.g. brighter), while the superlative compares the same quality to all others of its kind, implying that it is the best (e.g. brightest).

Here are some other examples:

Positive	Comparative	Superlative
hot	hotter	hottest
cold	colder	coldest
few	fewer	fewest
dark	darker	darkest
red	redder	reddest
large	larger	largest
short	shorter	shortest
old	older	oldest

Not all degrees of comparison follow the pattern of adding –er to the adjective for the comparative and –est for the superlative. Examples of ones to watch out for are:

Positive	Comparative	Superlative
good	better	best
bad	worse	worst
far	farther	farthest
little	less	least

Positive	Comparative	Superlative
much	more	most
real	more real	most real
important	more important	most important
happy	happier	happiest
late	later	last

Imagery

The other way of comparing things is to describe them in terms of something else. There are two ways of doing this in English: with **similes** and with **metaphors**.

A **simile** compares two different things using the words like or as.

> My dad was acting like a bear with a sore head.
> The giant was as tall as a tree.

A **metaphor** describes something as if it really were a completely different object, without saying that it is simply like that thing.

> My little boy can be a monkey at times.
> On seeing the beast bearing down on him, his legs turned to jelly.

An extended metaphor is one that is constructed using a number of different images in a longer piece of text. This might be achieved through the use of similes, metaphors and other images.

> The shark swam on, its gun-metal-grey skin camouflaging it against the gloom of the ocean. Its fins were blades slicing the water, its rudder tail keeping it on course as it closed on its target. Then, its body rigid, streaking through the waves like a torpedo, the killing machine struck.

✍ **English Idioms** ✍

English is a language overflowing with idioms. They appear constantly in written work and people use them daily, whether they realise it or not. But what is an idiom?

An idiom is a combination of words which has a sense beyond that which can be worked out precisely from the phrase itself. That particular phrase has come to denote something other than its literal meaning. For example, 'A penny for your thoughts' is a way of asking someone what's on their mind. You can work this out from the phrase, but in asking it you are not literally offering to give the person money in return for them telling you what they're thinking about.

Some idioms, however, have no literal meaning and only really make sense as an idiom. An example of this second kind would be 'to go Dutch'. There is no way that you could make any sense of what someone was saying if they suggested that you go Dutch, unless you already knew that it means to go halves on the bill after enjoying a meal together.

Listed below you will find a number of familiar English idioms which will either add colour and imagery to your own use of the language, or will help you work out what on earth it is other people are talking about.

Actions speak louder than words means that what people actually do is more important than what they say.

If something could be done by **any Tom, Dick or Harry**, it could be done by anyone.

Barking up the wrong tree means that you have either misunderstood something completely or you are utterly wrong.

If you have **butterflies in your stomach**, you are suffering from that nervous feeling you get before doing something that is important or stressful.

If someone asks, 'Has the **cat got your tongue**?' they mean that they think you should be speaking when you are not.

A **chip off the old block** is an expression which means that someone closely resembles one or other of their parents, usually in character as much as appearance.

If something is described as being a **different kettle of fish**, it is very different to whatever else is being talked about.

Something that is a total mess is sometimes called a **dog's dinner**.

If something happens only right at the last minute, it is said to happen at the **eleventh hour**.

Everything but the kitchen sink is an idiom which means that someone has considered – or packed, if they're going on holiday – every possible thing, whether they are really of use or not.

If you have a **face like thunder**, you are very angry or upset about something.

You are **fit as a fiddle** if you are in perfect health.

If you talk about something that has been bothering you, you **get it off your chest**.

If you are an able gardener who is good at making things grow, you are said to have **green fingers**.

If you abandon someone when they are in trouble, you **hang them out to dry**.

You **hold the fort** if you look after something for somebody while they are away.

Something is **hunky dory** if it is absolutely fine and all's well.

You make the outrageous claim, '**I'll eat my hat!**' if you are convinced that you are right and you want to let the other person know that there is no possibility of you being wrong.

The **icing on the cake** refers to something good happening that merely adds to an already excellent situation. However, it can equally mean the opposite when used sarcastically.

An **Indian summer** is the period of warmer weather that sometimes comes about in late autumn.

If you start something before you're supposed to, you are said to **jump the gun**.

Something is **just what the doctor ordered** if it is exactly what is needed by someone at that time.

Keen as mustard is an expression used to mean that someone is very enthusiastic.

You **know your onions** if you are well-informed about something.[17]

If someone – or even something – is in dire trouble they are said to be a **lame duck**.

Larger than life is a term that is used to mean that someone or something is over-the-top, excessive or exaggerated.

---

[17] And you should certainly know your onions now when it comes to idioms of the English language.

Someone who has the **Midas touch** makes a lot of money out of any project they put their mind to.

My hands are tied is something you might say if you were unable to do anything to help someone, for some reason.

A **nest egg** is a sum of money saved up for the future.

Not my cup of tea is an idiom that means you don't like something very much.

If you offer someone the **olive branch**, you are trying to make peace with them.

People are **on the same wavelength** if they share the same ideas and opinions.

A **paper tiger** is something or someone that, although it might appear powerful, is in fact weak.

You **put all your eggs in one basket** if you risk everything on one chance which could turn out to be a disaster.

A **queer fish** is a strange person.

Quick as a flash means that something happens incredibly quickly.

If it is **raining cats and dogs**, you have a torrential downpour on your hands.

If something happens without **rhyme or reason**, you cannot see the sense in it happening at all.

You **sail close to the wind** if you take risks and push the boundaries of what is safe or acceptable.

Something that is so easy that success is guaranteed can be described as being like **shooting fish in a barrel**.

The **thin end of the wedge** refers to something apparently small and insignificant which will, nonetheless, lead to bigger problems further down the line.

You **turn over a new leaf** if you change your behaviour for the better.

If someone dramatically changes their opinion about something, they are said to make a **U-turn**.

The upper classes and the establishment are sometimes referred to as the **upper crust**.

If you described someone as being a **velvet glove** you would be implying that despite appearing gentle, in truth, they were determined and inflexible underneath.

A **vicious circle** is a sequence of events that compound the problems that have gone before, simply making things worse. Family feuds in soap operas inevitably become vicious circles.

Someone who is dangerous despite appearing to be quite safe, or even innocent, is said to be a **wolf in sheep's clothing**.

If someone can't see the **wood for the trees**, it means that they are so caught up with the little details that they fail to see the bigger picture.

X marks the spot is a piratical term used to indicate where something is located or hidden.

If someone is said to be **yellow-bellied** it means they are a coward.

Someone who arrives with new ideas and a different, fresh approach is described as a **young blood**.

Zero hour is the time when something important is to begin.

✍ Literary Terms ✍

For a language that has produced some of the greatest literature in the world, English has inevitably spawned a whole host of **literary terms**, those names given to clever turns of phrase or ways in which a writer uses language to create a particular atmosphere or feeling. There are far too many for them all to be listed here. However, we have picked out some of the better known ones, just to give you a smattering of knowledge with which to impress your peers, or know-it-all kids.

Acrostic – a poem in which the initial letters of each line form a word or phrase when read down the page.

Alliteration – is the repetition of the same sound (usually an initial consonant) in a group of words, e.g. 'Around the rugged rocks the ragged rascal ran.'

Anti-hero (or **anti-heroine**) – the central character of a play or story who lacks the characteristics one would expect of a hero, such as nobility and a care for others.

Bathos – is when a writer who is trying to build up a dramatic mood ends up instead by lapsing into a sense of the ridiculous or trivial.

Blank verse – poetry that doesn't rhyme.

Canon – a recognised body of writings by authors considered to be the real deal.

Comedy – a form of literary composition, usually a play, which is written to amuse its audience. After various humorous mishaps and misunderstandings, things usually turn out all right in the end for the main characters. This is particularly true of

Shakespearian Comedy, which almost always ends in marriage for the nubile young protagonists.

Couplet – a pair of rhyming lines in a poem, which are usually the same length.

Dénouement – the climax of a story in which all the hanging plot threads are neatly tied up and any mysteries explained. Classic crime thrillers often end with a dramatic dénouement in which the detective reveals how the crime was committed and unmasks the culprit.

Didactic – a style of writing which is supposed to instruct or impart useful information to the reader (which is the style in which *Match Wits With The Kids* has been written).

Epic – a long poem that tells a story at the same time as celebrating the achievements of the legendary heroes that feature within it.

Episodic – a story written as a series of interconnected parts, rather than with one clear narrative plot. By their very nature, soap operas are episodic.

Fable – a short tale that is supposed to teach a moral lesson. It could be a poem or a piece of prose. The best-known are probably Aesop's fables (which were written by a slave in Ancient Greece in the 6th century BC).

Figure of speech – a way of saying something that adds variety and force to what is being said. A metaphor is one particular figure of speech.

Genre – the particular category that a piece of writing falls into. Romance, science fiction, fantasy, horror, biographical, historical, thriller, and comedy are all types of literary genre.

Haiku – a type of poem from Japan, which captures the essence of one thing within it. A haiku must always have a total of seventeen syllables arranged in three lines, which don't rhyme, with five in the first, seven in the second and five again in the third.

Hyperbole – exaggeration for the sake of emphasising something and not meant to be taken literally.

Irony – a humorous, sometimes sarcastic, way of expressing a particular meaning, usually by using language that actually means the opposite.

Jingle – a short set of verses that have a strong, repetitive rhythm which, as a result, stick in the mind. Many nursery rhymes feature jingles, as do television adverts, of course.

Limerick – a form of verse made up of five lines, in which the first, second and fifth lines rhyme with each other, and the third and fourth lines form a rhyming couplet. A limerick is usually a self-contained humorous poem.

Melodrama – a form of sensational drama that was particularly popular during the Victorian era. Soap operas are good examples of modern melodrama.

Monologue – a long speech made by a single character.

Mystery play – a once very popular form of medieval drama which recounted tales from the Bible.

Narrative – the recounting of a story, either of an actual event or one that has been made up. The person who tells the story is the narrator.

Novella – a fictional story that is more involved and longer than a short story and yet not as long or as complicated as a novel.

Ode – a formal poem that addresses a particular person or thing, and often goes on to praise that person or thing.

Onomatopoeia – the use of words that sound like the sounds they describe, e.g. whack, crash, fizz, pop.

Oxymoron – a figure of speech that combines two contradictory terms, e.g. love–hate, bittersweet, cold fire, living death.

Palindrome[18] – a word or phrase which is the same whether it is read forwards or backwards. Some examples of words that are palindromes are: pop, civic, level, madam, rotavator.

Parody – a mock version of a literary style which pokes fun at that style or a particular author.

Pathetic fallacy – this is the way in which natural phenomena reflect the emotions of a scene or a character, so that when someone is upset the clouds weep, while the sun shines when all is going well for our hero.

Pathos – the quality of a piece of writing which is able to evoke feelings of sadness or pity in the reader.

Proverb – a saying that either expresses some accepted truth or popular superstition. 'A stitch in time saves nine' and 'a bird in the hand is worth two in the bush' are examples of proverbs.

Quatrain – a verse of four rhyming (or unrhymed) lines which is the most popular type of stanza in English poetry. (The quintain is a stanza of five lines, as in a limerick.)

---

[18] A word that spells a different word or phrase backwards is called a semordnilap (which is itself 'palindromes' spelt backwards). Some examples are god, star and devil (dog, rats and lived).

Rhetoric – the art of using the spoken or written word effectively, often to persuade or impress.

Satire – a style of writing that points out the failings of individuals or institutions and then laughs at them.

Sibilance – a form of alliteration in which the 's' sounds within words are repeated to create a hissing effect, e.g. 'The **s**inuou**s** **s**nake**s** **s**lithered and **s**lipped acro**ss** the **s**wamp**s**.'

Sonnet – a poem made up of fourteen rhyming lines of the same length. William Shakespeare made the sonnet famous, writing 154 of them.

Stanza – a group of lines that forms part of a poem, both of which are sometimes referred to as a verse. The stanzas of a poem usually have the same structure.

Theme – an abstract idea that is highlighted within a piece of writing by the way in which the writer treats the subject matter. A particular theme can be carried on through several pieces of work.

Tragedy – a serious work which usually has the downfall of its central character at its heart. A tragedy does *not* have a happy ending! A popular sub-genre of tragedy is revenge tragedy, a form of drama in which the protagonist attempts to avenge the murder of a loved one. Typically, by the end of such a play virtually all of the main characters are dead, as is the case in Shakespeare's *Hamlet*.

Tragicomedy – a play that combines the elements of both a tragedy and a comedy. Unless a piece of work is either explicitly a tragedy or a comedy, it is probably a tragicomedy.

The **Uncanny** – the disturbing strangeness, or otherworldliness, that is created in horror and thriller fiction that leaves the reader on the edge of his or her seat.

Verisimilitude – an appearance or semblance of something being true or real within a literary work. Plays, stories and films work because people are prepared to believe that they are true for the duration of that particular piece of fiction.

Zeitgeist – literally 'the spirit of the time', used to refer to the current mood or outlook of any given time, but normally used to talk about the attitudes and feelings of the present time.

✒ English Literature ✑

Ask 100 people what the greatest works of English literature are, and you would probably end up with 100 different lists. However, there are certain texts which crop up again and again. Some you will have read or studied yourself, others you will have heard of, and some are more recent bestsellers.

To create a definitive list of the greatest works of literature is an impossible task, so instead of attempting that, we have produced a list of 50 of the best-known and most influential texts. Everything from poems to plays is included, along with epic gothic romances, children's books and even science fiction novels.

Starting with the first notable great work of English literature from the 7th century AD (recently given the big-screen Hollywood treatment), the list covers the centuries in between, bringing us all the way to where we are now at the beginning of the 21st century.

	Text	Author	Date	Type
1	*Beowulf*	Anonymous	c. 700 AD	Poetry
2	*The Canterbury Tales*	Geoffrey Chaucer	1387–90s	Poetry
3	*Le Morte D'Arthur*	Thomas Malory	1485	Poetry
4	*King Lear*	William Shakespeare	c. 1606	Drama
5	*Paradise Lost*	John Milton	1667	Poetry
6	*The Pilgrim's Progress*	John Bunyan	1678	Poetry
7	*Robinson Crusoe*	Daniel Defoe	1719	Novel
8	*Gulliver's Travels*	Jonathan Swift	1726	Novel
9	*Songs of Innocence and Experience*	William Blake	1789–94	Poetry
10	*The Rime of the Ancient Mariner*	Samuel Taylor Coleridge	1797	Poetry

	Text	Author	Date	Type
11	*The Prelude*	William Wordsworth	1805	Poetry
12	*Pride and Prejudice*	Jane Austen	1813	Novel
13	*Frankenstein*	Mary Shelley	1818	Novel
14	*Wuthering Heights*	Emily Brontë	1847	Novel
15	*Jane Eyre*	Charlotte Brontë	1847	Novel
16	*Great Expectations*	Charles Dickens	1861	Novel
17	*Alice's Adventures in Wonderland*	Lewis Carroll	1865	Novel
18	*Middlemarch*	George Eliot	1871	Novel
19	*Far from the Madding Crowd*	Thomas Hardy	1874	Novel
20	*Treasure Island*	Robert Louis Stevenson	1883	Novel
21	*The Jungle Book*	Rudyard Kipling	1894	Stories
22	*The Time Machine*	H.G. Wells	1895	Novel
23	*Dracula*	Bram Stoker	1897	Novel
24	*The Hound of the Baskervilles*	Arthur Conan Doyle	1902	Novel
25	*Heart of Darkness*	Joseph Conrad	1902	Novella
26	*Howards End*	E.M. Forster	1910	Novel
27	*Sons and Lovers*	D.H. Lawrence	1913	Novel
28	*The Waste Land*	T.S. Eliot	1922	Poetry
29	*Mrs Dalloway*	Virginia Woolf	1925	Novel
30	*Winnie-the-Pooh*	A.A. Milne	1926	Stories
31	*Brave New World*	Aldous Huxley	1932	Novel
32	*A Handful of Dust*	Evelyn Waugh	1934	Novel
33	*The Hobbit*	J.R.R. Tolkien	1937	Novel
34	*Rebecca*	Daphne du Maurier	1938	Novel
35	*Brighton Rock*	Graham Greene	1938	Novel
36	*Animal Farm*	George Orwell	1945	Novel
37	*Lord of the Flies*	William Golding	1954	Novel
38	*A Clockwork Orange*	Anthony Burgess	1962	Novel

	Text	Author	Date	Type
39	*The Spy Who Came in from the Cold*	John Le Carré	1963	Novel
40	*The French Lieutenant's Woman*	John Fowles	1969	Novel
41	*The Hitchhiker's Guide to the Galaxy*	Douglas Adams	1979	Novel
42	*The Secret Diary of Adrian Mole, Aged 13¾*	Sue Townsend	1982	Novel
43	*Money*	Martin Amis	1984	Novel
44	*His Dark Materials Trilogy*	Philip Pullman	1995–2000	Novels
45	*Harry Potter and the Philosopher's Stone*	J.K. Rowling	1997	Novel
46	*The No. 1 Ladies' Detective Agency*	Alexander McCall Smith	1998	Novel
47	*Atonement*	Ian McEwan	2001	Novel
48	*Brick Lane*	Monica Ali	2003	Novel
49	*The Da Vinci Code*	Dan Brown	2003	Novel
50	*Labyrinth*	Kate Mosse	2005	Novel

✍ Spot Test! ✍

Right, let's see how closely you were paying attention! It's the teacher's weapon of choice and well, what did you expect – you are here to learn, aren't you? Now stop grumbling, imagine you're being asked these questions by your kids, and let's see if you can help them with their homework.

Kids, you have to do this too. If you can answer these, you're on your way to being able to complete your assignments by yourself, allowing your knackered Mum and Dad to settle down with a bottle of wine and remember the good old days when it was just the two of them!

Answers at the bottom of the page, no peeking … time starts now!

1) What is an imperative sentence doing?
2) What is a group of jellyfish called?
3) What is the name given to verbs that can be used as either main verbs or auxiliary verbs?
4) What tense is the following sentence in? 'I am going to stop your pocket money tomorrow.'
5) What is the name of a phrase where the initial letters spell a word or give a sequence of letters related to something else? For a bonus point, what are the seven colours of the rainbow?
6) What is a homograph?
7) What does 'inflammable' mean?
8) If you vow to 'turn over a new leaf', what will you do?
9) What is a mystery play?
10) Who wrote *The Pilgrim's Progress*, and when?

---

1) *Giving an order.* **2)** *A smack of jellyfish.* **3)** *Primary verbs.* **4)** *Simple future.* **5)** *A mnemonic. The colours of the rainbow are red, orange, yellow, green, blue, indigo and violet.* **6)** *A word that is spelt the same as another, but has an entirely different meaning.* **7)** *Easily set on fire.* **8)** *Change your behaviour for the better.* **9)** *A form of medieval drama that recounts tales from the Bible.* **10)** *John Bunyan in 1678.*

Chapter Two

MATHEMATICS
Think of a Number

At its worst, mathematics is characterised by tedious equations being learnt out of context with no discernible purpose, apparently, other than to cause discomfort to the student. At its best, it is a thing of beauty that describes and shapes the world around us, from the uniqueness of every snowflake to the fractal pattern of ferns and the internal beauty of a nautilus shell.

If it wasn't for mathematics, humankind would never have got to the Moon and you wouldn't be able to check your emails or use your mobile phone – and imagine where we'd be without those!

⊞ As Easy As 1, 2, 3 ⊞

In this chapter we are going to be using a large number of technical terms to talk about the topic of **Number**. As there are so many, rather than explain them as we go along, it makes more sense to refresh your memory as to what they are right here.

Term	Definition	Example
Digits	The individual numbers used to make up all other numbers.	0, 1, 2, 3, 4, 5, 6, 7, 8, 9
Place value	Every digit that makes up a number has a specific place value. The value of the digit changes depending on its place in the number. Place value changes by a factor of 10 upwards as you move one column to the left, and by a factor of 10 downwards as you move one column to the right.	Consider the digit 8 in the following examples: 827 – here the digit 8 represents 800 as it is in the hundreds column. 1208 – here the digit 8 is 8 units.
Decimal point	The decimal point separates whole numbers in terms of place value (thousands, hundreds, tens, units) from fractions (tenths, hundredths, thousandths).	12.34
Integer	A whole number. It can be positive or negative.	5, 13, –179, 6893, –12345
Directed numbers	Another name for integers.	
Positive numbers	Numbers above zero.	6, 12, 24, 336
Negative numbers	Numbers below zero.	–3, –14, –60, –2049
Prime number	A prime number is one that can be divided only by itself and 1 (in other words it has only two factors). **N.B.** 1 itself is not a prime number.	The first fifteen prime numbers are: 2, 3, 5, 7, 11, 13, 17, 19, 23, 29, 31, 37, 41, 43, 47

Term	Definition	Example
Operation	An action or procedure which produces a new value from one or more values. Binary operations use two values and include addition, subtraction, multiplication and division.	$1 + 1 = 2$ $17 - 25 = -8$ $9 \times 12 = 108$ $36 \div 3 = 12$
Factors	The factors of a number are all those numbers that can divide into it without leaving a remainder.	The factors of 30 are: 1, 2, 3, 5, 6, 10, 15, 30
Prime factors	It is possible to break any number down into a list of prime numbers which, when multiplied together, will result in the original number.	140 expressed as a product of its prime factors = $2 \times 2 \times 5 \times 7$
Multiple	Multiplying one number by another results in a multiple of the first number. The multiples of a number are simply those numbers that appear in its multiplication table.	The multiples of 7 are: 7, 14, 21, 28, 35, 42, 49, 56, 63, 70, 77, 84, 91, 98, etc.
Highest common factor	Also called the HCF for short, it is the largest factor that two different numbers have in common.	The HCF of 28 and 98 is 14
Lowest common multiple	Also known as the LCM, it is the smallest number that is a multiple of two different numbers.	The LCM of 8 and 12 is 24 (i.e., $8 \times 3 = 24$ and $12 \times 2 = 24$)
Powers	A handy way of expressing how many times a number should be multiplied by itself.	$3^3 = 3 \times 3 \times 3 = 27$
Indices	Another name for powers (singular index).	

Term	Definition	Example
Square root	The square root of a number is the number that, when multiplied by itself, gives the number you started with. The symbol for a square root is $\sqrt{}$. (Something to the power $\frac{1}{2}$ is another way of asking for a square root.)	The square root of 81 is 9, or $\sqrt{81} = 9$, or $81^{\frac{1}{2}} = 9$
Cube root	The cube root of a number is the number that, when multiplied by itself three times, gives the number you started with. The symbol for a cube root is $\sqrt[3]{}$. (Something to the power $\frac{1}{3}$ is another way of asking for a cube root.)	The cube root of 125 is 5, or $\sqrt[3]{125} = 5$, or $125^{\frac{1}{3}} = 5$
Square numbers	These are whole numbers raised to the power 2 (in other words, a number times itself).	$10^2 = 10 \times 10 = 100$
Cube numbers	These are whole numbers raised to the power 3 (or a number times itself, times itself again).	$10^3 = 10 \times 10 \times 10 = 1000$
Significant figures	The first significant figure (sf) is the first digit of a number which is not zero. The second, third, fourth (and so on) significant figures follow after that and may be zero. Writing numbers to a certain sf may involve rounding off.	5.981 to 3 sf is 5.98 2899 to 2 sf is 2900

Did you know...?

The prime number 73,939,133 has a very peculiar property. If you keep removing a digit from the right-hand end of the number, each of the remaining numbers will also be a prime number. It is the largest number known that has this peculiar prime property.

The four rules of number

So, before we get bogged down in fractions, percentages and ratios, let's start with something straightforward, to get the old grey matter going.

The **four rules of number** are, quite simply, the four basic operations of **addition**, **subtraction**, **multiplication** and **division**.

N.B. The opposite operation of addition is subtraction and vice versa. The opposite operation of multiplication is division.

$12 + 7 = 19 \qquad 19 - 7 = 12$	$8 \times 11 = 88 \qquad 88 \div 11 = 8$

Multiplication tables

It's worth pointing out here that if you are going to be an efficient mathematician, you are going to have to know your **multiplication tables** (also called **times tables**). They're the sort of thing you once knew off by heart but now that you've become old and lazy, they've gone from your memory along with so much else.[19]

So, just to make things that little bit easier for you, the multiplication tables from 1 to 12 are presented on the next page for your convenience. Look closely and you'll start to see all sorts of patterns between them.

---

[19] Like where you left your car keys or when your wedding anniversary is.

$1 \times 1 = 1$	$1 \times 4 = 4$	$1 \times 7 = 7$	$1 \times 10 = 10$
$2 \times 1 = 2$	$2 \times 4 = 8$	$2 \times 7 = 14$	$2 \times 10 = 20$
$3 \times 1 = 3$	$3 \times 4 = 12$	$3 \times 7 = 21$	$3 \times 10 = 30$
$4 \times 1 = 4$	$4 \times 4 = 16$	$4 \times 7 = 28$	$4 \times 10 = 40$
$5 \times 1 = 5$	$5 \times 4 = 20$	$5 \times 7 = 35$	$5 \times 10 = 50$
$6 \times 1 = 6$	$6 \times 4 = 24$	$6 \times 7 = 42$	$6 \times 10 = 60$
$7 \times 1 = 7$	$7 \times 4 = 28$	$7 \times 7 = 49$	$7 \times 10 = 70$
$8 \times 1 = 8$	$8 \times 4 = 32$	$8 \times 7 = 56$	$8 \times 10 = 80$
$9 \times 1 = 9$	$9 \times 4 = 36$	$9 \times 7 = 63$	$9 \times 10 = 90$
$10 \times 1 = 10$	$10 \times 4 = 40$	$10 \times 7 = 70$	$10 \times 10 = 100$
$11 \times 1 = 11$	$11 \times 4 = 44$	$11 \times 7 = 77$	$11 \times 10 = 110$
$12 \times 1 = 12$	$12 \times 4 = 48$	$12 \times 7 = 84$	$12 \times 10 = 120$
$1 \times 2 = 2$	$1 \times 5 = 5$	$1 \times 8 = 8$	$1 \times 11 = 11$
$2 \times 2 = 4$	$2 \times 5 = 10$	$2 \times 8 = 16$	$2 \times 11 = 22$
$3 \times 2 = 6$	$3 \times 5 = 15$	$3 \times 8 = 24$	$3 \times 11 = 33$
$4 \times 2 = 8$	$4 \times 5 = 20$	$4 \times 8 = 32$	$4 \times 11 = 44$
$5 \times 2 = 10$	$5 \times 5 = 25$	$5 \times 8 = 40$	$5 \times 11 = 55$
$6 \times 2 = 12$	$6 \times 5 = 30$	$6 \times 8 = 48$	$6 \times 11 = 66$
$7 \times 2 = 14$	$7 \times 5 = 35$	$7 \times 8 = 56$	$7 \times 11 = 77$
$8 \times 2 = 16$	$8 \times 5 = 40$	$8 \times 8 = 64$	$8 \times 11 = 88$
$9 \times 2 = 18$	$9 \times 5 = 45$	$9 \times 8 = 72$	$9 \times 11 = 99$
$10 \times 2 = 20$	$10 \times 5 = 50$	$10 \times 8 = 80$	$10 \times 11 = 110$
$11 \times 2 = 22$	$11 \times 5 = 55$	$11 \times 8 = 88$	$11 \times 11 = 121$
$12 \times 2 = 24$	$12 \times 5 = 60$	$12 \times 8 = 96$	$12 \times 11 = 132$
$1 \times 3 = 3$	$1 \times 6 = 6$	$1 \times 9 = 9$	$1 \times 12 = 12$
$2 \times 3 = 6$	$2 \times 6 = 12$	$2 \times 9 = 18$	$2 \times 12 = 24$
$3 \times 3 = 9$	$3 \times 6 = 18$	$3 \times 9 = 27$	$3 \times 12 = 36$
$4 \times 3 = 12$	$4 \times 6 = 24$	$4 \times 9 = 36$	$4 \times 12 = 48$
$5 \times 3 = 15$	$5 \times 6 = 30$	$5 \times 9 = 45$	$5 \times 12 = 60$
$6 \times 3 = 18$	$6 \times 6 = 36$	$6 \times 9 = 54$	$6 \times 12 = 72$
$7 \times 3 = 21$	$7 \times 6 = 42$	$7 \times 9 = 63$	$7 \times 12 = 84$
$8 \times 3 = 24$	$8 \times 6 = 48$	$8 \times 9 = 72$	$8 \times 12 = 96$
$9 \times 3 = 27$	$9 \times 6 = 54$	$9 \times 9 = 81$	$9 \times 12 = 108$
$10 \times 3 = 30$	$10 \times 6 = 60$	$10 \times 9 = 90$	$10 \times 12 = 120$
$11 \times 3 = 33$	$11 \times 6 = 66$	$11 \times 9 = 99$	$11 \times 12 = 132$
$12 \times 3 = 36$	$12 \times 6 = 72$	$12 \times 9 = 108$	$12 \times 12 = 144$

Did you know...?

The largest number in mathematics is infinity (which is represented by the symbol ∞). The word 'infinity' comes from the Latin *infinitas* meaning 'unboundedness'. Despite being considered a number, in that it counts or measures things, infinity is not a real number.

Directed numbers

When you are adding or subtracting **directed numbers**, use a number line like the one below to help you:

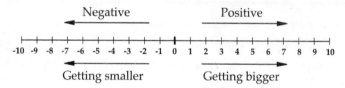

At 6:00pm the temperature outside is 5°C. Overnight there is a cold snap and the temperature drops by 7°C, so that at 6:00am the next morning it is a chilly –2°C.

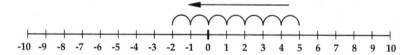

Addition and subtraction operations involving numbers which have like signs (i.e. a positive and a positive, or a negative and a negative) will produce a positive number for the answer. Unlike signs (i.e. a positive and a negative, or a negative and a positive) will give a negative.

$$4 + (-3) = 4 - 3 = 1$$
$$-9 - (-5) = -9 + 5 = -4$$
$$-7 + (-2) = -7 - 2 = -9$$
$$2 - (-6) = 2 + 6 = 8$$

When you are multiplying or dividing directed numbers, simply carry out the appropriate operation and then find the sign that will fit the answer, as you do when adding or subtracting them (like signs give a positive, unlike signs give a negative).

$-5 \times (-2) = 10$
$12 \times (-3) = -36$
$-24 \div 6 = -4$
$-18 \div (-6) = 3$

Did you know...?

There are 63,360 inches in a mile.

There are 86,400 seconds in one day.

There will be 8,765,832 hours in this millennium, from the start of 1 January 2000 until the end of 31 December 2999.

Indices[20]

An **index**, or **power**, is a quick way of expressing how many times a number (in this case called the base) should be multiplied by itself.

$8^5 = 8$ to the power of $5 = 8 \times 8 \times 8 \times 8 \times 8 = 32768$

Standard index form can be used to write very large or very small numbers much more succinctly.

$2.12 \times 10^6 = 2120000$ $\qquad$ $8.9 \times 10^{-3} = 0.0089$

---

[20] Because they are so useful for dealing with horribly large numbers, these should possibly be called super powers. After all, when you have them at your disposal, nothing can stop you!

Indices are governed by a set of laws that it is worth remembering.

- When multiplying powers, add them together.

  e.g. $4^3 \times 4^6 = 4^{3+6} = 4^9$

- When dividing powers, subtract them.

  e.g. $6^8 \div 6^2 = 6^{8-2} = 6^6$

- A number raised to the power 0 is 1 (as long as the number you start off with isn't zero).

  e.g. $9^0 = 1$

- A number raised to the power 1 is itself.

  e.g. $10^1 = 10$

- The number 1 raised to any power is still just 1.

  e.g. $1^{26} = 1$

- When one power is raised to another, multiply the powers.

  e.g. $(7^3)^5 = 7^{3 \times 5} = 7^{15}$

- A number raised to a negative power turns the number upside down, making the power positive.

  e.g. $5^{-3} = \frac{1}{5^3} = \frac{1}{125}$

- A power that is a fraction is really a root.

  e.g. $16^{\frac{1}{2}} = \sqrt{16} = 4$

Order of operations

If you have a calculation that requires a number of different operations to be used upon it (and quite possibly has some brackets thrown in there as well) and you don't know where to start, have no fear. Just remember the word **BIDMAS** and carry the operations out in the following order:

Brackets
Indices (or powers)
Division
Multiplication
Addition
Subtraction

Consider the following …
$(7 + 12) \times 5^2$

In this case, work out what's in the brackets first …
$7 + 12 = 19$

Then work out the indices …
$5^2 = 25$

There is nothing to divide, so multiply next …
$19 \times 25 = 475$

And as there is nothing to add or subtract, you're done. Easy, eh?
$(7 + 12) \times 5^2 = 475$

Fractions and decimals

Fractions are numbers that are parts of one whole. The top number of a fraction is called the numerator and the bottom number is called the denominator. A fraction whose numerator is smaller than its denominator is called a **proper fraction**. One that has a numerator larger than its denominator is an **improper fraction** (sometimes called a **top-heavy fraction**), and a fraction seen with an integer is a **mixed number**.

$$\frac{3}{4}$$

$$\frac{12}{9}$$

$$1\frac{3}{8}$$

A proper fraction   An improper fraction   A mixed number

Equivalent fractions, as their name would suggest, are ones which, although they may appear different, are actually equal in value. The following pairs of fractions are all equivalent fractions.

$$\frac{1}{2} = \frac{4}{8} \qquad \frac{2}{3} = \frac{6}{9} \qquad \frac{5}{8} = \frac{25}{40} \qquad \frac{1}{6} = \frac{8}{48} \qquad \frac{3}{5} = \frac{33}{55} \qquad \frac{7}{10} = \frac{21}{30}$$

A fraction can be **simplified** if its numerator and denominator have a factor in common.

e.g. $\frac{16}{20} = \frac{4}{5}$

4 is the HCF of both 16 and 20, and so the numerator and denominator are divided by 4 to produce the simplified fraction. This procedure is called cancelling down.

You can add or subtract fractions only if they have the same denominator. This means that you will often have to find equivalent fractions before you can carry out the operation (and then cancel down again afterwards to simplify the resulting answer if necessary).

e.g. $\frac{1}{3} + \frac{2}{7} = \frac{7}{21} + \frac{6}{21} = \frac{13}{21}$

Multiplying fractions is much more straightforward; just multiply the numerators together and then do the same for the denominators. If one of the fractions is a mixed number, turn it into an improper fraction first (and do the same with whole numbers as well).

e.g. $\frac{2}{3} \times \frac{1}{12} = \frac{2}{36}$ which cancels down to become $\frac{1}{18}$

When you need to divide fractions, turn the second fraction upside down[21] and then multiply the two fractions together as described above.

e.g. $\quad \frac{4}{5} \div \frac{5}{9} = \frac{4}{5} \times \frac{9}{5} = \frac{36}{25} = 1\frac{11}{25}$

To find the fraction of a quantity, multiply the fraction by the quantity.

e.g. Hyacinth plants 32 daffodil bulbs in her garden but only ¾ of them come up. How many daffodils it that?

$\quad \frac{3}{4} \times 32 = 32 \div 4 \times 3 = 24$

So, 24 bulbs flowered.

If you want to change a fraction into a decimal,[22] you must divide the numerator by the denominator.

e.g. $\quad \frac{1}{5} = 1 \div 5 = 0.2$

To change a decimal into a fraction, write out the decimal as a fraction with a denominator to the appropriate power of 10, dependent on how many decimal places it goes to (10, 100, 1000, etc), and then cancel down.

e.g. $\quad 0.6 = \frac{6}{10} = \frac{3}{5}$

When you multiply or divide a decimal by a power of 10, you simply move the decimal place accordingly. If you multiply by 100, for example, move the decimal point two places to the right.

e.g. $\quad 2.65 \times 100 = 265$

---

[21] This is called the reciprocal of the fraction.
[22] Which should really be called a decimal fraction anyway ...

Or you might divide by 1000, in which case you move the decimal point three places to the left.

e.g. $78.3 \div 1000 = 0.0783$

Percentages

The words *per cent* are Latin and mean 'part of a hundred', so a **percentage** is simply a fraction which has a denominator of 100.

To find the percentage of a given quantity, the easiest thing to do first is work out what 1% is. Then you simply multiply that figure by the number in front of the percentage sign (%).

e.g.   What is 25% of 700?
        1% of 700 = 7
        $7 \times 25 = 175$
        So, 25% of 700 is 175.

If you are asked to find one quantity as a percentage of another, all you have to do is divide the first quantity by the second and then multiply by 100, and don't forget to add the percentage sign at the end.

e.g.   9 out of 12 felines expressed a preference for the **MANGY** brand of processed meaty chunks. What percentage is that?
        $9 \div 12 = 0.75$
        $0.75 \times 100\% = 75\%$
        So, 75% of the cats preferred **MANGY** cat food.

You will often find that a change in value can be expressed as a percentage as well. This applies to profit and loss, or appreciation and depreciation, or even bargain discounts in the sales. It is worked out as follows:

$$\text{Percentage change} = \frac{\text{change}}{\text{original}} \times 100$$

e.g.   Tom bought a brand new motorbike, a year ago, for £3,000. However, over the course of that year it has depreciated in value and is now worth only £2,550. What is this depreciation expressed as a percentage?

$3000 - 2550 = 450$

$\frac{450}{3000} \times 100 = 0.15 \times 100 = 15\%$

Ratios

Ratios are really just another form of fractions (or decimal fractions, if you prefer), used to compare one quantity to another.

If you have 3 adults helping with a class of 30 children you have a ratio (of adults to children) of 3:30. In its simplest form this is a ratio of 1:10. Expressed as a fraction this is $\frac{1}{10}$ and as a decimal it's 0.1.

Proportion

Fractions, decimals and percentages are all different ways of expressing a **proportion** of something. As a result, it's worth just memorising some of the more commonly occurring fractions along with their equivalent decimals and percentages, so that you can see how closely related they are.

Fraction	Decimal (fraction)	Percentage
$\frac{1}{1}$	1.0	100%
$\frac{1}{4}$	0.25	25%
$\frac{1}{2}$	0.5	50%
$\frac{3}{4}$	0.75	75%
$\frac{1}{3}$	0.3333 recurring[23]	33.333% or 33⅓%
$\frac{2}{3}$	0.6666 recurring	66.666% or 66⅔%
$\frac{1}{5}$	0.2	20%
$\frac{2}{5}$	0.4	40%
$\frac{3}{5}$	0.6	60%
$\frac{4}{5}$	0.8	80%
$\frac{1}{6}$	0.1666 recurring	16.666% or 16⅔%
$\frac{5}{6}$	0.8333 recurring	83.333% or 83⅓%
$\frac{1}{8}$	0.125	12.5% or 12½%
$\frac{3}{8}$	0.375	37.5% or 37½%
$\frac{5}{8}$	0.625	62.5% or 62½%
$\frac{7}{8}$	0.875	87.5% or 87½%
$\frac{1}{10}$	0.1	10%

Did you know...?

Roman numerals were still used for mathematical calculations until the 13th century AD, when Leonardo da Pisa – more commonly known as Fibonacci – published his *Liber abaci*, or 'The Book of Calculations'. Fibonacci was the son of a Pisan merchant who served as a customs officer in North Africa. He travelled widely in Barbary (Algeria) and was later sent on trips to Egypt, Syria, Greece, Sicily and Provence. In 1200 he returned to Pisa and used the knowledge he had gained on his travels

---

[23] If a number is recurring, it simply means that when it is expressed as a decimal, it has a set of final digits that repeat an infinite number of times. Strangely, when such numbers are expressed as fractions, they do not recur.

to write *Liber abaci*. Through this magnum opus he introduced the Latin-speaking world to the decimal number system. The first chapter of Part 1 begins:

These are the nine figures of the Indians: 9 8 7 6 5 4 3 2 1. With these nine figures, and with this sign 0 which in Arabic is called zephirum, any number can be written, as will be demonstrated.

Fibonacci is best known for a simple series of numbers, introduced in *Liber abaci*, which are now known as the *Fibonacci sequence* in his honour.

The Fibonacci sequence

The **Fibonacci sequence** begins with the numbers 0 and 1. After that, this simple rule applies: *Add the last two numbers to get the next.*

0, 1, 1, 2, 3, 5, 8, 13, 21, 34, 55, 89, 144, 233, 377, 610, 987, etc.

A special value, closely related to the Fibonacci series, is called the **golden ratio**. This is said to exist for two quantities when the ratio between their sum and the larger amount is the same as the ratio between the quantities themselves. In terms of figures, this ratio is roughly 1.6180339887. Many artists and architects have proportioned their works to approximate the golden ratio, believing it to be aesthetically pleasing. Certainly the golden ratio can be found in the pyramids of Giza and the Parthenon at Athens.

Interestingly, the golden ratio is just as prevalent in the natural world and influences the shape of spiralling nautilus shells, while flowers often have a Fibonacci number of petals. For example, daisies can have 34, 55 or even as many as 89 petals.

If you look at the arrangement of the seeds in a sunflower you will see that they appear to be spiralling outwards, both to the left and the right. There is a Fibonacci number of spirals, and it is this arrangement that keeps the seeds uniformly packed, no matter how large the seed head of the sunflower.

⊞ **As Easy As A, B, C** ⊞

Algebra, eh? How could we cope without it?

If right now you're thinking, 'quite happily' or you're one of those people who, when you were younger, couldn't understand how something that had nothing to do with numbers could have anything to do with mathematics, then have no fear; this section's for you.

Many of the mathematical problems you face every day (wittingly or unwittingly) can be boiled down to a few simple algebraic equations. It's just a different way of looking at things. You'll encounter other equations when you read up on **Shape** and **Space**, or when you come to look at the chapters covering the sciences.

Algebra is simply the exercise of putting a mathematical problem, which could be written as a sentence, into an equation or formula. Letters are used as symbols, either in place of numbers or to represent other operations.

Many of the 'Think of a number' kind of brain-teasers can be written down as algebraic equations. For example, think of a number. Now double it and add two. Times the result by three and add another three. Take away the number you first thought of. Take four away from what's left. Now subtract five and divide the answer by five. You're back with the number you first thought of – am I right?

This complicated-sounding puzzle can be written down, if we use the letter n to denote the number you have to think of at the beginning. Going through the problem systemically, writing down each of the operations that have to be completed in order (making use of brackets where appropriate), we end up with the equation:

$$\frac{3(2n+2)+3-n-4-5}{5} = n$$

Try the puzzle again, this time writing out the equation, replacing the n with any number you care to think of. Amazing, isn't it?

There are a number of terms and expressions used in algebra which you just need to know.

Term	Definition	Example
Expression	Any arrangement of letter symbols and numbers.	$5x + 3y - 5$
Variable	A symbolic representation used to represent a quantity or expression. A variable often represents an unknown quantity that has the potential to change.	$5y = 45$ y is the unknown variable
Formula	This connects two different expressions containing variables, where the value of one variable depends on the values of the other variables, making use of an equals sign.	$b = c + d$
Equation	This is different from a formula because it connects two different expressions which include values which are unknown. Again, the two expressions are joined by an equals sign.	$2x + 3 = 9$
Identity	Similar to an equals sign in appearance (but with an extra bar, '$\equiv$'), an identity connects expressions involving unspecified numbers but which always remains true, regardless of which numerical values are put in place of the letter symbols.	$4(a + 5) \equiv 4a + 20$

Term	Definition	Example
Function	A function is the way in which two sets of values are connected so that a value from the first set matches up with a unique value in the second set.	$a = 5b - 3$ The value of a will vary according to the value of b
Substitution	This is the act of replacing a letter symbol in an algebraic equation with a number.	$x = 2y$ If $y = 3$ then $x = 6$
Simultaneous linear equations	These are two equations with two unknown variables.	$4c - d = 8$ $6c + 4d = 34$
Inequalities	There are four inequality signs used in algebra.	> means 'greater than' < means 'less than' $\geq$ means 'greater than or equal to' $\leq$ means 'less than or equal to'
Coefficient	The number that appears in front of a letter symbol.	$5n$ 5 is the coefficient of n

Algebraic expressions can be simplified if like terms (those that are represented by the same letter symbol) are joined together.

e.g. $4x - 2y + 7x - 3y = 11x - 5y$

or $6c + 3b + 2d + 4b - 1b + 5d = 6c + 6b + 7d$

They can also be simplified by multiplying together numbers, letters or brackets accordingly.

e.g. $8c \times 9d = 8 \times 9 \times c \times d = 72cd$

or $(a + 4)(a - 7) = a(a - 7) + 4(a - 7)$
$$= a^2 - 7a + 4a - 28$$
$$= a^2 - 3a - 28$$

When you are faced with having to simplify algebraic fractions, you just use the same rules that apply to any calculation involving fractions. With addition and subtraction of algebraic fractions, this means making sure that they have a common denominator.

This also applies to indices (or powers). The same laws that apply to them (that you read about in the section about Number) apply to algebra as well.

And when it comes to finally working out the equation, you can rearrange it so that the value you are trying to determine becomes the subject. For example, the formula for calculating the circumference of a circle is to multiply the diameter of the circle by Pi (represented by the symbol π and with a rough value of 3.14):

$$C = \pi \times D$$

But if you already know what the circumference is, you can work out the diameter by rearranging the formula so that D becomes the subject of the equation:

$$D = \frac{C}{\pi}$$

⊞ **Keeping in Shape** ⊞

When you were at school, you probably had to learn the names and properties of all sorts of interesting shapes (with just as interesting names) but now that you have other things to occupy your mind, you can't quite remember what they all were.

But never fear, everything you could possibly want to know about 2D and 3D shapes (and possibly even a little bit more than that) is presented for you right here.

Properties of angles

Before we go rushing into looking at shapes, we should really start by looking at angles. An **angle** is the amount of turning that takes place between the position of one line and the position of another. Angles are always measured in **degrees**.

There are several types of angles which you should know.

Type of angle	Picture	Definition
Acute		An angle between 0° and 90°.
Right angle		A right angle is always 90°.
Obtuse		An angle between 90° and 180°.
Reflex		An angle between 180° and 360°.

You can add to those a half turn, which is equal to 180°, and a whole turn, which equals 360°. Angles which are on a straight line will always add up to 180°, while angles about a point add up to 360°.

The angles inside a triangle also add up to 180°, but the angles inside a quadrilateral add up to 360°.

Vertically opposite angles will always be equal and an exterior angle of a triangle equals the sum of the opposite interior angles ($c = a + b$).

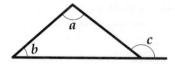

There are three different kinds of angles associated with **parallel lines**. **Alternate** angles (c and f) are equal, **corresponding** angles (b and f) are also equal and **interior** angles (d and f) add up to 180°.

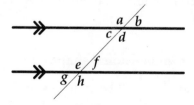

The angles inside a polygon (a shape with many sides) can be calculated as follows:

The sum of the interior angles of a polygon
= (the total number of sides – 2) × 180°

e.g.   The sum of interior angles of a hexagon = (6 – 2) × 180°
$$= 4 \times 180°$$
$$= 720°$$

Properties of one-dimensional shapes

A straight line is a **one-dimensional** shape, which means that it has only length and no height or depth.

Parallel lines (like railway tracks) travel in the same direction and are always the same distance apart (or equidistant). Parallel lines never meet. The point on the horizon where perspective means that parallel lines appear to meet is called the vanishing point.

Perpendicular lines are lines that are at right angles (90°) to one another.

Properties of two-dimensional shapes

Two-dimensional shapes (like triangles and rectangles) have length and height, meaning that they also have an area. However, all of the points on a 2D shape are within the same plane.

The distance around the outside of a shape is called the perimeter. To calculate the perimeter of a 2D shape, simply add together the lengths of all of its sides.

Some 2D shapes will be symmetrical. There are three different types of symmetry.

Type of symmetry	Definition	Example
Reflective	Where one half of a shape is a mirror image of the other. The mirror line is called the line (or axis) of symmetry. A shape can have more than one line of symmetry.	
Rotational	When a shape is turned and still looks exactly the same. The number of times the shape can be turned within 360° and still look the same is its order of rotational symmetry.	
Plane	A 3D solid has a plane of symmetry if the plane can divide the solid into two exact halves which are the mirror image of one another. Plane symmetry occurs only in 3D solids and a solid can have more than one plane of symmetry.	

Congruent shapes are ones which are exactly the same size and shape. Mirror images still count as being congruent.

A **tessellation** is a pattern made up of interlocking 2D shapes which fit together without leaving any gaps between them.

A **transformation** changes the position or size of a shape. There are four different types of transformation with which you should be familiar (see next page).

Transformation	What it does	What's affected
Reflection	Creates a mirror image of the shape.	Position *is* affected. Size and shape *are not* affected.
Translation	This moves a shape from one place to another. Vectors describe the distance and direction of the translation.	Position *is* affected. Size and shape *are not* affected.
Rotation	Turns a shape through an angle about a fixed point called the centre of rotation.	Position *is* affected. Size and shape *are not* affected.
Enlargement	Changes the size of an object, but not its shape. The point from which the enlargement happens is called the centre of enlargement, while the scale factor lets you know how many times the length of the original shape has changed.	Position and size *are* affected. Shape *is not* affected.

Shapes are described as being **similar** if they are the same shape (with equal corresponding angles, and corresponding lengths are to the same ratio) but are different sizes.

Properties of triangles

All **triangles** have **three sides** and **three internal angles**, which always add up to 180° in total. There are four different types of triangle to be aware of.

Type of triangle	Picture	Properties
Equilateral		All 3 sides are equal in length. All 3 angles are equal (60° each). Has 3 lines of symmetry and rotational symmetry order 3.
Isosceles		2 sides are equal. The 2 angles at its base are equal. Has 1 line of symmetry.
Scalene		None of the sides are the same length. All of the angles are different.
Right-angled		Has a right angle (90°). May be an **isosceles** triangle or a **scalene** triangle.

To find out the area of a triangle – any triangle – use the following formula:

$$\text{Area of a triangle} = \tfrac{1}{2} \text{ base} \times \text{vertical height}$$
$$A = \tfrac{1}{2} \times b \times h_v$$

To construct a triangle, simply draw the longest side, place the point of a compass at one end and draw an arc with a radius equivalent to one of the remaining two sides (see page 86 for definitions of these terms). Now place the compass point at the other end of the line and draw an arc with a radius the same as the other side of the triangle, making sure it bisects with the first arc. Draw two lines, one from each end of the longest side, culminating where the two arcs meet. *Voilà!* One triangle!

Pythagoras' Theorem

Pythagoras was a mathematician who first made a name for himself in Ancient Greece in the 6th century BC. However, he has lived on in the minds of millions thanks to his discovery which we now take for granted, and to which he gave his name: **Pythagoras' Theorem**.

Pythagoras' Theorem states that in a right-angled triangle, the square on the hypotenuse (the longest side, which is always opposite the right angle) is equal to the sum of the squares on the other two sides. This is normally expressed using the equation $a^2 + b^2 = c^2$, where c is the hypotenuse.

So, if we have a right-angled triangle with sides 3 m, 4 m and 5 m in length[24] (5 m being the hypotenuse) then:

$$3^2 + 4^2 = 5^2$$
$$9 + 16 = 25$$

Using Pythagoras' Theorem you can work out the length of any side on a right-angled triangle, as long as you know the lengths of the other two sides. Take the following example:

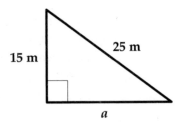

a

---

[24] A right-angled triangle where the sides are in the ratio of the integers 3:4:5 is an example of a Pythagorean triple, which is useful for quickly working out the length of a side when you already have the other two sides of the triple. This also works for a triangle with sides in the ratio of 5:12:13.

$$15^2 + a^2 = 25^2$$
$$a^2 = 25^2 - 15^2$$
$$a^2 = 625 - 225$$
$$a^2 = 400$$
$$a = \sqrt{400}$$
$$a = 20 \text{ m}$$

Properties of quadrilaterals

Quadrilaterals are shapes that have four sides and four internal angles, which add up to 360°. There are a number of different types of quadrilaterals with varying properties.

Quadrilateral	Picture	Properties
Square		All 4 sides are equal in length. Has 2 pairs of parallel sides. All 4 angles are right angles (90°). Has 4 lines of symmetry and rotational symmetry order 4. The diagonals are equal and bisect each other at right angles.
Rectangle		Has 2 pairs of parallel sides. Opposite sides are equal in length. All 4 angles are right angles (90°). Has 2 lines of symmetry and rotational symmetry order 2. The diagonals bisect each other, but not at right angles.
Rhombus (or Diamond)		All 4 sides are equal in length. Has 2 pairs of parallel sides. Has 2 lines of symmetry and rotational symmetry order 2. Opposite angles are equal, none of which are right angles. The diagonals bisect each other at right angles and bisect the corner angles.

Quadrilateral	Picture	Properties
Parallelogram		Has 2 pairs of parallel sides. Opposite sides are equal in length. Has rotational symmetry order 2. Opposite angles are equal, none of which are right angles.
Trapezium		Has 1 pair of parallel sides. Has 1 pair of non-parallel sides (which may or may not be equal in length). Has only 1 line of symmetry if it is an isosceles trapezium (like the one shown).
Kite		Has 2 pairs of adjacent sides which are equal. Has 1 line of symmetry. Diagonals cross at right angles but do not bisect each other.

To calculate the area of a quadrilateral, use the appropriate formula from the following:

Area of a rectangle (or a square) = length × width
$$A = l \times w$$

Area of a parallelogram (or a rhombus) = base × vertical height
$$A = b \times h_v$$

Area of a trapezium = average of parallel sides × distance between them
$$A = \frac{1}{2} \times (a + b) \times h$$

Properties of other regular polygons

A **polygon** is a 2D shape with multiple straight sides. In a **regular polygon** all of the sides are equal in length.

Regular polygon	Picture	Properties
Pentagon		Has 5 equal sides. All 5 angles are equal. Has 5 lines of symmetry and rotational symmetry order 5.
Hexagon		Has 6 equal sides. Has 3 pairs of parallel sides. All 6 angles are equal. Has 6 lines of symmetry and rotational symmetry order 6.
Heptagon		Has 7 equal sides. All 7 angles are equal. Has 7 lines of symmetry and rotational symmetry order 7.
Octagon		Has 8 equal sides. Has 4 pairs of parallel sides. All 8 angles are equal. Has 8 lines of symmetry and rotational symmetry order 8.
Nonagon		Has 9 equal sides. All 9 angles are equal. Has 9 lines of symmetry and rotational symmetry order 9.
Decagon		Has 10 equal sides. Has 5 pairs of parallel sides. All 10 angles are equal. Has 10 lines of symmetry and rotational symmetry order 10.

Properties of circles

A **circle** is unusual in that it is a one-sided shape, a closed curve (the interior of which is called a disk). In Euclidean geometry[25]

---

[25] Named after Euclid of Alexandria, a Greek mathematician now known as the 'father of geometry'.

it is defined as 'the set of all points in a plane at a fixed distance, called the radius, from a given point, the centre' – but don't let that put you off!

The circle has a number of properties peculiar to itself, which are as follows:

Term	Picture	Definition
Circumference		The distance around the outside of the circle.
Radius		A straight line from the centre of the circle to the circumference. The radius is half the diameter.
Diameter		A straight line passing through the centre of the circle that reaches the circumference at both ends. The diameter is twice the radius.
Arc		Part of the circumference.
Chord		A straight line that joins two points on the circumference (in other words, two ends of an arc). It does not go through the centre of the circle.
Segment		The part of a circle enclosed between an arc and a chord.
Sector		The shape enclosed by two radii of a circle and the arc between them.

Term	Picture	Definition
Secant		A line which cuts through a curve at one or more points.
Tangent		A line that touches the circle at only one point.
Perpendicular bisector		A straight line that cuts a chord (and hence a segment) in half, which passes through the centre of a circle.

Did you know...?

If you draw a triangle inside a semi-circle, using the diameter as the base line of the triangle, no matter where the opposite angle touches the curved edge of the semi-circle, it will always be 90°.

π

Pi or π is one of the most important mathematical constants. It is approximately equal to 3.14, and represents the ratio of any circle's circumference to its diameter in Euclidean geometry, which is the same thing as the ratio of a circle's area to the square of its radius. These are the two formulae you should learn connected to circles:

Area of a circle = π × the radius squared

$$A = \pi \times r^2$$

Circumference of a circle = π × diameter

$$C = \pi \times D$$

Did you know...?

Of all the shapes that have the same perimeter, a circle will have the largest area. While among all the shapes with the same area, the circle will have the shortest perimeter.

Properties of three-dimensional solids

Any three-dimensional shape has **volume** (also referred to as **capacity**), meaning that it has length, height and depth. 3D solids are made up of **faces** (the flat surfaces of a solid), **edges** (where two faces meet) and **vertices** (corners, where the edges meet).

3D solid	Picture	Properties
Sphere		Has two faces (but one of them is on the inside).[26] Has no edges or vertices.
Cube		Has 6 faces that are all the same. Has 12 edges and 8 vertices.
Cuboid		Has 6 faces which are 3 pairs of opposite equal faces. Has 12 edges and 8 vertices.
Triangular prism[27]		Has 5 faces, 3 rectangular, adjacent and the same, with 1 pair of opposite equal triangular faces. Has 9 edges and 6 vertices.

---

[26] This is something unusual to spheres and does not apply to other 3D solids. For example, a cube *does not* have 12 faces!

[27] A prism is a solid shape that can be cut into slices which are all the same shape – rather like seaside rock.

3D solid	Picture	Properties
Hexagonal prism		Has 8 faces, 6 rectangular, adjacent and the same, with 1 pair of opposite equal hexagonal faces. Has 18 edges and 12 vertices.
Regular tetrahedron		Has 4 faces, all triangular and all the same. Has 6 edges and 4 vertices.
Square-based pyramid		Has 5 faces, 4 of which are triangular and the same. Has 8 edges and 5 vertices.
Cylinder		Has 3 faces, 1 pair of which are equal circles. Has 2 edges and no vertices.
Cone		Has 2 faces, 1 of which is a circle. Has 1 edge and no vertices.

To calculate the volume of a solid, use the appropriate formula from the following:

Volume of a sphere = $\frac{4}{3}$ x π x the radius cubed

$$V = \frac{4}{3}\pi r^3$$

Volume of a cuboid (or a cube) = length × width × height

$$V = l \times w \times h$$

Volume of a prism = area of cross-section × length

$$V = A \times l$$

Volume of a cylinder = area of cross-section (which is a circle)
× height (or length)

$$V = \pi r^2 \times h$$

Volume of a cone = one third the area of the base × height

$$V = \tfrac{1}{3}bh$$

Did you know...?

There are only five regular polyhedra (polyhedra being the plural of polyhedron, which is a 3D geometric object with flat faces and straight edges). This fact was known to the Ancient Greeks and these five regular polyhedra are also known as Platonic bodies. They are the tetrahedron (which has 4 faces), the cube (with 6 faces), the octahedron (8 faces), the dodeca-hedron (12 faces) and the icosahedron (which has 20 faces). Other polyhedra have faces that are made up of more than just the one 2D shape.

Nets

The **net** of a 3D solid is a 2D shape which can be folded to form the 3D solid shape. The following are all different nets for a cube:

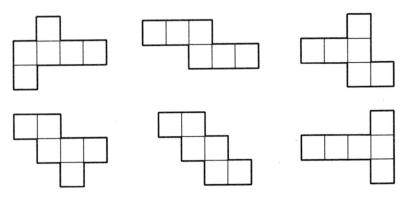

Coordinates

When you are working in three dimensions, as with solid shapes, every position on the 3D solid has **three coordinates** that denote its position in space, along an **x axis** (length), **y axis** (height) and a third direction indicated by the **z axis** (depth).

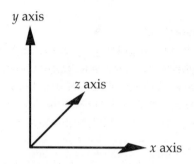

Did you know...?

A sphere has two sides, but there is such a thing as a one-sided surface, and it's called a Möbius strip. It was discovered by A.F. Möbius (1790–1868) and is made by taking a strip of paper, twisting one end through 180° (one half turn) and then gluing the ends together.

Units of measurement

Length, **weight** and **capacity** (or **volume**) are all forms of measurement. You encounter them every day, from the moment you step on the bathroom scales to when you fill up the car with petrol. And although Britain went metric decades ago, people will still happily talk about a pint of milk (a pint being an imperial measurement) while buying their orange juice by the litre (a metric measurement).

The table below gives some of the most common **units of measurement**[28] along with some rough comparisons, to give you an idea of how they measure up against each other.

	Metric	Imperial	Comparison
Length	10 mm = 1 cm 100 cm = 1 m 1000 m = 1 km	12 inches = 1 foot 3 feet = 1 yard	2.5 cm ≈ 1 inch 30 cm ≈ 1 foot 1 m ≈ 39 inches 8 km ≈ 5 miles
Weight	1000 mg = 1 g 1000 g = 1 kg 1000 kg = 1 tonne	16 ounces (oz) = 1 pound 14 pounds (lb) = 1 stone	25 g ≈ 1 ounce 1 kg ≈ 2.2 pounds
Capacity	1000 ml = 1 litre 100 cl = 1 litre 1000 cm³ = 1 litre	20 fluid oz = 1 pint 8 pints = 1 gallon	1 litre ≈ 1¾ pints 4.5 litres ≈ 1 gallon

mm = millimetres   mg = milligrams   ml = millilitres
cm = centimetres   g = grams   cl = centilitres
m = metres   kg = kilograms   l = litres
km = kilometres

Did you know...?

The metric system as we know it today was first introduced in the 18th century in France, after the French king, Louis XVI, charged a group of experts to develop a unified, natural and universal system of measurement to replace the various, and conflicting, systems in use at the time. The creators of this metric system, who included Lavoisier (the 'father of modern chemistry'), tried to choose units that were logical and practical. Their metric system was adopted in 1791 after the French Revolution. It was based on units of ten, because scientists, engineers and bureaucrats found it easier to carry out the complex unit conversions that their work so often required them to do.

---

[28] So no rods, chains or furlongs here.

⊞ **Lies, Damned Lies and Statistics**[29] ⊞

Day in and day out we are bombarded with information, from newspaper reports and television adverts through to the list of ingredients on the side of a cereal box and cinema listings. In mathematics we call this information data,[30] and it is by cunningly exploiting this data that we can have an influence over the world around us. Or, if we're not careful, someone else will use the data to control us.

Ever heard of Big Brother?[31] Well, Orwell's dystopian view of the future has arrived, the place is here, and the time is now. In this, the Information Age, we have easier access to an unprecedented amount of data. Learn to handle this effectively and interpret the information presented to you effectively, or face the consequences, Citizen Smith!

Handle with care

Statistics is the branch of mathematics to do with collecting, analysing, interpreting, explaining and presenting data. If you want to back up a particular point you are making, the addition of some suitable statistics can appear to add credence to your argument.

However, statistics is potentially a very dangerous area of maths because of the ease with which the actual figures themselves can be made up. As the American comedian Steven Wright put it, '47.3% of all statistics are made up on the spot'.

---

[29] To quote the famous American writer Mark Twain.
[30] Which is technically the plural form of 'datum' (meaning 'a reference from which measurements are made'), but which is more often than not used as a singular noun itself.
[31] As in the novel *Nineteen Eighty-four*, rather than the TV reality gameshow.

Statistics are often used to subtly mislead the public, because most people don't understand how they work. So, pay closer attention and you won't end up as one of those that George Carlin was referring to when he said, 'Think about how stupid the average person is; now realise half of them are dumber than that.'

Organising data

However it's been collected (whether it's been done discreetly or explicitly through a questionnaire) and for whatever purpose (as part of a survey or to test a hypothesis), data can be organised in any number of ways, depending on what findings those using it want to reveal, or the impression that they want to give.

Data that has been collected often appears first in the form of a tally chart (or frequency table). The tally chart shows how often an item occurs, the tallies themselves being the marks put down on the chart. (Every fifth tally is drawn across the preceding four to make a gate.) The tallies are then added up to find the frequency of each item.

Favourite subject	Tally	Frequency
English	卌 卌 ‖	12
Mathematics	卌 卌	10
Science	卌 ‖	7
History	卌 卌 ‖‖	14
Geography	卌 ‖‖	9
Modern Foreign Languages	卌	5
Classics	‖‖	3

This data can then be presented in various different forms. **Pictograms** use symbols or pictures to represent a certain number of items (meaning that one symbol does not necessarily have to represent one item). Charts that use pictograms always have each row labelled and require a key, with the symbols themselves being of equal size.

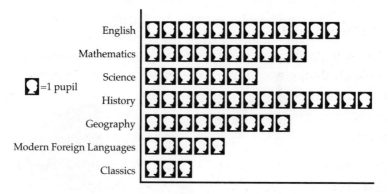

A **bar chart** uses bars or columns of equal width to present the information gathered. The height of a bar indicates the frequency of an item.

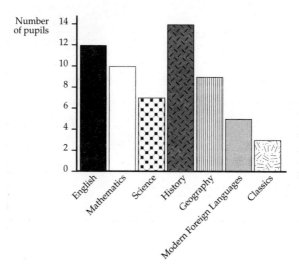

N.B. Be aware that the axes of a bar chart do not need to start at zero. For example, advertisers will often start the numbers on an axis further up the scale, to give the impression of there being a greater difference between the popularity of two products.

Pie charts are circular and show varying frequencies as differently sized portions of the 'pie'. To calculate the correct angles in order to work out how big each slice of the pie should be, divide 360° by the total number of items listed, and then multiply it by each frequency in turn.

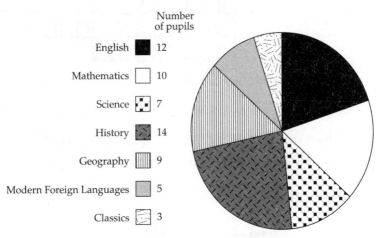

	Number of pupils
English	12
Mathematics	10
Science	7
History	14
Geography	9
Modern Foreign Languages	5
Classics	3

You can also present data using a **line graph**, which is simply a set of points joined by lines. They are useful for showing how things change over time, highlighting the highest point, but are possibly not the best format for representing data such as we are using here.

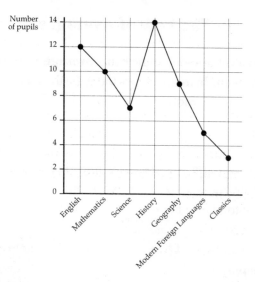

And then there is the **scatter graph**, which plots the information as a series of points. Again, they are useful for seeing if there is a correlation[32] between two different sets of data, but not so useful for comparing school pupils' favourite subjects.

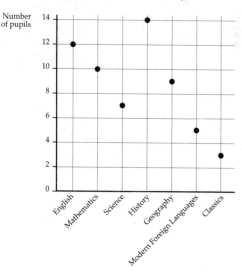

---

[32] In other words, a connection between them.

⊞ The Law of Averages ⊞

When you talk about something being **average**, what type of average do you mean? In mathematics there are three kinds: the **mean**, the **median** and the **mode**. We will deal with each one in turn.

Mean

This is what people are normally referring to when they talk about finding the average. You work out the **mean** by adding together the total number of a set of values (such as the number of goals scored by a football team) and dividing by the number of different values used (which in this case would be the number of matches played).

$$\text{Mean} = \frac{\text{the total sum of set values}}{\text{the number of values used}}$$

Take Footyville United. The team play ten matches, and end up with the following set of results.

Team played	Goals scored by Footyville Utd	Result
Somerset Town	4	Won
Shropshire City	2	Drew
West Midlands Villa	0	Lost
Yorkshire Wanderers	1	Lost
Rutland Forest	2	Drew
Norfolk Athletic	2	Lost
Devon Rovers	8	Won
Avon Albion	5	Won
Northumberland FC	4	Won
Hampshire United	2	Drew

To work out how many goals they scored on average per match (in other words to find the **mean**), we add all of the goals scored together and divide by 10, the number of matches played.

$$\text{Mean} = \frac{4+2+0+1+2+2+8+5+4+2}{10}$$

$$= \frac{30}{10}$$

$$= 3 \text{ goals were scored on average per match}$$

Median

When you rank a set of results in order of size, the **median** is the middle value. If we rank Footyville United's match results by size we get:

$$0, 1, 2, 2, \mathbf{2}, \mathbf{2}, 4, 4, 5, 8$$

As there isn't one middle number in this case we have to take the middle two, which are both 2, and so our median is 2. If the two scores were different we would have to take the middle value between them.

Mode

The **mode** of a set of data is merely the value which occurs most. In the case of Footyville's match scores, the mode is 2 as well.

Range

When you have a set of results such as these, you work out the **range** by subtracting the lowest value from the highest. Here it would be:

$$8 - 0 = 8$$

So Footyville United's range of goals scored would be 8.

⌗ **Probability** ⌗

Probability is simply the likelihood of something happening. In mathematics all probabilities are rated between 0 and 1, with 0 meaning it will definitely never happen and 1 meaning it is a certainty.[33] They can be written as fractions, decimals or percentages.

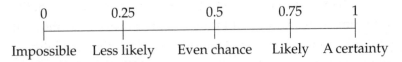

The probability, as I write this, of me being a tree (or indeed of you being a tree) is impossible and so has a probability of 0. However, if you are reading this chapter right now, then the probability of you being able to read is 1 – a certainty.

If you have all the necessary information at your disposal, you can work out the probability of something happening using the following formula:

$$\text{Probability (of an event)}^{34} = \frac{\text{number of ways of that event happening}}{\text{total number of possible outcomes}}$$

Imagine that you have a Scrabble bag with all of the letter tiles necessary to spell the word PROBABILITY (and only those letters) inside it. There are eleven letters in the word in total and each letter appears only once, other than B and I which both appear twice.

---

[33] In fact, the more you look into probability the more you realise that a sure thing is anything but. Very few things in life are certain, other than the old certainties of death and taxes!

[34] Sometimes written as P(event).

So, if you put your hand into the bag and pull out a tile, the chance of it being a Y is 1 in 11, whereas the chance of pulling out a B is 2 in 11. If we were to write these probabilities as fractions we would have:

P(Y) = 1/11
P(B) = 2/11

The probabilities of events which cannot possibly happen at the same time will always add up to 1. So, in the example above, if you only ever take out one letter tile at a time, the possibility of taking out a Y is 1 in 11, whereas the possibility of *not* taking out a Y is 10 in 11, and so is a much more likely outcome. We could also work this out using the following formula:

Probability (of an event not happening)
= 1 − Probability (that an event will happen)

For the example above we would write:

P(not Y) = 1 − P(Y)
10/11 = 1 − 1/11

You can estimate the probability of something happening simply by carrying out a number of **trials**. For example, if you were conducting a market survey to find out whether people preferred Brand A of tomato ketchup to Brand B, it would be impractical to ask every single person in the country.

However, you could carry out a trial using 100 people. This would be much more realistic. If 80 of the people in the trial said that they preferred Brand A, you could then work out the probability of anyone in the country preferring Brand A.

$$\text{Estimated probability} = \frac{\text{number of successful trials}}{\text{total number of trials}}$$

Which in this case would be:

$$\text{Probability of someone preferring Brand A} = \frac{80}{100}$$

You could then make the claim that 8 out of 10 people (or 80%) prefer Brand A!

If you are calculating the probability of something occurring which could happen in more than one way, you must remember to add all of the ways together to find the total probability.

People sometimes make the mistake of assuming that because one particular outcome has already occurred, a different outcome is more likely the next time. This is not necessarily the case!

Take, for example, tossing a coin. The first time you toss it, there is an even chance that it will be either heads or tails (a probability of 0.5, ½ or 50%). Say it lands heads up. The second time you toss the coin, there is still the same 50/50 chance that it will be either heads or tails: this is not affected by the fact that heads has already come up once. It doesn't matter how many times you toss the coin; the probability of it landing on heads or tails is always the same – 50/50.

✉ Spot Test! ✉

Pythagoras did what with a hippopotamus now? Maybe you were daydreaming about chocolate cake while reading the *Keeping in Shape* section? Or perhaps you've been counting sheep instead of numbers?

Time's ticking and either your kids are pulling away or your parents are catching up. Anyway, we hope you were memorising your times tables carefully – you're about to be put to the test!

Prove us wrong. Quick as you can now, answer the following questions:

1) Write out the next eight numbers of the Fibonacci sequence: 0, 1 …
2) What's $\frac{3}{7} \div \frac{7}{9}$?
3) What is 100 cubed?
4) What is the symbol for infinity?
5) What is 30% of 1200?
6) Calculate $(23 – 13) \times 3^3 – 14$
7) If you have a bag containing a marble for each colour of the rainbow, what is the probability of your pulling out the red marble?
8) Express π to three significant figures.
9) List the factors of 45.
10) What is the formula for working out the volume of a cone?

1) *1, 2, 3, 5, 8, 13, 21, 34* **2)** $\frac{27}{49}$ **3)** *1,000,000* **4)** ∞ **5)** *300* **6)** *256* **7)** $\frac{1}{7}$ **8)** *3.14*
9) *1, 3, 5, 9, 15, 45* **10)** $\frac{1}{3}$ *base × height*

103

Chapter Three

BIOLOGY
That's Life!

The science curriculum studied in schools these days has changed quite dramatically from that once taught by lab-coated schoolmasters who always carried the odour of mysterious chemicals about them. This is in part due to continuing advances being made within the sciences, and in part thanks to a general namby-pambiness that now pervades educational establishments.

For example, in the area of biology, the intention is for children at secondary school level to gain an understanding of how the human body works, how plants work, how living things are classified and grouped together, how creatures evolve and their relationship with their environment. Much of this you will have covered yourself during your school days, although students of science today aren't expected to cut up formaldehyde-soaked rats and dead frogs. Long gone are the days when your biology teacher would bring out the scalpel and dissection board, like some desperate wannabe Dr Frankenstein.

While we would encourage a thorough dissection of all the sciences for academic study, we wouldn't actually want you to chop up the neighbour's cat and cut yourself with your best Sunday roast carving knife in the process. And we certainly wouldn't recommend such an approach while using this book: bodily juices can leave such a nasty stain.

✝ Life and Living Processes ✝

What you would have known as **biology**, school students today are just as likely to encounter in the form of 'Life and Living Processes'. As you will remember, this subject covers everything to do with any living thing (that has existed on the planet) from protozoa, fungi and fish, through to reptiles, birds and mammals – even ourselves.

Cells

Every living thing is made up of **cells**. All cells have inside them a nucleus, which determines how the cell behaves (except for red blood cells which have no nucleus), a mixture of chemicals (which include the cell's nutrition and resultant waste products) called cytoplasm, and a cell membrane through which nutrients and waste can pass.

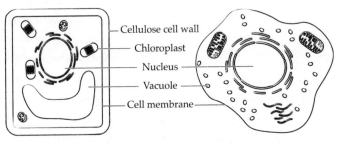

Cellulose cell wall
Chloroplast
Nucleus
Vacuole
Cell membrane

A plant cell and an animal cell

If you take a look at the illustration above, you will see that the main difference between animal and plant cells is that plant cells also have a cell wall (which compensates for the lack of a skeleton and helps the plant keep its shape) and chloroplasts. The chloroplasts contain chlorophyll, a green chemical which absorbs energy from the sun. It is the chlorophyll that allows the process called photosynthesis to occur, by which green plants make their own food.

Did you know...?
The biggest cell in humans is the ovum, or female sex cell, at a full 1 mm in diameter. After that comes the nerve cell. The smallest human cell is the male sperm cell. So who says size matters?

Tissue and organs

Just as a flat-packed build-it-yourself kitchen is made up of all manner of different components, so a huge variety of cells is needed to make up an animal or plant. Cells of the same type group together to form **tissue** (such as muscles, tendons and nerves, each of which has their own purpose), while several different tissues combine to make up an **organ**.

🕷 🕷 🕷

The Human Animal

It can be easy to forget, with everything that goes on in our busy lives, that humans are animals – highly-evolved animals, but animals all the same.[35] This means that there are certain characteristics and physical needs which we share with all other living creatures: we breathe, we move, we reproduce, our bodies have to stay healthy – and then we die. As the saying goes, all good things must come to an end.

---

[35] Although in the movie *The Matrix*, Agent Smith compares the human race to a virus because it has spread across the globe unchecked, devouring and destroying all the natural resources it comes into contact with!

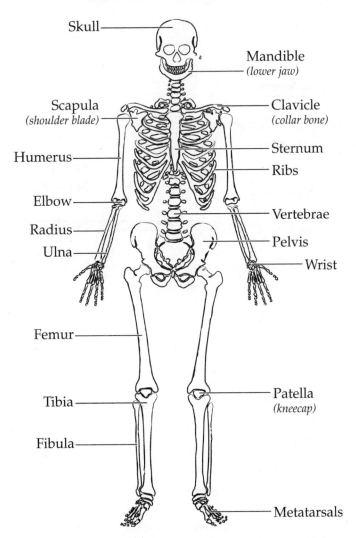

The human skeleton

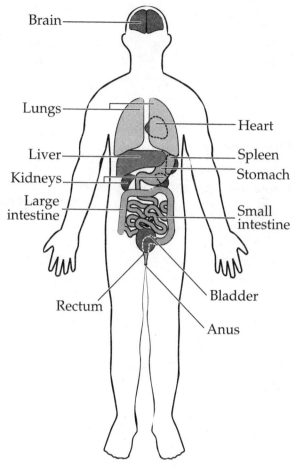

The human body

Did you know...?

The adult human body contains 206 bones. You are born with closer to 300, but many of these fuse together during childhood. The largest (and longest) bone in the human body is the femur, which extends from the hip to the knee. The smallest is the stirrup bone, one of three tiny bones which transmit sound from the eardrum to the inner ear. It is less than 3 mm long.

Did you know…?

Almost all mammals have the same number of vertebrae in their necks, from humans to giraffes to blue whales to mice. And the magic number? Seven.

Getting your breath back

Two other factors that make us just like every other animal on the planet are **breathing** and **respiration**. These are two distinctly different processes. They are closely connected – it is, in part, the action of breathing that allows respiration to occur – but they are not the same.

It might sound obvious, but breathing is the mechanical process by which we get oxygen into our bodies, and that is ultimately needed by our cells to keep them alive. The lungs transfer oxygen (from the air we breathe) into the bloodstream and also get rid of carbon dioxide expelled by our cells.

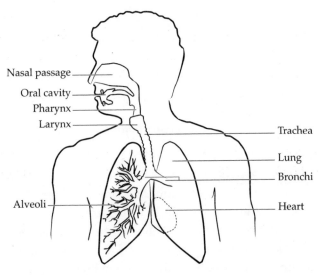

The human respiratory system

When you inhale, the intercostal muscles of the chest move the ribcage upwards and outwards. This enlarges the chest cavity (also called the thorax) and air fills the lungs as the air pressure inside is reduced.

Air enters the lungs and ends up inside the alveoli, tiny sacs only one cell thick. There are millions of alveoli, giving the inside of your lungs a massive surface area.[36] Oxygen is able to pass through this thin wall into blood capillaries which then transport it throughout the body to where it is needed.

When you exhale, the intercostal muscles move the ribcage down and in again, reducing the size of the chest cavity so that the pressure increases, forcing air out through the nose and mouth. It is perhaps surprising that we exhale most of the oxygen that we inhale in the first place. The air that we breathe in is roughly 21 per cent oxygen. The air that leaves our lungs again as we exhale is still 17 per cent oxygen.

Respiration, on the other hand, is the process by which all cells within the body produce energy from a combination of glucose (a sugar) and oxygen, which are carried to the cells in the blood supply. Respiration produces carbon dioxide and water as waste products, and these are then carried away from the cells, again through the blood.

glucose	+ oxygen	$\rightarrow$	carbon dioxide	+	water
$C_6H_{12}O_6$	+ $6O_2$	$\rightarrow$	$6CO_2$	+	$6H_2O$

---

[36] An adult's lungs have a surface area of approximately 140 m^2, which is roughly the same size as a tennis court!

Getting around

The fact that we are able to move at all is down to four things: **bones**, **muscles**, **ligaments** and **tendons**. (Although of course our brain has its part to play as well.) The point where two or more bones meet is called a joint. A joint allows movement of the skeleton, and most allow for a considerable amount of movement. Two of these synovial joints, as they are called (ones which allow for a considerable degree of movement), are hinge joints (as found in the knee) and ball and socket joints (as are found in the hips and shoulders).

At a joint, the different bones are held together by ligaments, but it is the muscles which actually control the movement of these joints. They are attached to the bones by tendons. There are many pairs of muscles all over the body that work in opposite directions to move limbs backwards and forwards. These are called antagonistic muscle pairs and they work as follows.

When a muscle contracts it gets shorter and fatter, and pulls on the bone. When it relaxes, it gets longer and does not tug on the bone any more; another muscle on the other side of the joint is needed to pull the bone in the opposite direction, again by contracting. If you think of your arm, when you flex your muscles your bicep stands out because it has contracted, getting shorter and fatter, and so shows up more. The tricep is the muscle on the underside of your arm which pulls it straight again, once you've finished showing off your fine athletic physique. The bicep and tricep, therefore, are working together as a pair; when one is contracted, the other is relaxed.

Getting lucky

All humans reproduce sexually.[37] During sexual reproduction a sperm cell (a male sex cell) joins with an egg, or ovum (a female sex cell), and a new living being is created.

Before human beings are able to reproduce, however, they undergo adolescence, whereby a child becomes an adult. The release of hormones (testosterone in boys and oestrogen in girls) required for this transition triggers physical changes known as puberty. Boys' voices typically deepen and girls develop both larger breasts and wider hips as gender differences begin to display themselves through body shape. Both sexes experience growth in bodily hair, as well as the more unwanted teenage side effects of greasy hair, body odour, spots and a general sense of being misunderstood. Also during this stage the reproductive organs grow to maturity and start producing sex cells of their own.

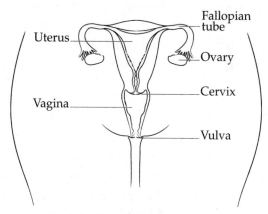

The female reproductive system

---

[37] Although some plants and animals can reproduce asexually (without the need for sex). An example of asexual reproduction in plants would be the taking of a cutting from a plant in order to grow another, identical specimen. Many invertebrates, such as sea stars and sea anemones, reproduce asexually, whereby an individual organism produces offspring that are genetically identical to itself.

When a woman is sexually mature, her body will undergo a monthly **menstrual cycle**. As part of this cycle, she will release a single egg from one of her ovaries (although in the case of twins,[38] triplets and so on, more than one egg is released at the same time). This is called ovulation.

This egg, which has the potential to become another human being if it is fertilised, travels slowly along the fallopian tube. At the same time, the fleshy lining of the uterus thickens, as the womb prepares itself to receive a fertilised egg, just in case. If the egg arrives in the uterus unfertilised, the lining falls away and is expelled from the body, along with the egg, through the vagina, resulting in a period (which is also called menstruation).

For the egg to become fertilised, sexual intercourse needs to take place so that a male sperm cell can be introduced to the female ovum. During intercourse, the erectile tissue of the man's penis becomes engorged with blood, so that it swells until it is erect. The penis is inserted into the vagina and sperm, produced in the testes, flows along the sperm tube and out of the urethra in a process called ejaculation, usually entering the woman's body at the cervix, the entrance to the uterus.

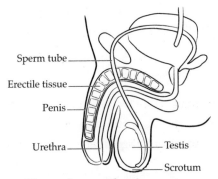

Sperm tube

Erectile tissue

Penis

Urethra

Testis

Scrotum

The male reproductive system

---

[38] Identical twins occur when a single egg is fertilised, but then divides into two separate embryos. Non-identical (or fraternal) twins occur when two fertilised eggs develop in the womb at the same time.

Did you know...?

All embryos start life as female with internal female organs. If the baby is to be a boy, from six weeks the genes on the Y chromosome cause the foetus to develop testicles which then produce the male hormone testosterone. It's this testosterone that makes the male organs grow. The clump of cells in the embryo that would have developed into ovaries then travel downwards to become the testes instead.

Fertilisation takes place inside the fallopian tubes where the swimming sperm meet the egg. Of all the millions of sperm that are released into the womb during ejaculation, only one little chap will make it through the outer membrane of the ovum.[39] The nuclei of the two sex cells then fuse. This one cell (now known as a zygote) then divides several times before it reaches the womb, becoming an embryo.

On reaching the uterus, the fertilised egg embeds itself in the thickened lining that has been prepared for it. It is here that the embryo develops into a foetus, joined to the placenta by the umbilical cord. The growing baby receives all the oxygen and food it needs from its mother via the umbilical cord, and waste materials are also passed back along it. The foetus is surrounded by amniotic fluid, a watery liquid that is much like a warm bath for the baby that also protects it from shock.

Pregnancy in humans lasts for nine months. In mice it lasts only 18–20 days, whereas the gestation period of an elephant is 22 months! By comparison, the blue whale is pregnant only for about a year.

---

[39] A man ejaculates between 1 and 5 ml of semen in one go, the average being 2–3 ml. The popular myth that a man ejaculates 9 cc is precisely that: a myth. And it's nothing compared to an adult wild male boar which produces half a litre in one go!

Incredibly, the embryos of many vertebrates (and not just mammals) start out looking very similar, possibly demonstrating just how closely related we are to our animal friends. However, as the foetuses develop, the differences become much more apparent.

Getting fit and healthy

How fit you are, or otherwise, is measured in terms of how capable you are of performing certain physical tasks and how quickly your body recovers afterwards. No matter what the latest faddy diet might suggest, there are only two things that you need to do to keep fit and healthy: eat a balanced diet and exercise regularly. You also need to keep away from drugs which can have a serious effect on the body. This includes nicotine and alcohol.

Eating a healthy, balanced diet provides your body with everything it needs to help it grow, repair itself and have enough energy to perform all the various activities required of it. Humans need to drink enough water, and to eat a combination of proteins, carbohydrates, fats,[40] vitamins, minerals and fibre to stay healthy.

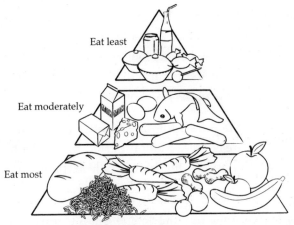

Eat least

Eat moderately

Eat most

Healthy eating pyramid

---

[40] Yes, weight watchers, even fats!

Proteins provide amino acids which are necessary for building up the body as well as repairing it. They are found in foods like meat, fish, milk and cheese.

Carbohydrates provide energy and include both sugars and starch, which are found in bread, potatoes, pasta and rice.

Fats, found in butter, oil, margarine and food cooked in these products, are needed by the body to store energy and keep it warm.

Saturated fats are normally solid at room temperature and are usually derived from animal products. They contain the maximum number of hydrogen atoms (they are 'saturated' with hydrogen atoms) and eating a diet high in these has been linked to an increased risk of coronary heart disease.

Unsaturated fats, on the other hand, come from vegetable sources. They are usually liquid at room temperature and are considered to be better for you, particularly if you are watching your cholesterol.

Small amounts of vitamins are also needed to keep the body healthy. They are found in abundance in fruit and vegetables. Small amounts of minerals are also required and are again found in fruit. However, the best sources of minerals tend to be green vegetables.

The insoluble fibre that we eat – which comes from foods such as fruit, vegetables, wholegrain cereals, bread and pasta – is not digested by the body but instead is needed to help keep things running smoothly within the digestive tract – more specifically assisting in clearing it out through the production of faeces.

The water we drink is vitally important. After all, we are approximately 60 per cent water ourselves! It is a natural solvent and is used to carry substances around the body. It also provides the right medium wherein certain important reactions can take place.

Digestion is the term used to describe the process by which the body breaks down food into molecules[41] that the body can absorb. It starts with chewing, where food is crushed and partially liquefied in the mouth. Saliva contains an enzyme[42] called amylase which starts to break down starch.

Most of the work is done in the stomach, where food is kept for some hours and mixed with gastric juices. Stomach acid contains hydrochloric acid which is powerful enough to kill most harmful bacteria. Enzymes called proteases break down proteins in the food.

Digestion continues after the food leaves the stomach. In the small intestine, stomach acid is neutralised with alkaline juices, and fats are broken down at this stage. The intestines also absorb the useful chemicals produced by the digestive process. It is not until it reaches the large intestine that water is absorbed into the blood. Whatever's left afterwards can't be used by the body and so is formed into faeces. These are stored inside the rectum before eventually being passed out through the anus.

Getting ill

Of course, no matter how careful you are with what you put into your body and how regularly you exercise, it is almost inevitable that at some point you are going to get ill. This is because there

---

[41] The building blocks of a cell.
[42] Enzymes are proteins that accelerate chemical reactions.

are all sorts of other living things out there which seem to think that human beings make the perfect breeding grounds and have everything that the aspiring bacteria need to get on in life.

Various kinds of micro-organisms – everything from bacteria to viruses, and even fungi – can cause ill-health. They can enter the body through any orifice, as well as through a cut in the skin (the huge organ that covers the outside of your body). Bacteria make you sick because they produce toxins, whereas a virus damages the cells themselves.

Did you know...?
Bacteria are the most successful living organisms in existence! They are found in all sorts of hostile environments, from the bottom of the ocean to the bottom of your gut, and, in the end, they eat every other living thing on the planet.

Bacteria and viruses differ in a number of important ways. A bacterium[43] has a cell wall and a cell membrane while a virus has a coating of protein. A bacterium has genes and cytoplasm, but no nucleus, while a virus has both genes and a nucleus, but no cytoplasm. Bacteria can reproduce outside of living cells (meaning they can breed quite happily on your kitchen chopping board) and are destroyed by antibiotics, but viruses can reproduce only inside living cells and antibiotics don't have any effect on them. This is why when you go to the doctor because you are feeling terrible, and he tells you that you have a virus, there is absolutely nothing he can prescribe to make you feel any better!

The body does its best to stop you getting ill to begin with in a number of ways. Firstly, the skin acts as a barrier to stop anything nasty getting inside. Secondly, the organs used for

---

[43] The singular form of 'bacteria'.

breathing produce a sticky mucus which traps harmful microbes. And thirdly, blood platelets are produced to seal off any cuts or grazes.

If something unpleasant does get into the bloodstream, the white blood cells come into play. They engulf microbes and then produce natural antibodies which destroy them. They also manufacture antitoxins to counter the effects of any poisons that the microbe might emit. In the end, the white blood cells digest the miscreant.

Once you've had one disease, your body knows how to counter it the next time you might succumb to the same disease, and so is more likely to be able to stop it before you get ill. As a result, you may become immune.

Did you know...?
The green colour of the mucus that appears on your handkerchief when you blow your nose comes from immune cells called neutrophils. When you get a cold, neutrophils engulf the bacteria and destroy them using digestive enzymes, some of which (such as *lactoferrin*) need iron to be active. Ferrous iron compounds are green and so that's why snot is green. And have you ever wondered why snot is so appetising to children? It's because it has basically the same ingredients as junk food: complex sugars, sodium and water!

🕷 🕷 🕷

Flower Power

Of course **plants** are living organisms too, but they vary from human beings and other animals in some very important ways. For a start, they do not have organs (although they are made up of different types of tissue) and they do not have skeletons.

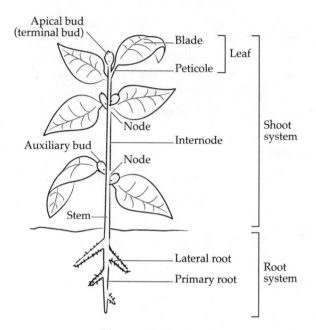

The parts of a plant

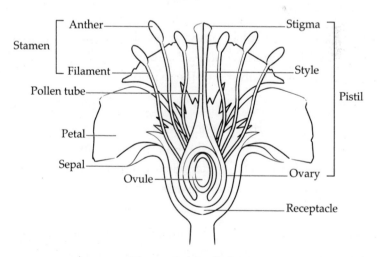

The parts of a flower

Did you know...?

A mature oak tree can draw up 50 gallons or more of water from the soil through its roots each day. Oak trees can live for up to 500 years, and by the time a tree is 100 years old, it produces up to 2,200 acorns annually.

Photosynthesis

Unlike animals, green plants are able to produce food for themselves via the process of **photosynthesis**. This occurs inside the leaves and involves a chemical reaction taking place between water drawn up into the plant from the soil by its roots and carbon dioxide absorbed by the leaves from the air.

$$\text{carbon dioxide} + \text{water} \xrightarrow[\text{chlorophyll}]{\text{light}} \text{glucose} + \text{oxygen}$$

$$6CO_2 + 6H_2O \rightarrow C_6H_{12}O_6 + 6O_2$$

The process takes place only in sunlight, with the green-pigmented chlorophyll contained within the cells in the plant's leaves acting as a catalyst[44] for the reaction.

So that they can absorb as much sunlight as possible, leaves usually have a large surface area.[45] They are also thin so that carbon dioxide is easily absorbed. The CO_2 enters through stomata (most of which are on the underside of the leaf), and it is through these that oxygen and water are expelled by the plant.

---

[44] A substance that accelerates the rate of a chemical reaction.

[45] A noticeable exception are conifers, the leaves of which have evolved to become needles to cope with the cold conditions in which these trees normally grow.

The surface of a leaf is called the cuticle and has a waxy exterior to stop water evaporating from it. Beneath this is a layer of cells called the epidermis, and below that the palisade cells. These contain a large number of chloroplasts, which contain the chlorophyll and so are where photosynthesis actually occurs.

As well as being helpful to the plant, because it provides it with food, photosynthesis is also vitally important to the rest of the planet, as it helps to replace the oxygen in the atmosphere.

Did you know...?
The Amazon rainforest covers an area of over 1.2 billion acres, two-fifths of the whole of South America. With 2.5 million square miles of rainforest, the Amazon represents 54 per cent of the total rainforests left on the planet. The Amazon rainforest has been described as the 'Lungs of the Planet' because more than 20 per cent of the world's oxygen is produced by the plants growing there.

However, plants don't need just photosynthesis for healthy growth. As well as taking up water, the roots that keep a plant secure in the soil also absorb the minerals dissolved within the water. Phosphorous is vital for effective root growth, nitrogen is needed to help leaves and stems grow, and without potassium the plant couldn't produce flowers, which are an indispensable part of the reproductive process.[46] Essential minerals, such as these, can be provided by adding fertilisers to the soil in which the plant is growing.

Sulphur, calcium and magnesium are also needed by the plant, but only trace amounts of each. Magnesium is essential for photosynthesis to occur, as without it the plant cannot produce enough chlorophyll.

※ ※ ※

---

[46] Just as they can aid human reproduction, on occasions.

Variety is the Spice Life

All humans form one species, meaning that although we all differ from one another, we still share certain characteristics. These include having one head, two arms and two legs, being designed to walk upright, reproducing sexually and breathing using our lungs. However, there are just as many ways in which everyone differs from everyone else, such as in terms of eye colour, weight, skin tone and so on. These differences between species and individuals of the same species are referred to as **variation**.

Whether a living organism is one species or another is determined by the genetic information stored in its DNA.[47] In your case, this information was inherited from your parents and was contained in both the sperm cell and ovum that fused to create you. It determines everything about you from your gender and your hair colour, to your height and your body shape.

> 'People are DNA's way of making more DNA.'
> (Edward O. Wilson, 1975)

That same information can be found in any one of the trillions of cells that make up your body, contained within their nuclei. So, in theory, an identical copy of you could be created from any one of your cells, assuming you had a handy home-cloning kit lying around.

Did you know...?

Chimpanzees share around 98 per cent of their DNA with us – but then that's hardly surprising when you consider how all of our major organs work in the same way. And besides, humans share 50 per cent of their DNA with bananas!

---

[47] DNA = Deoxyribonucleic acid.

Classification

All living things, including plants, animals and human beings, are classified into different taxonomic groups. **Taxonomy** is the science of classifying plants and animals.

It was Carl Linnaeus (1707–78) who introduced the system of classifying species of organisms into certain groups. With great forethought he gave these taxonomic groups scientific Latin names, allowing people to use the same system all over the world.

The main categories into which living things are divided, from the broadest groups to the most detailed, are as follows:

Kingdom
Phylum, division
Class
Order
(Superfamily, stirps)
Family
Genus
Species
(Subspecies, variety, race, stock, strain, breed)
Individual

Every living thing belongs to one of five different kingdoms, based on what the organism's cells are like.

Kingdom	Examples
Protoctists	Organisms such as amoebae and paramecia.
Prokaryotes	Bacteria and blue-green algae.
Fungi	Mushrooms, moulds and yeast.

Kingdom	Examples
Plants	All green plants, including algae, plants that do not produce seeds (such as ferns and mosses), as well as plants that are seed producers (such as conifers and flowering plants).
Animals	All multi-cellular animals from jellyfish and worms, through molluscs and amphibians to fish, birds and mammals.

The animal kingdom is subdivided again into vertebrates (creatures that have backbones) and invertebrates (those without backbones).

Vertebrates are then divided again into either reptiles, amphibians or fish (all cold-blooded animals), and birds or mammals (which are warm-blooded).

Did you know...?
Cold-blooded creatures are unable to control their own body temperatures and so are as warm or as cold as their surroundings. However, by means of internal processes, warm-blooded animals can keep their body temperatures the same whatever the temperature of their surroundings.

Invertebrates are divided into coelenterates, flatworms, annelids, molluscs, echinoderms and arthropods.

There are four smaller groups within arthropods, depending on the number of legs they have. These are: centipedes and millipedes (creatures with more than twenty legs), crustaceans (those with ten to fourteen legs), arachnids (that have eight legs) and insects (with only six legs). Although they do not have a backbone, arthropods do have a tough outer coating called an exoskeleton.

Different species of creatures can be grouped into different phyla within the animal kingdom.

Animal Kingdom

Phyla	Features	Examples
Protozoa	Organisms made up of a single cell	Amoebae
Sponges	Animals made of similar cells joined together loosely	Sponges
Cnidaria	Creatures with body walls made of only two layers of cells	Sea anemones Jellyfish
Flat worms	Having a flattened, worm-like shape	Tape worms
Annelida	Worms with segmented bodies	Earthworms
Arthropoda	Animals with jointed legs and segmented bodies	Insects (insecta) Spiders (arachnida) Centipedes (myrapoda)
Mollusca	Having no segments but rather a fleshy pad on which to crawl	Slugs Snails Razor shellfish
Echinodermata	Having a star-shaped body and spiny skin	Starfish
Fish	Creatures with paired fins and gills	Salmon Sharks Minnows
Amphibia	Animals with slimy skin, which spend some of their lives in water and lay their eggs in water	Frogs Toads Newts Salamanders
Reptilia	Creatures with dry, scaly skin, which lay their eggs on land	Snakes Lizards Chameleons

Phyla	Features	Examples
Aves	Animals with feathers and which lay their eggs on land[48]	Sparrows Penguins Ostriches
Mammalia	Having hair and giving birth to live young, which they then feed with milk excreted from special glands	Rabbits Horses Whales Gorillas Humans

Different species of plants can be grouped within the plant kingdom in a similar way. One of the means of dividing plants is as follows:

Plant Kingdom

Plants without seeds					Plants with seeds	
Algae	Mosses	Fungi	Ferns	Lichens	Conifers	Flowering plants

Here are four examples of how very different living things can all be classified according to Carl Linnaeus's system:

	Meadow buttercup	Great white shark	Common kestrel	Human being
Kingdom	*Plantae*	*Animalia*	*Animalia*	*Animalia*
Phylum, division	*Magnoliophyta*	*Chordata*	*Chordata*	*Chordata*
Class	*Magnoliopsida*	*Chondrichthyes*	*Aves*	*Mammalia*
Order	*Ranunculales*	*Lamniformes*	*Falconiformes*	*Primates*
Family	*Ranunculaceae*	*Lamnidae*	*Falconidae*	*Hominidae*
Genus	*Ranunculus*	*Carcharodon*	*Falco*	*Homo*
Species	*Ranunculus acris*	*Carcharodon carcharias*	*Falco tinnunculus*	*Homo sapiens*

---

[48] In other words, birds.

Inheritance

Genetic information is passed from one generation of living things to the next by means of threads of **DNA** stored within chromosomes which are themselves found inside the nuclei of cells.[49]

There are 23 pairs of chromosomes found in most human cells: 22 of these are ordinary pairs and the last remaining pair are sex chromosomes. If these sex chromosomes are alike (called XX) the person is female. If they are different (XY) they are male.

Genes are the instructions carried by a chromosome which determine every characteristic of a human being, from eye and hair colour to a person's blood group. There are two copies of each gene in a normal body cell, one in each chromosome, so one gene comes from the mother and one from the father.

Variation between siblings (as in variation between entirely different species) is the result of mutation, as much as it is down to having a different mix of genes.

Did you know...?
Dogs have the greatest range of variation of any animal species. All kinds of dogs – from chihuahuas and Rottweilers to Great Danes and poodles – are all the same species!

Discontinuous variation is the way in which the population can be separated according to clearly distinguishable groups, such as by blood group. Continuous variation applies to things which cannot be separated into clearly different groups, such as height and weight.

---

[49] Except for red blood cells, of course.

Mutation happens when a mistake occurs during the process of copying chromosomes when cells divide. Radiation and certain chemicals can also cause cells to mutate. Most mutations are considered to be harmful but good mutations are also possible. For example, blue eyes (which many people find very appealing) are a mutation. Originally our human ancestors all had brown eyes!

Selection

Natural selection – an expression popularised by the work of Charles Darwin (1809–82) – is the process by which favourable traits, which can be inherited, become more common generation after generation. As this occurs, those traits which would be considered unfavourable become less common. It's also referred to as **evolution**.

However, mankind has also forced certain species of animals and plants to evolve in a particular way, mainly through selective breeding. By choosing to breed only animals that display certain desirable characteristics, farmers have changed the way that certain domesticated species have developed. They have done the same with particular strains of plant.

🕷 🕷 🕷

Living Things in their Environment

Every living thing is affected by the environment in which it lives, including the other organisms that share its **habitat** (the place where it lives, feeds and reproduces). The habitat will provide everything that the organism needs to survive, including shelter as well as food and a place to reproduce.

For example, a pond and its surroundings presents a frog with all of these things, while a pile of rotting leaves under a hedge furnishes an earthworm with food, shelter and somewhere to produce young.

Any animal will have adapted to exist comfortably within in its environment. For example, a fish has gills, a tail and fins, all of which allow it to live in water. Plants adapt in the same way. Bluebells grow in woodland and flower in the spring, before the trees block out the sun when summer arrives.

And of course all animals need to eat to stay alive. Plants that take carbon dioxide and water from their immediate surroundings to produce their own food, in the form of glucose, effectively end up making all of the food that animals in a food chain need to survive. Because of this, plants are called producers. The animals which eat the plants (such as slugs and pond snails) are the primary consumers. Other animals which eat these primary consumers (such as shrews and sticklebacks) are called secondary consumers. Tertiary consumers (like stoats and pike) feed off the secondary consumers.

Animals can be grouped according to what they eat. Herbivores consume only plants. Carnivores devour meat. Animals which are quite happy eating both plants and meat (such as humans) are called omnivores (meaning 'eats all').

Did you know...?

There are other even more specialised feeders. Mosquitoes, leeches and ticks are like vampires, in that they are haemovores and so feed off blood. Insectivores, like bats and spiders, are specialised carnivores which live off insects. There are even things which clear up the waste of other creatures – by eating it. Organisms that do this, such as dung beetles, are called coprovores.

Food chains and food webs

Here is an example of a simple **food chain**, in which grass is the producer.

$$sun \rightarrow grass \rightarrow zebra \rightarrow lion$$

Grass photosynthesises glucose during the hours of daylight. Herds of zebra then eat the grass and these animals are, in turn, preyed upon by lions.

However, in reality the feeding relationships between creatures sharing a habitat are much more complex. They can be shown most clearly using a food web, which is made up of a number of food chains joined together.

In the case of a food web which has an oak tree as the producer, due to the complex web of interconnecting feeding relationships, it soon becomes clear how the loss of a habitat or a dramatic change within it can affect everything living in that habitat as well. For example, if the oak were to be cut down, the animals that feed directly from it, like squirrels, beetles and aphids, could no longer survive. This in turn would lead to the disappearance of the secondary consumers that feed on them, such as woodpeckers and swallows. As a direct result of this, the kestrel would be deprived of its diet. So the loss of the tree could ultimately lead to the loss of the kestrel.

Predator–prey relationships

Predator–prey relationships follow a clear pattern which sees the populations of both the predators (carnivorous animals) and their prey increase and decline directly according to the status of the other.

For example, on a piece of land there is a colony of rabbits. Foxes arrive and hunt the rabbits as their prey. As the rabbit population declines, due to being hunted by the foxes, the fox population increases, as a consequence of having a plentiful food supply. However, the more foxes there are, the more rabbits they need to catch in order to survive. When the rabbit population declines past a certain point, the foxes no longer have enough food to sustain them, and so they die off as well. The more foxes that die in this way, the fewer predators there are to prey on the rabbits, and so the rabbit population increases again.

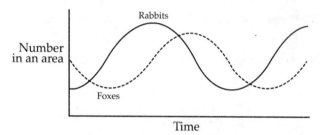

The predator–prey relationship

As can be seen, the prey population is at its lowest not long after the predator population has been at its greatest. Conversely, when there are the fewest predators around, that is when the prey's numbers will rise to their highest.

⚦ Spot Test! ⚦

Surprise, surprise, here's another quick quiz to see what you can remember from the last chapter. You should've seen this one coming really, so we expect great things from you.

Parents, could you calmly (and accurately) explain the facts of life to your kids? And kids, next time you spot a creepy crawly, could you safely say which taxonomic group you should put it in?

There's only one way to find out! Eyes down and start writing.

1) Which part of the flower consists of the anther and the filament?
2) What is the largest (and longest) bone in the human body?
3) What are the sex chromosomes for a male?
4) What is the singular form of bacteria?
5) In a predator–prey relationship, when there are lots of rabbits, what will happen to the fox population?
6) Who first developed the system of taxonomy?
7) Name the tiny sacs, only one cell thick, in your lungs that help oxygen get into your bloodstream.
8) What does DNA stand for?
9) What acid can be found in the stomach?
10) What is the term to describe an organism that can reproduce without the need for sex?

Chapter Four

CHEMISTRY
Elementary, My Dear Watson[50]

Chemistry has long had a strange, alluring hold over school pupils. It seems that they just can't wait to enter the lab – which they envision being like something out of a Hammer horror film – to mix together highly improbably coloured compounds. In the best tradition of such mad scientist-style experiments, the chemistry student secretly harbours the hope that these will result in some kind of dramatic explosion or produce a bubbling elixir which would make Dr Jekyll proud.

The reality in the modern classroom, of course, is often a lot less dramatic. And yet the potential that lies in grasping the concepts of chemistry is no less exciting!

---

[50] As Sherlock Holmes *never* said during any of his escapades, as related by Sir Arthur Conan Doyle.

☠ Materials and their Properties ☠

Chemistry, or 'Materials and their Properties' as it is now also known, is the subject that examines the very building blocks that everything else is constructed from – atoms, molecules and elements. It is also the subject that studies what happens when two volatile substances react in the presence of one another.[51]

Elements, Compounds and Mixtures

Everything in the world around us is made from different **materials**, such as stone, wood, glass and plastic. These are themselves made from **elements**, the most basic building materials, which are in turn broken down into **atoms**.

Atoms are made up of three sub-atomic particles: protons, neutrons and electrons.[52] Protons have a relative charge of +1 and electrons have a relative charge of –1 (*neut*rons have a *neut*ral charge of 0). An equal number of protons and electrons means the atom is electrically neutral overall. The nucleus of an atom is made up of the neutrons and protons. The electrons, on the other hand, 'orbit' the nucleus, a bit like our solar system.

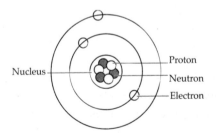

The structure of an atom

---

[51] Rather like the participants of reality TV shows like *Wife Swap* and *Big Brother*.
[52] Atoms were first suggested as a philosophical concept in Ancient Greece. The Greek word, *atomos*, literally meant 'the smallest indivisible part of matter'. Which as you've just found out, isn't quite correct.

Did you know...?

Atoms are mostly made of ... nothing! There is a large amount of space (comparatively) between the nucleus of the atom and the electrons orbiting it. In fact, if the nucleus was a pea in the middle of a cricket pitch, the electrons would be as far away as the furthest seats.

There are roughly 100 known elements. Each one is represented by a different chemical symbol. These symbols are the same no matter where you are in the world.

Most elements are classed as metals. There are many more metals than non-metals. To complicate matters, there are some elements that display properties which put them between metals and non-metals.

Metals share certain characteristics, as do non-metals. Metals are solid at room temperature (with the exception of mercury,[53] gallium, caesium and francium), shiny, have a high density, conduct both heat and electricity and are malleable (meaning they can be shaped) or ductile (drawn out into thin wires).

Non-metals are solid, liquid or gas at room temperature, have a dull finish, a low density, do not conduct heat and electricity (other than graphite, a form of carbon[54]) and are brittle.

All of the elements can be found on the Periodic Table of the chemical elements, the invention of which is usually credited to Dmitri Mendeleev, a Russian chemist who came up with the

---

[53] Mercury has a melting point of –38.83°C which is why it is used in thermometers and barometers. Mercury used to be called quicksilver, and its chemical symbol Hg originates from the Greek word *hydrargyrum*, meaning 'liquid silver'.

[54] Other forms of carbon are coal and diamonds! In fact, the parts of *us* that aren't water are mainly carbon.

Atomic number — Symbol — Name

6
C
Carbon

1 H Hydrogen																	2 He Helium
3 Li Lithium	4 Be Beryllium											5 B Boron	6 C Carbon	7 N Nitrogen	8 O Oxygen	9 F Fluorine	10 Ne Neon
11 Na Sodium	12 Mg Magnesium											13 Al Aluminium	14 Si Silicon	15 P Phosphorus	16 S Sulphur	17 Cl Chlorine	18 Ar Argon
19 K Potassium	20 Ca Calcium	21 Sc Scandium	22 Ti Titanium	23 V Vanadium	24 Cr Chromium	25 Mn Manganese	26 Fe Iron	27 Co Cobalt	28 Ni Nickel	29 Cu Copper	30 Zn Zinc	31 Ga Gallium	32 Ge Germanium	33 As Arsenic	34 Se Selenium	35 Br Bromine	36 Kr Krypton
37 Rb Rubidium	38 Sr Strontium	39 Y Yttrium	40 Zr Zirconium	41 Nb Niobium	42 Mo Molybdenum	43 Tc Technetium	44 Ru Ruthenium	45 Rh Rhodium	46 Pd Palladium	47 Ag Silver	48 Cd Cadmium	49 In Indium	50 Sn Tin	51 Sb Antimony	52 Te Tellurium	53 I Iodine	54 Xe Xenon
55 Cs Caesium	56 Ba Barium	57 La Lanthanum	72 Hf Hafnium	73 Ta Tantalum	74 W Tungsten	75 Re Rhenium	76 Os Osmium	77 Ir Iridium	78 Pt Platinum	79 Au Gold	80 Hg Mercury	81 Tl Thallium	82 Pb Lead	83 Bi Bismuth	84 Po Polonium	85 At Astatine	86 Rn Radon
87 Fr Francium	88 Ra Radium	89 Ac Actinium	104 Rf Rutherfordium	105 Db Dubnium	106 Sg Seaborgium	107 Bh Bohrium	108 Hs Hassium	109 Mt Meitnerium	110 Ds Darmstadtium	111 Rg Roentgenium	112 Uub Ununbium	113 Uut Ununtrium	114 Uuq Ununquadium	115 Uup Ununpentium	116 Uuh Ununhexium	117 Uus Ununseptium	118 Uuo Ununoctium

58 Ce Cerium	59 Pr Praseodymium	60 Nd Neodymium	61 Pm Promethium	62 Sm Samarium	63 Eu Europium	64 Gd Gadolinium	65 Tb Terbium	66 Dy Dysprosium	67 Ho Holmium	68 Er Erbium	69 Tm Thulium	70 Yb Ytterbium	71 Lu Lutetium
90 Th Thorium	91 Pa Protactinium	92 U Uranium	93 Np Neptunium	94 Pu Plutonium	95 Am Americium	96 Cm Curium	97 Bk Berkelium	98 Cf Californium	99 Es Einsteinium	100 Fm Fermium	101 Md Mendelevium	102 No Nobelium	103 Lr Lawrencium

The periodic table

idea in 1869. Mendeleev wanted the table to illustrate recurring trends in the properties of the different elements. As new elements have been discovered, the layout of the table has been refined and extended.

Chemical compounds

A **compound** is something that is made by combining different elements. Water is one (two hydrogen atoms combined with one oxygen atom to make H_2O, technically hydrogen oxide) and another, albeit a rather more complex compound, is glucose $(C_6H_{12}O_6)$ – in other words, sugar. A chemical compound may have different properties from the elements that combined to create it and it is impossible (or at least very hard) to separate them again.

Our homes are full of different chemical compounds. You might be surprised to learn how familiar some of these are.

Compound	Scientific name	Chemical formula	Number of atoms it is made from
Table salt	Sodium chloride	NaCl	1 sodium + 1 chlorine
Toothpaste	Sodium fluoride (active ingredient)	NaF	1 sodium + 1 fluoride
Chalk (a form of limestone)	Calcium carbonate	$CaCO_3$	1 calcium + 1 carbon + 3 oxygen
Baking soda	Sodium bicarbonate	$NaHCO_3$	1 sodium + 1 hydrogen + 1 carbon + 3 oxygen
Milk of Magnesia (indigestion remedy)	Magnesium hydroxide	$Mg(OH)_2$	1 magnesium + 2 oxygen + 2 hydrogen

Compound	Scientific name	Chemical formula	Number of atoms it is made from
Refined sugar	Sucrose	$C_{12}H_{22}O_{11}$	12 carbon + 22 hydrogen + 11 oxygen
Soap	Sodium stearate	$C_{17}H_{35}COONa$	17 carbon + 35 hydrogen + 1 carbon + 1 oxygen + 1 oxygen + 1 sodium
Epsom salts	Magnesium sulphate heptahydrate	$MgSO_4.7H_2O$	1 magnesium + 1 sulphur + 4 oxygen *combined with* 14 hydrogen + 7 oxygen
Anti-dandruff shampoo	Zinc pyrithione (active ingredient)	$C_{10}H_8N_2O_2S_2Zn$	10 carbon + 8 hydrogen + 2 nitrogen + 2 oxygen + 2 sulphur + 1 zinc
Washing soda	Sodium carbonate	Na_2CO_3	2 sodium + 1 carbon + 3 oxygen

Did you know...?

If a compound is made up of two different elements, such as carbon dioxide (CO_2), its chemical name will always end with the letters –ide. Compounds that contain three different elements (one of them being oxygen) always end in –ate, such as sodium carbonate ($NaCO_3$).

Did you know...?

Simply by combining carbon, hydrogen and oxygen in different proportions, you end up with testosterone, vanilla, aspirin, glucose, vinegar and alcohol, which are all made from just those three elements.

Mixtures

A **mixture** is something made from a number of elements or compounds but which have not reacted together to create a new substance. The elements and compounds that make up mixtures are usually easy to separate and still possess the same properties that they did before being combined. Mixtures often have impurities mixed in with them.

An obvious example of a mixture is air, the composition of which depends on where you are. It is generally accepted that air is composed of approximately 79 per cent nitrogen (N_2) and 21 per cent oxygen (O_2), but with tiny quantities of other gases in the mix, such as argon (Ar), neon (Ne), methane (CH_4), hydrogen (H_2), helium (He) and krypton (Kr), as well as 0.04 per cent carbon dioxide (CO_2).

However, in a crowded space or on a motorway, there will be greater proportions of gases such as carbon dioxide (CO_2) and carbon monoxide (CO).

Did you know...?

Carbon monoxide (CO) is a colourless, odourless gas that is also highly toxic to humans. It is the most common type of fatal poisoning in many countries, and usually occurs in the home, due to faulty gas appliances. However, it is highly useful in modern technology. For example, it is carbon monoxide that helps packed meat appear fresher for longer, and it has many applications in bulk chemicals manufacturing, being a principal component of syngas, which is often used for industrial power.

Some other common mixtures are sea water, petrol and alloys[55] like brass and steel. The elements and compounds that make them up can all be separated, either through distillation or other processes that often involve cooling and melting.

Some of the common chemicals found in your home shouldn't be mixed together. Bleach mixed with acid toilet bowl cleaners can result in toxic, potentially deadly fumes. Bleach mixed with vinegar (another type of acid) produces toxic chlorine vapour, while bleach mixed with ammonia will also produce toxic, and potentially lethal, fumes.

Did you know...?

Gunpowder (first discovered by the Chinese in the 9th century) is a mixture of several elements and compounds. First comes charcoal, which is carbon (C), then sulphur (S), once called brimstone, and lastly saltpetre, which is actually potassium nitrate (KNO_3). A simplified chemical equation for the combustion of gunpowder is:

$$10\ KNO_3 + 3\ S + 8\ C \longrightarrow 2\ K_2CO_3 + 3\ K_2SO_4 + 6\ CO_2 + 5\ N_2$$

States of matter

Substances can also be grouped as **solids**, **liquids** or **gases**; the three states of matter.[56] At room temperature (which is taken to be 20°C) a solid is a substance which has a melting point above

---

[55] An alloy is a mixture of metals, such as the nickel–chrome alloy used for dental fillings.

[56] There are in fact more like fifteen states of matter, at the last count. They are: solid, amorphous solid, liquid, gas, plasma, super-fluid, supersolid, degenerate matter, neutronium, strongly symmetric matter, weakly symmetric matter, quark-gluon plasma, fermionic condensate, Bose-Einstein condensate (or 'bec') and strange matter. However, students studying chemistry at GCSE level and below need to worry only about the standard three.

20°C, a liquid is a substance which has a melting point below 20°C but a boiling point above 20°C, and a gas is a substance which has a boiling point below 20°C.

All substances are made from tiny particles (atoms or molecules) but it is the arrangement of these that determines whether it is a solid, a liquid or a gas. In a solid the particles are packed together tightly, allowing for very little movement, no more than minute vibrations. In a liquid the particles are still close together but not so regularly arranged as in a solid. This allows for greater freedom of movement. However, in a gas the particles are spaced widely apart and are continually moving rapidly in all directions.

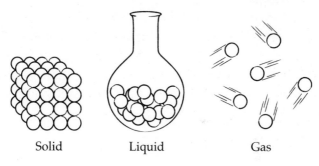

Solid   Liquid   Gas

Phases of matter

Solids are also either soluble (meaning that they can be dissolved) or insoluble (meaning that they can't). If a solid (such as table salt) is dissolved in a solvent (something in which something else can be dissolved – in this example, water) a solution is produced (in this case, salt water). If more and more of the solid is added to the solution, there will come a point where it becomes a saturated solution, meaning that nothing more can be dissolved within it.

Mixtures that have been made by dissolving solids in a solution can be separated again by a variety of means. Sometimes (as in the case of salt water) evaporation (whereby molecules in a liquid state spontaneously become gaseous, leaving the dissolved solid behind) is enough. Another method of separating mixtures is by a process called distillation (a method of separating chemical substances based on differences in their boiling points). Chromatography (which relies on the molecules in mixtures having different characteristics so that they travel at different speeds when pulled along a piece of paper by a solvent) can also be used to separate mixtures made by combining a substance with water.

☠ **Geological Changes**[57] ☠

The classic, almost cartoon-ish, image of the chemist is that of a bespectacled scientist combining brightly coloured liquids from strangely shaped glass flasks which inevitably explode, leaving his clothes and face covered in soot and his hair sticking straight up as a result.

However, as well as describing what substances are made up of, a large part of the chemist's role is working out how substances can be combined and changed to either create something else or to cause a desired reaction to occur.

But it is not only scientists who do this. Reactions are continually occurring in the world around us, and often they have little or nothing to do with the influence of human beings.

Rock 'n' Roll

The Earth is constantly in a state of flux: its shape is altered by the internal workings of the planet, the movement of its tectonic plates, and the very rocks from which it is formed suffer the effects of the elements.[58]

The rocks are thousands of millions of years old, first forming when the planet itself took shape, as spinning particles of space debris were caught in the gravitational field of our sun and joined together to become the Earth.

---

[57] Geology is the science and study of the solid matter that constitutes the Earth, so obviously there is a cross-over with geography, which is the study of the Earth and its features, inhabitants, and phenomena.

[58] That is sun, wind and rain, rather than carbon, sulphur, hydrogen and the rest – although such elements do have their part to play in the weathering process.

Like everything else, **rocks** are made from chemical compounds which, in this case, are called **minerals**. These minerals can take the form of crystals and/or grains (which are packed tightly together).

The Earth is made up of three types of rock, **sedimentary**, **metamorphic** and **igneous**.

Type of rock	How it is formed	What it is like	Examples
Sedimentary (*formed from sediment*)	Rocks are eroded or weathered and break up into pieces. These pieces are transported to the sea where they sink to the bottom as sediment. This sediment is then crushed under the weight of other rocks until it is cemented together.	Made up of grains. May contain fossils.	Limestone Chalk Sandstone Breccia
Metamorphic (*changed in form*)	Formed when sedimentary rock is subjected to very high temperatures and pressures.	May contain crystals but can also be non-crystalline.	Slate Marble Schist Quartzite
Igneous (*formed by fire*)	Created when magma from inside the Earth is cooled and crystallises (as during a volcanic eruption).	The size of crystals formed depends on how quickly the magma cools. If it is quickly, the crystals are small; slowly, and the crystals are larger.	Basalt Granite Pumice Obsidian

Did you know...?
Chalk (calcium carbonate) is formed from the skeletal remains of tiny sea creatures that lived at the bottom of Earth's pre-historic oceans millions of years ago. However, the chalk your teachers at school used to write on the blackboard – or threw at you in annoyance – is not chalk at all but gypsum (hydrated calcium sulphate). 75 per cent of all gypsum is used in building, as it is an essential ingredient of concrete, cement and plaster.

Weathering

Over time, rocks are broken down by the effects of **weathering**. This weathering takes three forms. **Mechanical weathering** occurs when rocks are heated up during the day by the sun and then cooled down again at night. As the rock gets hotter it expands. As it cools, it contracts. This causes stresses within the rock which eventually lead to cracks forming. Water can then enter these cracks, and if it gets cold enough for the water to freeze, the expanding ice accelerates the destructive process. The repeated freezing and thawing effect that causes rocks to break down is called freeze-thaw.

Rocks can also be broken down by chemical reactions and this is known as **chemical weathering**. Rain can cause chemical weathering as rain water is actually a weak acid called carbonic acid (H_2CO_3), since it has carbon dioxide dissolved in it. This acid reacts with limestone ($CaCO_3$), from which many buildings are made, to form calcium hydrogen carbonate ($Ca(HCO_3)_2$), which is also water-soluble. This means that they are effectively being washed away. But don't worry, you're not going to see Big Ben floating off down the Thames any time soon.

The third form of weathering is **biological weathering**. It is caused by the action of plants working on the rocks. For example, when a tree grows on a cliff top, its roots penetrate the rocks, causing stresses which can lead to the rocks being broken up.

Many buildings are effectively made from rock, just like much of the landscape around us. As a result they are susceptible to the effects of weathering as well. These effects have been exacerbated by industrial pollution and acidic compounds dissolved in rain water literally eating away the stones that buildings are constructed from.

The Rock Cycle

As you can see, the substance of the Earth is constantly being eroded away and recycled by the planet, so that new rock is also being formed at the same time. This effect is described by the rock cycle (see opposite).

Igneous rocks are produced by crystallising magma (which is molten rock) and either come to the surface of the planet during volcanic eruptions, or as a result of something called **slow uplift**. These rocks are then broken down by weathering and erosion, eventually becoming sediment. This sediment is transformed into sedimentary rocks which can then become metamorphic rocks, if the conditions are right. Some rock also returns to the magma beneath the Earth's crust and thus completes the cycle.

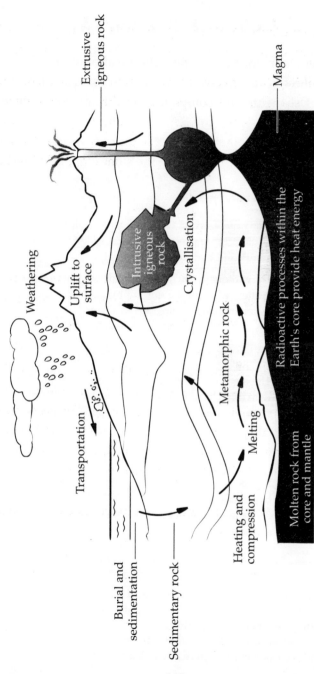

Extrusive
igneous rock

Magma

Weathering

Uplift to
surface

Intrusive
igneous
rock

Crystallisation

Transportation

Metamorphic rock

Radioactive processes within the
Earth's core provide heat energy

Melting

Heating and
compression

Burial and
sedimentation

Sedimentary rock

Molten rock from
core and mantle

The rock cycle

149

☠ Chemical Reactions ☠

New materials are formed during a **chemical reaction**. Through studying these reactions, scientists have found that there are a number of elements and compounds which always react in a similar way.

Combination of elements and compounds	Chemical reaction	Example
Metal + acid	Many metals react with dilute acids to produce a salt[59] and hydrogen gas.	zinc + sulphuric acid $Zn + H_2SO_4 \rightarrow ZnSO_4 + H_2$
Metal carbonate + acid	The carbonate reacts with dilute acid to form a salt, water and carbon dioxide gas.	calcium carbonate + hydrochloric acid → calcium chloride + water + carbon dioxide $CaCO_3 + 2HCl \rightarrow CaCl_2 + H_2O + CO_2$
Metal oxide + acid	The metal oxide[60] reacts with dilute acid to form a salt and water.	copper(II) oxide + sulphuric acid → copper(II) sulphate + water $CuO + H_2SO_4 \rightarrow CuSO_4 + H_2O$
Metal hydroxide + acid	In this case the metal hydroxide reacts with dilute acid to form a salt and water.	sodium hydroxide + hydrochloric acid → sodium chloride + water $NaOH + HCl \rightarrow NaCl + H_2O$

[59] A salt is a compound formed when an acid reacts with a metal, metal oxide, metal hydroxide or metal carbonate. Chlorides, carbonates, nitrates and sulphates are all classed as salts. Hydrochloric acid is used to make chlorides, sulphuric acid makes sulphates and nitric acid makes nitrates.
[60] Metal oxides are sometimes referred to as bases.

Combination of elements and compounds	Chemical reaction	Example
Metal + water	A metal reacts with water (hydrogen oxide) to produce a salt and hydrogen gas.	calcium + water → calcium hydroxide + hydrogen $Ca + 2H_2O \rightarrow CaOH + H_2$
Metal + oxygen *Combustion* *(burning)*	When some metals burn they use up oxygen in the air and form oxides.[61]	magnesium + oxygen → magnesium oxide $2Mg + O_2 \rightarrow 2MgO$

Reactivity

Some metals will burn in air or react with water more quickly than others. They are ranked in order of reactivity from highest to lowest within the **reactivity series**. The reactivity of a number of common metals is as follows:

Metal	Reactivity
Potassium	Highly reactive (reacts with water)
Sodium	
Calcium	
Magnesium	Reactive (reacts with acids)
Aluminium	
Zinc	
Iron	
Nickel	
Tin	
Lead	
Copper	Highly unreactive
Mercury	
Silver	
Platinum	
Gold	

---

[61] An oxide is a compound of a metal and oxygen.

Different types of reactions

The reactivity series is a useful aid to predicting what will happen during a chemical reaction. If a metal higher in the reactivity series meets a metal that is lower, a **displacement reaction** takes place, with the two metals swapping places.

A good example of a displacement reaction is the **Thermite reaction**:[62]

iron(III) oxide + aluminium → aluminium oxide + iron
$$Fe_2O_3 + 2Al \rightarrow Al_2O_3 + 2Fe$$

An **exothermic reaction** is one during which energy is released, which in turn causes a rise in temperature.

An **endothermic reaction** is one which takes energy from its surroundings, causing a resultant drop in temperature.

When a chemical reaction takes place, there is no gain in mass. The final total mass of the products of the reaction is always the same as the masses of the reactants that were used. If there is a change in mass, it is only an apparent one.

If mass does seem to have been lost, it means that something (for example a gas) has been released during the reaction, and if there seems to be an increase in mass, it is because something – again, usually a gas – has been gained during the reaction.

Did you know...?
Unreactive metals are often precious metals like gold, platinum and silver. As well as looking shiny and pretty, their very unreactivity makes them ideal for creating jewellery, as other metals would react with air or water and tarnish.

[62] Which has the practical application of being used to weld together lengths of railway track.

Acids and alkalis

Acids and alkalis make up many of the substances in the world around us. They are found in fruit, the rain, our stomachs and cleaning products, as well as in medicine cabinets and kitchen cupboards.

Every substance in the world has a pH value[63] between 0 and 14. This indicates how acidic or alkaline a substance is. Strong alkalis can be just as harmful to living creatures, like us, as strong acids. Pure water is equally acid and alkaline and so is considered neutral. A substance that is neutral in this way has a pH rating of 7.

It is **acid** that gives vinegar its distinctive flavour and that tells you if an apple is sour and not good to eat. Strong acids have a pH of 1–4, while weak acids have a pH of 5–6. Some common acids are:

Acid	Chemical formula	Found in...
Citric acid	$H_3C_6H_5O_7$	Citrus fruits, lemon juice (pH 2)
Acetic acid (a.k.a. ethanoic acid)	CH_3COOH	Vinegar (pH 3), paints and adhesives
Nitric acid	HNO_3	Explosives, fertilisers, aged pine and maple
Hydrochloric acid	HCl	Stomach acid (pH 2), metal treatments
Sulphuric acid	H_2SO_4	Car batteries, industrial processes to refine petroleum, treat metal and make fertilisers
Phosphoric acid	H_3PO_4	Soft drinks, rust removers
Oxalic acid	$H_2C_2O_4$	Rhubarb, car cooling systems
Formic acid (a.k.a. methanoic acid)	$HCOOH$	Stings and bites of ants and other insects
Carbonic acid	H_2CO_3	Rainwater (pH 5.5)

---

[63] The concept of pH was first introduced by Danish chemist S.P.L. Sørensen at the Carlsberg Laboratory in 1909. In English the letters pH stand for 'the potential of hydrogen'.

Alkalis are almost the opposite of acids and will often neutralise them (which is why they are used in remedies designed to relieve heartburn and acid indigestion). Strong alkalis have a pH of 10–14, while weaker alkalis have a pH of 8–9. Some common alkalis are:

Alkali	Chemical formula	Found in...
Sodium hydrogen carbonate	$NaHCO_3$	Bicarbonate of soda (pH 8)
Magnesium hydroxide	$Mg(OH)_2$	Milk of Magnesia (pH 10), other antacid indigestion remedies
Sodium carbonate	$Na_2CO_3.10H_2O$	Washing soda
Sodium hydroxide	$NaOH$	Caustic soda (pH 14), oven cleaners
Hydrogen peroxide	H_2O_2	Hair bleach
Potassium hydroxide	KOH	Chocolate and cocoa processing, ice cream, pretzels, fungicide, wart treatments, alkaline batteries
Calcium hydroxide (*lime*)	$Ca(OH)_2$	Fertiliser, lime kilns
Nitrogen hydroxide (*ammonia*)	NH_3	Fertiliser, disinfectant (pH 12), large-scale refrigeration units

Indicators are substances which change colour depending on how acid or alkali something is. Common indicators used in laboratories are litmus, litmus papers and Universal indicator (which changes through a spectrum of colours from red to purple depending on acidity or alkalinity). However, there are plenty of other effective indicators in the natural world, including red cabbage!

☠ Spot Test! ☠

Well done – you've reached the end of chemistry. But were you paying attention to every last detail? Let's hope so because it's test time again!

Parents, if we find you've been chattering at the back of the class while your children soak it all up, there'll be trouble. And kids, we know Dmitri Mendeleev may have lived and died before your time but he's still important. The only question is … do you know who he is?

Ten questions with which to test your wits. Off you go!

1) What is the chemical formula of chalk?
2) What is the most common chemical element in air?
3) Complete the following equation: $Fe + H_2SO_4 \rightarrow$
4) What is the pH value of pure water?
5) Give an example of an igneous rock.
6) What is a saturated solution?
7) An acid and a metal will react together to make what?
8) What's the first element in the periodic table?
9) What are the three states of matter?
10) Name the three types of weathering that can happen to rocks.

Chapter Five

PHYSICS
Ye Cannae Change the Laws of Physics![64]

Physics. It's a word that strikes many people cold and conjures up images of geeks, or brainy boffins in motorised chairs. And yet if it wasn't for physics there would be no computers, no cars, no gravity and no universe!

It's the subject that everyone loves to hate, mainly because it involves a fair bit of complicated mathematics and deals with some rather challenging topics. But don't worry, we'll try to keep things as simple as possible.

---

[64] As Scotty would say on *Star Trek*, usually just before somebody (or something) on board the Starship *Enterprise* did precisely that!

⸎ Physical Processes ⸎

'Physical Processes', as modern secondary school students now refer to the subject formerly known as just 'physics', covers everything from forces and the miracle of electricity through to the wonders of the solar system and the microchip.

In an effort to show you that there is much not only to marvel at within the realm of physics, but also to love, we're going to start with something close to everyone's heart: the rules of attraction!

Magnetism: The Rules of Attraction

A **magnetic field** is the region surrounding a magnet (a magnet such as the solid iron and nickel core of planet Earth) where it has an effect on magnetic objects.

Magnets have been used (pivoted on needles) in ships' compasses for centuries in order to help sailors navigate. If it is able to turn freely, a magnet will always point towards magnetic north, with its north-seeking (or just north) pole.[65]

You can make a new magnet simply using a nail and a permanent magnet. Take an iron nail and stroke it repeatedly with a good, strong magnet, in the same direction each time, quickly and 50 to 100 times. The nail will now be magnetised and will be able to pick up smaller metal objects, such as a paper clip. You can also create a magnet using an electric current. Wrap a length of wire tightly around an iron nail, attach the two ends of the wire to the terminals of a battery – *voilà*! A magnet always has two poles (its strongest parts) – a north pole and a south pole.

---

[65] The opposite pole of a magnet is, of course, its south-seeking (or simply south) pole.

Magnets will attract ferrous metals such as iron or those alloys that contain iron (like steel), and nickel. However, they have no influence over non-ferrous metals, like magnesium, copper, chrome and zinc, nor alloys made of these non-ferrous metals, like brass.

The pole of one magnet will attract the opposite pole of another magnet, while repelling a similar pole. So, north attracts south and south attracts north, but north repels north and south repels south.

Placing a magnet on a tray covered with iron filings will allow you to see the magnetic field surrounding the magnet, creating a magnetic field pattern. Using iron filings in this way you can also study the attractive and repulsive fields that exist between a pair of magnets.

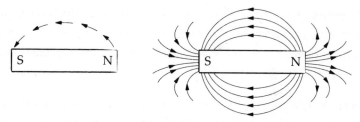

The magnetic field lines of a bar magnet

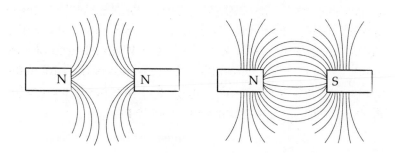

Attractive and repulsive magnetic fields

N.B. Magnetic field patterns are always drawn with the arrows pointing away from the north pole of the magnet and towards its south pole.

Did you know...?
Scientists believe that, on average, the Earth undergoes a geo-magnetic reversal – when its north and south magnetic poles flip – every 250,000 years. However, according to the geological record, the latest flip is severely overdue. It has been 750,000 years since the last one!

Electromagnets

An electric current produces its own magnetic field. These fields are normally very weak, but using this knowledge, powerful **electromagnets** can be constructed by wrapping a **coil** of wire around an iron core. A current is passed through the wire, which magnetises the iron. As soon as the electric current is switched off, the magnet is effectively switched off as well. Electromagnets are found inside washing machines, lawn mowers, loudspeakers, doorbells, relay switches, computers, cars and other vehicles.

Did you know...?
The world's largest superconducting electromagnet, the Barrel Toroid, is constructed from eight 5 m × 25 m rectangular coils cooled to –269°C and carrying a current of 20,000 amps. When switched on, the energy in its coils is equivalent to approximately 10,000 cars travelling at 70 kph (44 mph). The Barrel Toroid forms part of the Large Hadron Collider (LHC) experiment, being run at the international high-energy physics lab CERN, in Geneva. It is used to bend the paths of particles formed from the collision of protons or lead ions accelerated to near-lightspeeds in one of the most powerful particle accelerators ever built.

✶ ✶ ✶

Energy Resources

Everything we do requires **energy**, whether it is walking down to the local shops to buy the morning newspaper, turning on a light, or keeping our homes warm in the bitter depths of winter. Most of the energy we use within our homes and work places is provided by electricity, which is generated in the first place by burning fuel in a power station.

A fuel is something which burns in air to release energy largely in the form of heat, and includes things like wood, coal, oil and gas. Wood is easy to replace, as it literally grows on trees, but the other three are all **fossil fuels**, produced from dead prehistoric plants and animals over the course of millions of years. They cannot be replaced and are steadily running out.

As a result of this, it is vital that we increase our use of **renewable** sources of energy which include **wind** power, **hydroelectric** power (made by the movement of water), power generated by **waves and tides**, **solar** energy (from the sun) and **geothermal** energy (energy pumped up from deep inside the boiling heart of the Earth).

Energy is measured in joules (J). One joule is the energy needed to lift 1 kilogram a height of 1 metre. To boil a kettle of water uses up to 600,000 joules. That's the same as a shelf-stacker setting out 600,000 bags of sugar on a shelf 1 metre high. That's a lot of energy!

Electric circuits

For an electric current to pass through a **circuit**, all of its components must be connected, creating a path for the current to follow from the positive terminal of the power supply (which might be a battery) to the negative terminal.

Materials which are conductors (like copper wire) will allow a current to pass through them. Insulators (like the plastic sheath on the copper wire) are the opposite of conductors (called non-conductors) and so will cause a break in a circuit.

Electrical circuits can be represented in diagrammatical form. Such diagrams use a common set of symbols.

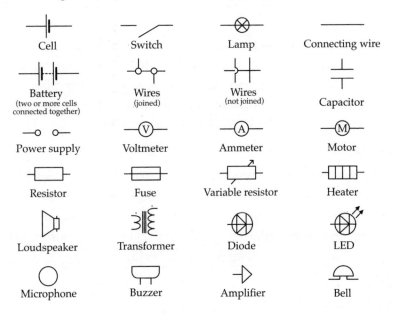

Some of the most common circuit symbols

There are of course many different types of circuit, depending on the complexity of an electrical system (for example inside a stereo or the wiring of a house), but generally they all break down into one of two types.

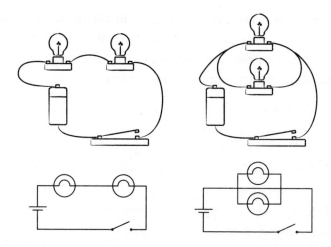

A series circuit and a parallel circuit

In a series circuit, the current from the cell passes through each lamp in turn. In a parallel circuit the current splits at the junction, before it reaches the lamps, and then rejoins at the junction afterwards.

How bright a lamp is also tells you how strong a current is passing through a circuit. The brighter it is, the greater the current; the duller it is, the weaker the current. The addition of a variable resistor to a circuit will allow you to vary the size of the current and hence the intensity of the light. As well as being used in dimmer switches, variable resistors also have practical applications in volume controls and adjusting motor speeds.

The size of an electrical current is measured in amps (A) by means of an ammeter. For them to work properly, ammeters always need to be arranged in series in a circuit. By using ammeters you can see quite clearly that the current is the same no matter where it is measured in a series circuit. It is not the current that gets used up by an electrical product, but energy.

The energy is transferred around a circuit, through its metal components, by electrons (negatively charged particles) moving from negative to positive. However, just to confuse things, the direction of a current is always shown as being from positive to negative.

The size of a current is dependent on two factors: the voltage of the battery or other power source supplying it (the higher the voltage, the greater the current) and the resistance of the circuit (the more resistance, the smaller the current). For example, adding more lamps to a circuit in series will increase the resistance, whereas adding more lamps in parallel would have no such effect.

Voltage is measured in volts (V), using a voltmeter. To work properly, a voltmeter needs to be connected in parallel with whatever is being assessed. Voltage is a measure of the energy transfer to and from charged particles carrying the electrical current in a circuit.

Resistance, which is a measure of how greatly an object opposes an electric current passing through it, is measured in ohms (Ω), using an ohmmeter.

Energy transfer

The energy required for any action exists in a number of different states.

Type of energy	What this means
Electrical	As in lightning, or what travels along power lines.
Kinetic	Movement energy. Sound is kinetic energy produced by vibrating air particles.

Type of energy	What this means
Gravitational potential	The energy that exists simply due to the effects of gravity. If an object falls, its gravitational potential energy is released when it hits something.
Light	As in the light we see coming from the sun or other sources of illumination.
Heat	As in the heat given off by a naked flame, a light bulb or a warm computer.
Chemical	This type of energy is used in a battery, which relies on chemical changes taking place within it to release energy.

Anything that happens requires an **energy transfer**, where one type of energy is turned into another. For example, when you strike a match, the chemical energy stored inside the match's tip is turned into both heat and light.

Energy is neither created nor destroyed, it merely changes state. This fact is known as the principle of the conservation of energy.

Heating and cooling are both processes in which a transfer of energy takes place. An object that is warmer than its surroundings, such as a hot cup of cocoa on a cold day, will cool down as a result of conduction taking place between the cocoa and the air. Something that is colder than its surroundings, such as an ice lolly enjoyed at the beach on a hot summer's day, will warm up, again as a result of conduction.

What happens in conduction is that the particles in something that is warm have more energy than those in something that is cold. This causes them to vibrate more vigorously. Energy is then transferred via these vibrations from particle to particle. The slower-moving (or colder) particles speed up, while the faster-moving (or hotter) ones slow down, until they are all moving at the same speed, having reached an equilibrium (in other words they are at the same temperature).

When an object emits radiant energy (like the cup of cocoa mentioned above), that object is cooled down. If something absorbs radiant energy (like the ice lolly), it is heated up.

Heating and cooling create convection currents in the air (as well as in liquids) whereby warmed air expands and so becomes less dense, causing it to rise, while cooler air (which is more dense) is drawn in to replace it. After all, nature abhors a vacuum.

Of course, though, there is a rather large vacuum through which heat does pass – space. The sun's heat energy cannot travel via conduction or convection as both of these require the presence of particles. It moves instead by means of infrared radiation, which is a wave along the electromagnetic spectrum. In fact all objects emit some level of heat radiation whether in vacuum or not, and this is most commonly used in household objects such as electric bar fires and oven grills.

Something which makes a good conductor is efficient at passing energy from one particle to another. Objects made of metal are a good example of this, because the particles in metals are packed together tightly.

A good insulator is something that reduces the energy transfer that takes place between an object and its surroundings. This means a good insulator will keep cold things cold and hot things hot, like a Thermos flask or a cool bag. Air, so long as it is contained so that convection currents cannot form, makes a good insulator because it is very poor at conducting heat energy.

N N N

Feel the Force

Everywhere you look in the world around you, you will witness forces in action: things pushing or pulling other things, causing things to stop or start or change direction, or even change shape. This is evidence of **forces** in action. As Obi Wan Kenobi would say, 'Use the Force, Luke'.[66]

When you are describing a force, you always describe it as:

Object A pulls/pushes on Object B

In diagrams, an arrow is included to show the direction of the push or pull being exerted.

Within the field of physics, weight has a very specific definition. It is the force that pulls an object towards the Earth and is measured in newtons (N). Weight is affected by gravity, but mass[67] (kg) stays the same. This means that on the Moon, where the pull of gravity is weaker, you would weigh less, even though there is still the same amount of you there.

Every object on the Earth is constantly being affected by the force of the Earth pulling it. This means that for something to appear to be still, there must be another force working on it to balance the Earth's pull.

An object that floats on water (like a lily pad on top of a pond) is actually being pushed up by the water, whereas something that sinks to the bottom (like a stone) must have a weight greater than the upward push of the water.

---

[66] Physicists traditionally are drawn to sci-fi, if only so that they can point out all of the scientific inaccuracies. They are not, however, traditionally comedians.

[67] When you refer to the mass of something in physics, you are basically talking about how much matter there is in an object.

Another force that objects have to contend with, especially ones travelling at speed, is air resistance. This is a resistive force, meaning it opposes the driving force needed to push something along. To make something move, or stop moving, forces need to become unbalanced, otherwise the object won't go anywhere.

This tendency of an object to remain at rest or to keep moving uniformly in a straight line (unless acted upon by some external force) is called inertia.

Friction is another resistive force that specifically prevents surfaces slipping or sliding over each other by acting in the opposite direction to any sliding motion. When you try to push the vacuum cleaner over the carpet, it is friction which will slow it down and stop it, if you don't keep pushing. Of course, the smoother the surface, the less friction there is.

When an object is affected by a driving force and starts moving, we are able to measure how fast it is travelling, as long as we know how far it has travelled and how long it has taken to cover that distance. The result of working out this equation gives us its average speed.

$$\text{average speed } (v) = \frac{\text{distance travelled } (s)}{\text{time taken } (t)}$$

Monsieur Rapide is competing in the Tour de France. He completes one 180-metre stretch in 60 seconds. If we apply the above equation, we can work out that his speed is (180 m ÷ 60 s) = 3 m/s. Not bad.

Of course, variations of this formula can also be used to determine the time taken when we know the speed and the distance, or the distance travelled if we know the speed and time taken instead.

Plotting distance and time on a graph is another way of determining speed, which in this case is represented on the graph by the slope (or gradient) produced.

When a force is exerted on something – for example, when your toe is trodden on by a lady wearing stiletto heels – this creates pressure at the point of contact. In the case of the clumsy stiletto-wearer, a large pressure is applied to a small area, resulting in a lot of pain!

The formula for calculating pressure is:

$$\text{pressure } (P) = \frac{\text{force } (F)}{\text{area } (A)}$$

Pressure is measured in newtons per metre squared[68] (N/m^2) or Pascals[69] (Pa).

This equation can also be rewritten to work out the force (where you have the area and the pressure) and the area (if you already know the pressure and the force being applied).

Turning forces

In our everyday lives we are constantly applying **turning forces**, to open a door, turn on a tap or wind down a car window.[70] The point around which something turns is called the **pivot**, and the effect that a force has in turning something round is called the **moment** (of the force). The moment is affected by how much

---

[68] Or centimetre squared if only a small area is involved.

[69] After Blaise Pascal (1623–62) who, among other things, made the first digital calculator (the 'Pascaline') to help his father with tax collection. A man you can equally praise and revile!

[70] Only if your car doesn't have electric windows, of course.

force is being applied and how far away from the pivot the application is taking place.

moment = force × perpendicular[71] distance to pivot

If two opposing moments of force balance each other out (as they do in a seesaw, for example), this is an example of the principle of moments.

The Principle of Moments

If an object is balanced, the sum of the clockwise moments about a pivot is equal to the sum of the anticlockwise moments about the same pivot.

---

[71] Perpendicular means exactly upright or vertical, in other words at right angles to the given surface.

⸸ Light ⸸

As you probably know, light travels in straight lines, which is why a shadow is formed when something opaque (meaning light can't pass through it) gets in the way of the beams of light. Because light from many different sources will usually be streaming towards an object, the intensity of the shadow depends on where it falls. The darkest part of the shadow is called the umbra. Where the light is only partially blocked, a partial shadow, called the penumbra, is formed.

Light travels much faster than sound,[72] which is why when an aircraft flies overhead and you look to see where the sound is coming from, you will not see the plane at that point; it has travelled further ahead.

The **speed of light** is approximately 300,000,000 m/s (or metres per second), whereas the speed of sound is only 330 m/s. If the aeroplane is flying at a height of 6,600 metres, it takes twenty seconds for the sound to reach your ears. However, it takes only a split second for the light bouncing off the plane to reach your eyes, so there is no discernible delay between an event happening and it being observed.

Even though light travels at such an incredible speed, it still takes rays from the sun eight-and-a-half minutes to reach the Earth. Light from Proxima Centauri (our *next* nearest star) takes four years to get here, and when we observe nebulae far off in space, using radio telescopes, we are seeing the after-effects of a star going supernova thousands, if not millions, of years in the past.

---

[72] Almost a million times faster!

N.B. Never look directly at the sun, to avoid damaging your eyes. To protect their eyesight when they are making space walks, the visors of astronauts' suit helmets have a thin layer of gold sealed between the inner and outer layers.

Seeing is believing

When we see something, light from the sun or artificial light sources (such as lamps, candles and TV screens) is scattered from the surface of the object, and some of it is reflected into our eyes. The eyes then send electrical signals along the optic nerve to the brain, which is where we really 'see' the object.

Did you know...?

Our brain actually sees the image upside down, due to the image being inverted as light passes through the lenses of our eyes. However, the brain compensates for this and turns the image the right way up again.

For us to be able to see objects in three dimensions, we need signals in the form of electrical nerve impulses from both eyes, so that we can accurately determine where something is in relation to other objects.

Through the looking glass

Something which does not **reflect** light in all directions is a **mirror**: light is reflected from a mirror at the same angle as it hits it.

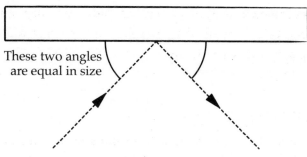

Light being reflected by a mirror

When you observe yourself in a mirror, your mind is actually playing tricks on you. You see a virtual image apparently formed right behind the mirror, the same distance as you are in front, when in reality the image cannot possibly be where you are seeing it at all.

Mirrors have many practical applications because of this property (beyond that of revealing every tiny fault about you to yourself). They are used in periscopes to turn light round corners, as light hitting a mirror at 45° is reflected at the same angle and so actually turns through 90°. Mirrors are also used in the construction of telescopes and lasers.

Did you know...?

The word laser is actually an acronym. The letters L-A-S-E-R stand for Light Amplification by Stimulated Emission of Radiation.

Refraction

As well as being reflected by mirrors, light is also **refracted** by glass and water. This means it changes direction slightly on entering either medium because it travels more slowly through both than it does through air (unless it strikes the boundary between the air and the glass or water at 90°).

Speed of light

In air	In water	In glass
300,000,000 m/s	230,000,000 m/s	200,000,000 m/s

It is refraction which creates the illusion that a straw in a glass of water is bent, or that the floor of a swimming pool is closer to the surface than it is in reality (and is another example of a **virtual image** being formed). Once the light re-enters the air, it speeds up again and changes direction once more.

Light passing through glass at different angles

Colour

Light, or **white light** as it is also called, is made up of the full **spectrum** of colours. This can be demonstrated by passing a ray of white light through a **prism**.[73] The light emerges from the prism split into the different colours of the rainbow. If this spectrum is then passed back through another prism, it will re-combine to become white light again.

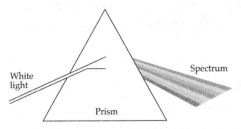

Light passing through a prism

---

[73] As seen on the cover of Pink Floyd's seminal prog-rock album *Dark Side of the Moon*.

A **rainbow** is formed when white light is dispersed by raindrops in the air which all act like tiny prisms.

When we see something white (like the dazzlingly pure laundry on a washing powder advert) all the colours in the light are reflected and so we see it as white.

However, when that same white light hits a coloured object, only that colour of light is reflected; all the others are absorbed. So if white light strikes a blue ball, all of the colours apart from blue are absorbed by the ball and only the blue light wavelength is reflected, giving the ball the appearance of being blue.

The effect of re-combining coloured light to make white light again is used in colour televisions. The **primary colours** of light are red, green and blue. When you watch TV you see the effect of combining these three colours. The secondary colours of yellow, magenta and cyan are made by combining two of the primary colours. Combine all three and white light is made.

This process is, understandably, called colour addition.

Non-luminous objects like the whiter-than-white laundry and the ball appear to be a particular colour because only one colour of light is reflected back from them while the rest are absorbed. This is called colour subtraction. Coloured filters also work by absorbing particular colour ranges of light.

While something that is white reflects all the colours in light, something that is black reflects none of the colours and absorbs them all.

The visible light spectrum is only part of the whole electromagnetic spectrum. It includes infrared, ultraviolet light and X-rays, and extends from below the frequencies used for modern radio transmissions (at the long-wavelength end) to gamma radiation (at the short-wavelength end). It covers wavelengths thousands of kilometres long, down to those which are a fraction of the size of an atom.

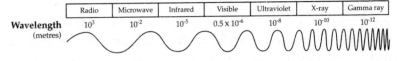

	Radio	Microwave	Infrared	Visible	Ultraviolet	X-ray	Gamma ray
Wavelength (metres)	10^3	10^{-2}	10^{-5}	0.5×10^{-6}	10^{-8}	10^{-10}	10^{-12}

The electromagnetic spectrum

⏷ **Sound** ⏷

Sound is produced when something vibrates, such as a loud-speaker on a stereo, the air inside a trumpet, or a tuning fork. In fact, sound can travel through anything that has particles that can vibrate. Where the particles are very close together, in solids like concrete, the vibrations travel very quickly. In liquids they do not travel quite so quickly, and they travel slowest of all through gases, such as air.

This means that where there is a vacuum, like the void of space, there is nothing to vibrate to transmit sound and so silence reigns.[74]

Sound waves travelling through air have three stages to them. First there is **compression**, where the particles are forced close together. This is followed by a **rarefaction** where the particles are stretched further apart. The **amplitude** of a vibration is the greatest distance the air particles move across each wave.

It is the frequency of the waves, in other words how many waves there are per second, which is responsible for the pitch of a sound. Frequency is measured in hertz[75] (Hz), with 1 Hz equal to one wave per second.

---

[74] Next time you watch a film in which spaceships are firing at each other through the void of space, you can tell the television with confidence that you should not be able to hear the *zzaps* and *kerpows* of the laser-bolts striking. A film which does get it right is *2001: A Space Odyssey*. However, if movies like *Star Wars* were scientifically accurate they probably wouldn't be so enjoyable.

[75] Named after Heinrich Hertz (1857–94), a German scientist who was the first to demonstrate the existence of electromagnetic waves.

So, the greater the amplitude of a sound, the greater its volume, whereas the greater the frequency of a sound, the higher its pitch. Sound waves can be visualised using an oscilloscope.

Did you know...?
The human ear can detect sounds ranging in frequency from 20 Hz to 20,000 Hz, although, as you get older, the upper end of this range is reduced. Frequencies higher than this are referred to as ultrasonic, while frequencies below it are referred to as infrasonic. Dogs and bats are among those animals capable of hearing ultrasound, while larger animals like whales, elephants and giraffes communicate using infrasound.

⚓ Spaceship Earth ⚓

Planet Earth is just one of nine planets[76] that make up our **solar system**. It travels through space at thousands of metres per second, rotating once about its axis every 24 hours, and takes roughly 365 days to travel around the sun.

Early astronomers used to think that the sun revolved around the Earth, because we do not feel our planet's movement from our position on its surface. However, this apparent movement of the sun is an effect of the Earth spinning in an anti-clockwise direction on its axis once a day.

The changing seasons, as well as the varying hours of daylight and darkness between summer and winter, are all due to the Earth's axis[77] being tilted.

All of the planets are named after Roman gods, except for the Earth. They move around the sun in the same direction, travelling in **elliptical orbits**. They are also all very nearly on the same **plane**, apart from Pluto. Pluto's inclined orbit, which is also more of a pronounced ellipse, means that Pluto sometimes gets closer to the sun than Neptune.

Did you know...?
The term 'planets' come from the Greek word *planetes*, meaning 'wanderers'.

The makeup of our Solar System, starting at the centre, is as follows:

---

[76] At least *traditionally* there are nine. Most astronomers seem now to agree that Pluto isn't a planet, meaning that there are only eight. But then others believe that objects such as the collection of icy bodies located beyond Neptune (belonging to the Kuiper Belt) should also be called planets, which would put the total number of planets orbiting our sun into the hundreds, if not the thousands, or even millions!

[77] Which always points towards Polaris, the Pole Star.

Heavenly body	Type	Appearance	What's it like?	Relative mass compared to the Earth (Earth = 1)	Distance from the sun (in millions of km)	Number of satellites (and names of principal moons)	Time taken to orbit the sun
The sun (*Sol, the sun god*)	A medium-sized, third-generation star	Brilliant bright white	A ball of burning hydrogen and helium.	333,000	0	n/a	n/a
Mercury (*messenger of the gods*)	Planet	Similar to our Moon	Its surface is covered with impact craters and can get as hot as 430°C.	0.06	58	0	0.24 Earth year, or 88 days
Venus (*goddess of beauty*)	Planet	Orange	A similar structure to Earth but covered by a dense atmosphere of carbon dioxide.	0.82	108	0	0.61 Earth year, or 225 days

Heavenly body	Type	Appearance	What's it like?	Relative mass compared to the Earth (Earth = 1)	Distance from the sun (in millions of km)	Number of satellites (and names of principal moons)	Time taken to orbit the sun
Earth	Planet	Blue-green	Largest of the terrestrial planets, 71 per cent of its surface is covered by the oceans. It is the only planet in our solar system capable of supporting life as we know it.	1.00	150	1 The Moon (*Luna*)	1 Earth year
Mars (*god of war*)	Planet	Blood-red	Coloured red by iron oxides on its surface, it is a terrestrial planet with a thin atmosphere.	0.11	228	2 Phobos, Deimos	1.88 Earth years

Heavenly body	Type	Appear-ance	What's it like?	Relative mass compared to the Earth (Earth = 1)	Distance from the sun (in millions of km)	Number of satellites (and names of principal moons)	Time taken to orbit the sun
Asteroid belt	Debris field		Rocky debris left over from the formation of the solar system 4.6 billion years ago. Despite some of the asteroids being 100 km in diameter, the larger ones are spaced roughly 2,000,000 km apart.	n/a	420	n/a	n/a

Heavenly body	Type	Appearance	What's it like?	Relative mass compared to the Earth (Earth = 1)	Distance from the sun (in millions of km)	Number of satellites (and names of principal moons)	Time taken to orbit the sun
Jupiter (*king of the gods*)	Planet	Swirling multi-coloured atmosphere with a huge red spot	A gas giant, more massive than all the other planets put together. Jupiter's Great Red Spot is actually a storm that could easily swallow the Earth three times over.	318	778	16+ Metis, Adrastea, Amalthea, Thebe, Io, Europa, Ganymede, Callisto, Leda, Himalia, Lysithia, Elara, Ananke, Carme, Pasiphaë, Sinope	11.86 Earth years

Heavenly body	Type	Appearance	What's it like?	Relative mass compared to the Earth (Earth = 1)	Distance from the sun (in millions of km)	Number of satellites (and names of principal moons)	Time taken to orbit the sun
Saturn (the Titan father of Jupiter)	Planet	Bright yellow (banded globe)	The second-largest planet in the solar system, it's encircled by more than 100,000 rings of dust, rock and ice. It is mainly composed of hydrogen, with small proportions of helium.	95	1427	21+ Mimas, Enceladus, Tethys, Dione, Rhea, Titan, Hyperion, Iapetus, Phoebe	29.50 Earth years

Heavenly body	Type	Appearance	What's it like?	Relative mass compared to the Earth (Earth = 1)	Distance from the sun (in millions of km)	Number of satellites (and names of principal moons)	Time taken to orbit the sun
Uranus (*god of the sky*)	Planet	Green-blue	An ice giant, its colour is the result methane clouds in its atmosphere.	14.6	2875	15+ Cordelia, Ophelia, Bianca, Cressida, Desdemona, Juliet, Portia, Rosalind, Belinda, Puck, Miranda, Ariel, Umbriel, Titania, Oberon, Caliban, Sycorax, Prospero, Setebos, Stephano, Trinculo	84 Earth years

Heavenly body	Type	Appear-ance	What's it like?	Relative mass compared to the Earth (Earth = 1)	Distance from the sun (in millions of km)	Number of satellites (and names of principal moons)	Time taken to orbit the sun
Neptune (*god of the sea*)	Planet	The blue planet	Similar to Uranus in size and make-up, it is encircled by faint rings of methane ice crystals.	17.2	4496	8+ Naiad, Thalassa, Despina, Galatea, Larissa, Proteus, Triton, Nereid	164.8 Earth years
Pluto (*god of the underworld*)	Planet	Brown-grey	A tiny, icy body, it is no longer considered to be a planet but the largest member of the Kuiper Belt.[82]	0.002	5900	3 Charon (about half the size of Pluto itself), Nix, Hydra	248.4 Earth years

Did you know...?

The distance of the Earth from the sun is the accepted value of the AU, or astronomical unit. So 1 AU is equal to 150 million km!

---

[78] Pluto was downgraded in status in August 2006, having only just had two new moons discovered in 2005.

> **Did you know...?**
>
> All of the moons of the principal planets of our solar system are named after figures from classical myth, like the planets themselves, with the exception of Uranus (and some of the more recently discovered moons of other planets, such as those of Saturn[79]). The seventh planet's moons, named after characters from Shakespeare's plays and Alexander Pope's *The Rape of the Lock*, were christened by the astronomer William Lassell (1799–1880) and John Herschel (1792–1871), the son of William Herschel who discovered Uranus.

There is a handy mnemonic that can be used as an aide memoire to help recall the names (and correct order of) the traditional nine planets of the solar system:

My **V**ery **E**asy **M**ethod: **J**ust **S**et **U**p **N**ine **P**lanets
Mercury, **V**enus, **E**arth, **M**ars, **J**upiter, **S**aturn, **U**ranus,
Neptune, **P**luto

The serious matter of gravity

There is a popular quote on this subject which goes, 'Gravity is a myth … the Earth sucks!' However, **gravity** is a very serious subject because everything in the universe is influenced by it (or at least by **gravitational force**), from planets and moons, to people and even space-time. The Moon stays in orbit around our planet due to the Earth's gravitational pull upon it, just as it is gravity that keeps the Earth circling the sun, along with the rest of the planets of the solar system.

There are four things you need to remember about gravitational forces.

---

[79] A number of which are named after figures from Inuit mythology.

1. They are attractive, and never repulsive; they always pull, never push.
2. They act between all objects that have mass.
3. They increase in strength as mass increases.
4. They decrease in strength the further away the masses are from each other.

⏸ Spot Test! ⏸

Bet you've been expecting this one! But were you looking forward to it? Well, that rather depends on whether you can tell your ammeter from your elliptical orbit. As always, answers are to be found at the bottom of the page – but if you're found cheating, you'll be at the bottom of the class.

How have you been doing so far, parents? Are you that far ahead of the kids, that you're past Pluto while they're still stuck back on Earth? Or do you need to use a periscope to see them, they're so far around the corner?

Whether you're pulling away or playing catch-up, your time starts now!

1) Name three sources of renewable energy.
2) What unit is energy measured in, and how is it defined?
3) What is the formula for calculating pressure?
4) What is the speed of light in air?
5) What does LASER stand for?
6) What lies between Mars and Jupiter, 420 million km from the sun?
7) The greater the amplitude of a sound, the greater its …
8) How could an electromagnet be made?
9) What colours would a black wall reflect?
10) The resistance of a circuit is measured in what?

---

1) *Wind power, hydroelectric power, wave and tidal power, solar energy and geothermal energy.* 2) *Energy is measured in joules. One Joule is the energy needed to lift a mass of 1 kg by a height of 1 metre.* 3) *pressure (P) = force (F) ÷ area (A).* 4) 3×10^8 *m/s.* 5) *Light Amplification by Stimulated Emission of Radiation.* 6) *An asteroid belt.* 7) *Volume.* 8) *By wrapping a coil of wire around an iron core. A current is passed through the wire which magnetises the iron.* 9) *None.* 10) *Ohms (Ω).*

189

✅ 70 Scientists Who Changed The World ✅

Ever since man first wondered about the world around him, there have been those who have not only wanted to understand it, but to control it and use it. Those listed below often made their advances inspired by the work of other scientists and inventors who came before them. As the saying goes, 'Standing on the shoulders of giants …'

Some of the individuals listed might not, at first, seem like the most obvious candidates for a hit-parade of scientific achievements but their inventions, discoveries and feats of engineering all fall within the different fields of science.

	Name	Dates	From	Inventions/Discoveries
1	Archimedes	287–212 BC	Syracuse, Sicily	Famous for jumping out of the bath and shouting 'Eureka!', his achievements included the invention of Archimedes' Screw (a machine for raising water) and Archimedes' Principle, which states that when a body is wholly or partially immersed in a fluid, it experiences an upward force equal to the weight of the fluid it displaces. So, the weight of fluid displaced by an object is equal to the weight of the object. He also explained how levers worked and how geometry could be used to measure circles.

	Name	Dates	From	Inventions/Discoveries
2	Hero of Alexandria	1st century AD	Alexandria, Egypt	A mathematician and engineer who invented the first steam turbine, but didn't see the practical application of it. Described how levers, pulleys and screws worked.
3	Roger Bacon	1214–94	England	Also known as Doctor Mirabilis, he was a monk who made lenses to improve eyesight, as well as gunpowder.
4	Nicolaus Copernicus	1473–1543	Poland	Proposed the theory that the Earth orbits the sun.
5	Andreas Vesalius	1514–64	Belgium	A physician by training, he was the author of *De humani corporis fabrica* ('On the Workings of the Human Body'). As a result he is often referred to as the founder of modern human anatomy.
6	Galileo Galilei	1564–1642	Italy	The first *real* scientist, Galileo was a mathematician, astronomer and physicist. He studied pendulums, falling objects and the movements of celestial bodies. He devised the Law of Accelerated Motion which states that falling bodies accelerate at a rate which is not affected by either their weight or composition.
7	Blaise Pascal	1623–62	France	Devised the first digital calculator (operated by a system of gears and wheels) and was a pioneer of hydraulics and pneumatics.

	Name	Dates	From	Inventions/Discoveries
8	Robert Boyle	1627–91	Ireland	Noted for his work in physics and chemistry, he is best known for the formulation of Boyle's Law, which states that for a fixed amount of gas kept at a fixed temperature, pressure and volume are inversely proportional (while one increases, the other decreases).
9	Christian Huygens	1629–95	Holland	Invented the first working pendulum clock. He also discovered the polarisation of light, and that light was made up of waves.
10	Antoine van Leeuwenhoek	1632–1723	Holland	Invented the first accurate and powerful single-lens microscope, which resulted in microscopic study becoming possible.
11	Isaac Newton	1642–1727	England	Responsible for theories of gravity, rules of calculus, Newton's Laws of Motion. His work *Opticks* explained that white light is made up of a spectrum of colours.
12	Thomas Newcomen	1663–1729	England	Newcomen's Engine, the first practical steam engine, devised to pump water out of Cornish tin mines.
13	Benjamin Franklin	1706–90	USA	His famous (and dangerous) kite experiment proved that lightning is a discharge of electricity. He invented the first lightning conductor and bifocal glasses.

	Name	Dates	From	Inventions/Discoveries
14	Carl Linnaeus	1707–78	Sweden	The 'father of modern taxonomy', he introduced the system of classifying species of organisms into specific groups.
15	Richard Arkwright	1732–92	England	Invented the water-frame spinning machine, which helped bring about the Industrial Age.
16	James Watt	1736–1819	Scotland	The first efficient steam engine and 'horsepower' as a measure of engine power are down to him.
17	Antoine Lavoisier	1743–94	France	Created the modern method of defining chemical elements and helped introduce the metric system.
18	Alessandro Volta	1745–1827	Italy	Discovered that contact between two different metals produces electricity and went on to invent the electric battery.
19	Edward Jenner	1749–1823	England	The 'father of immunology', he administered the first vaccination against smallpox.
20	Charles Macintosh	1766–1843	Scotland	A chemist, he invented weatherproof fabric (using latex and naphtha) upon which the raincoat which bears his name was based.
21	George Stephenson	1781–1848	England	Locomotive No. 1, the first engine to run on a public railway. His son Robert built the *Rocket*, the fastest engine of its time.

	Name	Dates	From	Inventions/Discoveries
22	John Walker	1781–1859	England	A chemist who invented the sulphur friction match, by accident.
23	William Sturgeon	1783–1850	England	A physicist and inventor, he made the first electromagnets and invented the first practical electric motor.
24	Karl Drais	1785–1851	Germany	Patented the first recognisable modern bicycle – the wooden, pedal-less *Draisienne*.
25	Jacob Bigelow	1786–1879	USA	Actually a botanist, he coined the modern definition of the word 'technology'.
26	Michael Faraday	1791–1867	England	The son of a blacksmith, he was one of the greatest pioneers of electricity and magnetism, inventing both the dynamo and the transformer. He was also responsible for the first electric-run lighthouse.
27	Charles Babbage	1792–1871	England	A mathematician, he invented the mechanical Analytical Engine – the world's first computer – having built a Difference Engine, which was a calculator.
28	William Fox Talbot	1800–77	England	Invented the negative–positive photographic process.

	Name	Dates	From	Inventions/Discoveries
29	Richard Owen	1804–92	England	A biologist, comparative anatomist and palaeontologist, he coined the word 'dinosaur' and was the driving force behind the establishment of the British Museum of Natural History in London.
30/31	Matthias Schleiden & Theodor Schwann	1804–81 & 1810–82	Germany	Between them, these two men described the differences between animal and plant cells, discovered the organic nature of yeast, and invented the term metabolism.
32	Isambard Kingdom Brunel	1806–59	England	One of the greatest civil and mechanical engineers the world has ever seen, he built the first tunnel under the Thames, designed the Clifton Suspension Bridge in Bristol and devised the largest steamships the world had ever seen.
33	Charles Darwin	1809–82	England	He proposed, and provided scientific evidence to prove, that all species of life have evolved over time from one or a few common ancestors, through the process of natural selection.
34	Elisha Otis	1811–61	USA	Designed the safety elevator, which paved the way for the development of the skyscraper.

	Name	Dates	From	Inventions/Discoveries
35	Samuel Colt	1814–62	USA	Developed a hand-held revolver that could fire six bullets without having to be reloaded. He also implemented the first use of remote control with electrically-controlled naval mines.
36	Crawford Williamson Long	1815–78	USA	A physician and pharmacist, he performed the first surgical operation which used ether to anaesthetise the patient.
37	Ada Countess Lovelace	1815–52	England	Daughter of the poet Lord Byron. Having corresponded with Charles Babbage, she wrote the first computer program which, had Babbage's Analytical Engine worked, would have been able to calculate a sequence of Bernoulli numbers.
38	Edwin Drake	1819–80	USA	Drilled the first productive oil well, using a steam engine to drive the drilling tool.
39	Francis Galton	1822–1911	England	A true polymath, he, among other things, devised a method for classifying fingerprints that proved useful in forensic science.
40	Louis Pasteur	1822–95	France	Discovered that germs cause disease and created the first vaccine for rabies.

	Name	Dates	From	Inventions/Discoveries
41	Etienne Lenoir	1822–1900	Belgium	Designed the first practical internal combustion engine and developed electric motors, telegraphy and railway signals.
42	Joseph Lister	1827–1912	England	Developed antiseptic, used in the surgical operations he carried out. He also introduced the idea of wearing white operating garments.
43	John Pemberton	1831–88	USA	The inventor of Coca-Cola, a beverage he created while trying to find a way to stop headaches and calm nervousness.
44	Alfred Nobel	1833–96	Sweden	The creator of dynamite, his substantial personal fortune founded the now-famous Nobel prizes.
45/46	Gottlieb Daimler & Karl Benz	1834–1900 & 1844–1929	Germany	Between them, these two brought the motor car to the mass market.
47	Thomas Edison	1847–1931	USA	Invented the first machine to record and play back sound, along with light bulbs and celluloid, used in America's early motion picture industry.
48	Alexander Graham Bell	1847–1922	Scotland	The telephone was his invention.
49	Konstantin Tsiolkovsky	1857–1935	Russia	Dubbed the 'father of space', he worked out that rockets (powered by liquid fuel) were the only means of propulsion that would work in the vacuum of space.

	Name	Dates	From	Inventions/Discoveries
50	Frederick Hopkins	1861–1947	England	He discovered vitamins, which are an essential aspect of nutrition, required for good health.
51/52	Auguste & Louis Lumière	1862–1954 & 1864–1948	France	They developed the cinematograph motion picture camera.
53	Leo Baekeland	1863–1944	Belgium	He invented Bakelite, which heralded the beginning of the plastic age.
54	Marie Curie	1867–1934	Poland	A physicist and chemist, she was a pioneer in the field of radioactivity, discovering polonium and radium. She died from aplastic anaemia (whereby bone marrow does not produce enough new cells to restock blood cells), almost certainly as a result of exposure to radiation.
55/56	Wilbur & Orville Wright	1867–1912 & 1871–1948	USA	Pioneers of aviation, they invented the 'Flyer III' in 1905, which was the first practical aeroplane.
57	Guglielmo Marconi	1874–1937	Italy	A physicist and electrical engineer, he invented the radio.

	Name	Dates	From	Inventions/Discoveries
58	Albert Einstein	1879–1955	Germany, Switzerland and USA	His Special Theory of Relativity showed that the speed of light cannot be exceeded and his General Theory of Relativity show that light passing a heavenly body is bent by its gravitational pull. He also discovered that an atom of an element losing mass can convert this mass into a phenomenal amount of energy, which led to the invention of nuclear power.
59	John Logie Baird	1888–1946	Scotland	The inventor of the television.
60	Laszlo Biro	1900–85	Hungary	Gave his name to his world-changing invention, the Biro, or ball-point pen.
61	Enrico Fermi	1901–54	Italy	A physicist, he built the first atomic reactor, using uranium to create the first nuclear chain reaction.
62	J. Robert Oppenheimer	1904–67	USA	The 'father of the atomic bomb', he is almost as famous for quoting from the *Bhagavad Gita*, 'Now I am become Death, the destroyer of worlds.'
63	Frank Whittle	1907–96	England	He built the first jet engine.
64	Rosalind Franklin	1920–58	England	A biophysicist and X-ray crystallographer, she made important contributions to the understanding of the fine structures of DNA and viruses, as well as coal and graphite, both of which are different forms of carbon.

	Name	Dates	From	Inventions/Discoveries
65	Theodore Maiman	1927–2007	USA	A physicist who made the first working laser. Lasers are now used in everything, from missiles and medical treatments to printers and CD players.
66/67	James D. Watson & Francis Crick	1928– & 1916–2004	USA & England	Molecular biologists who discovered that the structure of the DNA molecule is a double-helix.
68	Hugh Everett III	1930–82	USA	He was the physicist who first proposed the 'many-worlds interpretation' of quantum physics – what he called his 'relative state' formulation, but which most people know as the concept of parallel worlds or universes.
69	Marcian Hoff	1937–	USA	Inventor of the microprocessor, without which there would be no modern computers, mobile phones, washing machines, traffic lights, etc.
70	Stephen Hawking	1942–	England	A world-renowned theoretical physicist, he is known for his contributions to the fields of cosmology and quantum gravity, especially with regard to black holes.

Chapter Six

HISTORY
History Today

How history is taught in schools today is very different to how it was taught in the days of yesteryear. Rather than learning reams of dates, students are now encouraged to study original source documents, bearing in mind the bias and objectivity of the author where relevant. They are even expected to find the answers to specific questions about life in the past, and not merely regurgitate facts in return for marks.

Nor are students restricted to learning about the history of Britain and the impact of its nearer European neighbours. Children are now introduced to cultures and civilisations beyond those merely of the West, and they learn about historical figures important to a wide variety of peoples.

Although this, it could be argued, is a great improvement on the way history used to be taught in British schools, the down side is that children rarely study different historical eras or notable figures in any kind of chronological context.

So in this chapter, you will be presented with a potted history of the British and the British Isles, along with some other useful facts such as who ruled this country and when, as well as a list of famous battles that every history scholar should really know – just to remind you, of course, of what you already know, being the magnificent history scholar that you are.

❀ History is Written by the Winners ❀

A word that gets mentioned a great deal when talking about the study of history is 'sources'. These are the sources of information from which we can learn about the past. They can be primary (meaning they were written by someone who was there at the time, or made at that time) or secondary (created after the event as a replica, or written at a later date, such as this chapter).

They can be anything from examples of written evidence (newspaper articles, diaries, official documents, government records), through pictorial evidence (paintings, photographs), to actual artefacts from the time (coins, pottery, pieces of machinery) and the spoken word of people who were really there.

In this last sense, we are all sources of historical evidence. Everything that has happened to us before this point – yes, right now, as you read these words – is in the past and hence, history.

However, when you examine a piece of historical evidence it is very important to think carefully about who wrote it/said it/made it, and why. In other words, you must bear in mind how objective a viewpoint it represents and whether it is biased. A perfect example of biased historical sources being created today are newspapers, with most of the tabloids and broadsheets having an obvious leaning.

Taking an example from another historical period, it is now considered that the image of Richard III as a villainous, hunchbacked, prince-murdering tyrant was the creation of Tudor historians. And you have to remember that it was Henry Tudor – later Henry VII – who trounced Richard III at the Battle of Bosworth. Had Lord Stanley and his men not proved turncoats that day in 1485 (and changed sides), and had Henry lost the battle rather than Richard, what sort of impression of Richard III would the public have today?

So, when you are judging the value of a piece of evidence, in terms of how impartial an opinion it provides, it is best to collect a variety of sources and then weigh them against each other.

Remember: History is written by the winners.

❀ The Passage of Time ❀

Now, unless you're Doctor Who, Marty McFly or the Terminator, time passes in a linear direction, only ever going forwards. As William Shakespeare put it in *Macbeth*:

> To-morrow, and to-morrow, and to-morrow,
> Creeps in this petty pace from day to day,
> To the last syllable of recorded time.

BC or AD?

Events are dated as either being **BC** or **AD**. If the initials BC appear after a date, then you know it occurred before the birth of Christ, or simply **'Before Christ'** (hence BC).

If the letters AD are connected to a date, then that means it is a date after Christ's birth. AD is an abbreviation of the Latin phrase ***Anno Domini***, meaning 'in the year of our Lord' (and does not mean 'After Death', which is a commonly held misconception).

Traditionally the abbreviation BC should go after the year number, whereas the abbreviation AD should be placed before it. This is the convention that we have followed in *Match Wits With The Kids*. The reason for it is obvious, if you consider the origin of the two abbreviations. Take, for example, the following:

> 54 BC = 54 years Before Christ
> AD 2008 = Anno Domini [in the year of our Lord] 2008

Normally, a year which comes after the birth of Christ does not have to have an abbreviation connected to it at all; it is just assumed that the date is AD.

BCE and CE

Of course, the whole idea of BC and AD is based on the Christian religion and there is now a growing trend to use the abbreviations **BCE** and **CE** in their place. BCE stands for **'Before the Common Era'** and therefore CE just means **'Common Era'**. CE is often preferred by those who want to use a term that is unrelated to any religious idea of time.

However, since this is a book about all the things that the older generation were taught at school, we have not followed this convention, but have instead stuck to the traditional (and possibly less PC) dating system of BC and AD.

Centuries and Millennia

The last thing to bear in mind about historical dates is the numbering of **centuries**[80] and (if you study a long enough period of history) **millennia**.[81] It can appear slightly confusing when you consider that 1485 is in the 15th century, or that 1666 is in the 17th century. However, if you try to remember that the 1st century AD began with the year AD 1 and went through to AD 99, it suddenly makes a lot more sense. The same applies when you travel backwards through time. So, 3500 BC is in the 36th century BC.

And the same is also true of the millennia. In the year 2008 we are in the eighth year of the 3rd millennium, since the 1st millennium covered the period AD 1 to AD 999, and the 2nd millennium was from AD 1000 to AD 1999.

---

[80] From the Latin *centum* meaning 100, hence one century = 100 years.
[81] From the Latin *mille* meaning 1,000, so one millennium = 1,000 years.

✿ Kings and Queens of England ✿

What we know of as British history is generally accepted as covering the period from 1066 and the Norman Conquest through to the present day. However, if we include all the kings and queens, from the known rulers of tribal Britain through to those of the United Kingdom at the beginning of the 21st century, there have actually been over 300 monarchs of the British Isles.

British school children were once expected to know the kings and queens of England, from the arrival of William the Conqueror through to our current monarch, Queen Elizabeth II. When you were at school you may have been introduced to a poem, and a long one at that, designed to help you remember the long list of kings and queens. In case you've forgotten it, here it is again:

> Willie, Willie, Harry, Stee,
> Harry, Dick, John, Harry Three,
> One Two Three Neds, Richard Two,
> Harrys Four Five Six ... then who?

> Edwards Four Five, Dick the Bad,
> Harrys twain, Ned Six the lad,
> Mary, Bessie, James you ken,
> Then Charlie, Charlie, James again ...

> Will and Mary, Anne of Gloria,
> Georges Four, Will Four, Victoria,
> Edward Seven next, and then
> Came George the Fifth in 1910.

> Ned the Eight soon abdicated,
> So George Six was coronated,
> [or a George was reinstated]
> Then number two Elizabeth.
> And that's all folks, until her death ...

However, the above poem is notable for not including Lady Jane Grey, otherwise known as the Queen for Nine Days. Some academics accept that, as her name suggests, she ruled England for only nine days in 1553, between the reigns of Edward VI and Mary I, until her reign was cut short, as it were, by the headman's axe.

The poem also ignores the existence of a whole other royal dynasty which ruled in England before the arrival of Guillaume le Conqueror, who was, after all, French.

Since the Battle of Hastings and the foundation of the Norman dynasty of kings, there have been another five royal houses up to today. What follows is a full list of the kings and queens of the English, England and Britain, from AD 802[82] through to 2008, which also divides the rulers by royal house, where appropriate.

N.B. Not sure what the Roman numerals after a monarch's name mean? Then check out the section about Roman numerals in the chapter on Classics (page 354).

HOUSE OF WESSEX
Egbert (802–39)
Ethelwulf (839–55)
Ethelbald (855–60)
Ethelbert (860–66)
Ethelred I (866–71)
Alfred the Great (871–99)
Edward the Elder (899–924)

---

[82] We have started with Egbert because he was the first King of Wessex to have much of England under him as overlord.

Elfward (924)[83]

Athelstan (924–39)

Edmund I the Magnificent (939–46)

Eadred (946–55)

Eadwig the Fair (955–59)

Edgar the Peaceable (959–75)

Edward the Martyr (975–78)

Ethelred II the Unready (978–1016)

Edmund II, Ironside (1016)

HOUSE OF DENMARK

Canute (1016–35)

Harold I, Harefoot (1037–40)

Harthacanute (1040–42)

HOUSE OF WESSEX (restored)

Edward the Confessor (1042–66)

Harold II (1066)

HOUSE OF NORMANDY

William I the Conqueror (1066–87)[84]

William II, Rufus (1087–1100)

Henry I (1100–35)

Stephen (1135–54)

---

[83] Elfward was an illegitimate son of Edward the Elder. His reign lasted for less than a month.

[84] We might know him as William the Conqueror but, at the time, the English called him William the Bastard. It's not hard to understand why.

Did you know...?

Having seized the English throne on Henry I's death, despite having sworn fealty to the old king's daughter Matilda when she was declared as heir, Stephen had to battle his cousin, the Empress Maud, to keep control of the throne. The resulting civil war divided the country and lasted for the entirety of Stephen's reign, with Matilda even briefly ruling as queen herself for a time from 7 April–1 November 1141.

HOUSE OF PLANTAGENET

Henry II (1154–89)

Richard I, the Lionheart (1189–99)

John, Lackland (1199–1216)

Henry III (1216–72)

Edward I, Longshanks (1272–1307)

Edward II (1307–27)

Edward III (1327–77)

Richard II (1377–99)

Henry IV, Bolingbroke (1399–1413)

Henry V (1413–22)

Henry VI (1422–61, 1470–1)

Edward IV (1461–70, 1471–83)

Edward V (1483)

Richard III (1483–5)

Did you know...?

The House of Plantagenet was actually divided into two groups, the Houses of York and Lancaster. It was between the Yorkists (whose symbol was the white rose) and the Lancastrians (whose symbol was the red rose) that the Wars of the Roses were fought. These were a series of intermittent civil wars fought between 1455 and 1487 for control of the English throne. These two warring houses ruled England as follows:

House of Lancaster (1399–1461; 1470–1)

House of York (1461–70; 1471–85)

HOUSE OF TUDOR

Henry VII (1485–1509)
Henry VIII (1509–47)
Edward VI (1547–53)
Lady Jane Grey (1553)
Mary I (1553–8)
Elizabeth I (1558–1603)

HOUSE OF STUART

James I (1603–25)
Charles I (1625–49)

THE COMMONWEALTH

Did you know...?

During the time of the Commonwealth, following the execution of Charles I in 1649, there was no reigning monarch in England. However, during this time two men effectively ruled as Lords Protector. They were Oliver Cromwell (1653–58) and his son Richard Cromwell (1658–9). 1660 saw the Restoration of the monarchy when Charles II was invited to become king.

HOUSE OF STUART (restored)

Charles II (1660–85)
James II (1685–8)
William III & Mary II (1689–94)
William III (1694–1702)
Anne (1702–14)

Did you know...?

Incredibly, during her life Queen Anne gave birth to seventeen children! However, sadly none of them survived beyond infancy other than one son, the Duke of Gloucester, and he died when he was twelve. When Anne died on 1 August 1714 she was so vastly obese that she had to be buried in a square-shaped coffin.

HOUSE OF HANOVER

George I (1714–27)
George II (1727–60)
George III (1760–1820)
George IV (1820–30)
William IV (1830–7)
Victoria (1837–1901)

HOUSE OF WINDSOR

Edward VII (1901–10)
George V (1910–36)
Edward VIII (1936)
George VI (1936–52)
Elizabeth II (1952–)

Did you know...?

The sharp-eyed among you will have noticed that Edward VII ruled as the first of a different royal house to his mother, Queen Victoria. Such was the strength of anti-German feeling during the First World War, that the Royal Family, German in origin since the Hanoverian Settlement (see page 215), felt obliged to abandon all titles held under the German crown. On 17 July 1917, George V made a royal proclamation announcing that all descendants of Queen Victoria would now be members of the House of Windsor, taking the new title as a personal surname. So now you know.

❀ Prime Ministers ❀

Although kings and queens had a 900-year head-start, it some-times seems as though there have been almost as many prime ministers as English monarchs. However, generally a prime minister's term of office is considerably shorter than a monarch's reign (although not always), and a number of Britain's prime ministers have held that title on more than one occasion.

And of course, although Robert Walpole is widely accepted as being the first *de facto*[85] prime minister, technically he wasn't. Sir Henry Campbell-Bannerman *was*, in that he was the first to be officially given the title of Prime Minister in a Royal Warrant dated 10 December 1905. Up until that time, Walpole and his suc-cessors were First Lords of the Treasury, which means that there have actually been only nineteen prime ministers in total (includ-ing the current incumbent, Gordon Brown). The list below, how-ever, includes all those previous First Lords of the Treasury.

Who?	When?	Which party?
Robert Walpole, 1st Earl of Orford	1721–42	Whig
Spencer Compton, 1st Earl of Wilmington	1742–3	Whig
Henry Pelham	1743–54	Whig
Thomas Pelham-Holles, 4th Duke of Newcastle	1754–6	Whig
William Cavendish, 4th Duke of Devonshire	1756–7	Whig
Thomas Pelham-Holles, 4th Duke of Newcastle	1757–62	Whig
John Stuart, 3rd Earl of Bute	1762–3	Tory
George Grenville	1763–5	Whig

---

[85] Not sure what *de facto* means? Then quickly thumb forward to the Modern Latin Phrasebook that can be found in the chapter on Classics (page 332).

Who?	When?	Which party?
Charles Watson Wentworth, 2nd Marquess of Rockingham	1765–6	Whig
William Pitt the Elder	1766–8	Whig
Augustus Fitzroy, 3rd Duke of Grafton	1768–70	Whig
Frederick North, 2nd Earl of Guildford	1770–82	Tory
Charles Watson Wentworth, 2nd Marquess of Rockingham	1782	Whig
William Petty, Earl of Shelburne	1782–3	Whig
William Cavendish Bentinck, 3rd Duke of Portland	1783	Whig
William Pitt the Younger	1783–1801	Tory
Henry Addington	1801–4	Tory
William Pitt the Younger	1804–6	Tory
William Grenville, 1st Baron Grenville	1806–7	Whig
William Cavendish Bentinck, 3rd Duke of Portland	1807–9	Whig
Spencer Perceval	1809–12	Tory
Robert Banks Jenkinson, 2nd Earl of Liverpool	1812–27	Tory
George Canning	1827	Tory
Frederick Robinson, Viscount Goderich, 1st Earl of Ripon	1827–8	Tory
Arthur Wellesley, 1st Duke of Wellington	1828–30	Tory
Charles Grey, 2nd Earl Grey	1830–4	Whig
William Lamb, 2nd Viscount Melbourne	1834	Whig
Robert Peel	1834–5	Tory
William Lamb, 2nd Viscount Melbourne	1835–41	Whig
Robert Peel	1841–6	Tory
Lord John Russell, 1st Earl Russell	1846–52	Whig
Edward Stanley, 23rd Earl of Derby	1852	Conservative
George Hamilton-Gordon, 4th Earl of Aberdeen	1852–5	Tory

Who?	When?	Which party?
John Temple, 3rd Viscount Palmerston	1855–8	Liberal
Edward Stanley, 23rd Earl of Derby	1858–9	Conservative
John Temple, 3rd Viscount Palmerston	1859–65	Liberal
Lord John Russell, 1st Earl Russell	1865–6	Liberal
Edward Stanley, 23rd Earl of Derby	1866–8	Conservative
Benjamin Disraeli, 1st Earl of Beaconsfield	1868	Conservative
W.E. Gladstone	1868–74	Liberal
Benjamin Disraeli, 1st Earl of Beaconsfield	1874–80	Conservative
W.E. Gladstone	1880–5	Liberal
Robert Cecil, 3rd Marquess of Salisbury	1885–6	Conservative
W.E. Gladstone	1886	Liberal
Robert Cecil, 3rd Marquess of Salisbury	1886–92	Conservative
W.E. Gladstone	1892–4	Liberal
Archibald Primrose, 5th Earl of Rosebery	1894–5	Liberal
Robert Cecil, 3rd Marquess of Salisbury	1895–1902	Conservative
A.J. Balfour	1902–5	Conservative
Henry Campbell-Bannerman	1905–8	Liberal
H.H. Asquith	1908–16	Liberal
David Lloyd George	1916–22	Liberal
Andrew Bonar Law	1922–3	Conservative
Stanley Baldwin	1923–4	Conservative
Ramsay MacDonald	1924	Labour
Stanley Baldwin	1924–9	Conservative
Ramsay MacDonald	1929–35	Labour
Stanley Baldwin	1935–7	Conservative
Neville Chamberlain	1937–40	Conservative
Winston Churchill	1940–5	Conservative
Clement Attlee	1945–51	Labour
Winston Churchill	1951–5	Conservative
Anthony Eden	1955–7	Conservative
Harold Macmillan	1957–63	Conservative

Who?	When?	Which party?
Alec Douglas-Home	1963–4	Conservative
Harold Wilson	1964–70	Labour
Edward Heath	1970–4	Conservative
Harold Wilson	1974–6	Labour
James Callaghan	1976–9	Labour
Margaret Thatcher	1979–90	Conservative
John Major	1990–7	Conservative
Tony Blair	1997–2007	Labour
Gordon Brown	2007–	Labour

Whig – Whig was originally used to describe those people opposed to the religious policies of Charles II. However, the Whigs later supported the Hanoverian settlement (which, in 1714, allowed the Elector of Hanover in Germany to succeed to the British throne as George I). They believed in a constitutional monarchy, opposed the monarch's right to absolute rule, and favoured reform.

Tory – By the 19th century the Tories were the Whigs' parliamentary rivals. They supported the established Church and the traditional political structure, being keen monarchists.

Liberal – The Whigs steadily evolved into the Liberal Party.

Conservative – The Tories eventually became the Conservative Party.

Labour – The Labour Party wasn't established until 1900, when it became apparent that there was a need for the interests of the increasing numbers of the working classes to be represented by a political party.

❀ **Famous Battles** ✿

No matter how much we might try to escape from the fact, the modern world has been shaped by conflict more than anything else. War has necessitated advances in medicine and technology that might not have otherwise been achieved so quickly. Even Leonardo Da Vinci designed machines of war (when he wasn't busy planting clues about the nature of the Holy Grail in paintings for Tom Hanks to discover later).

Something which is sadly lacking from the knowledge of many young people today is the record of many of the famous (or you could argue *infamous*) battles that have had such a huge impact on the British Isles and the world beyond. To help reacquaint you with some of the facts that you may well have come across during your own school days, with which you can then better inform today's ill-educated younger generations, we present here a list of twenty of what should be the most famous battles fought by the British on British soil and beyond.

The Battle of …	When?	Where?	Who?	Why?	Who won?
1 Hastings	14 October 1066	Battle, East Sussex	King Harold of England's Saxons V Duke William of Normandy's Normans	Edward the Confessor died without an heir. Although Harold had previously sworn an oath to William that he could be king on Edward's death, Harold took the throne for himself instead. William invaded in order to take the crown of England by force.	The Normans

	The Battle of …	When?	Where?	Who?	Why?	Who won?
2	Arsuf	September 1191	Holy Land (modern-day Palestine/Israel)	Richard the Lionheart's English crusaders V The armies of Salah al-Din Yusuf ibn Ayyub, Sultan of Egypt and Syria (a.k.a. Saladin)	Arsuf was one of the many battles that made up the Crusades (1095–1291). Richard defeated Saladin's forces at Arsuf and almost reached Jerusalem, the crusaders' goal. However, he had to return to England to deal with problems caused by Prince John. Richard concluded a three-year pact with Saladin, which retained a narrow coastal strip of land for the crusaders and allowed pilgrims to enter Jerusalem.	The English Crusaders
3	Bannockburn	23–24 June 1314	Bannockburn, Stirlingshire	Robert Bruce's Scots V King Edward II's English	Bruce had rebelled against the English. He laid siege to Stirling as part of his struggle for Scottish independence. Edward II retaliated.	The Scots

	The Battle of ...	When?	Where?	Who?	Why?	Who won?
4	Agincourt	25 October 1415	Agincourt, France (40 miles south of Calais)	King Henry V's English army V The French army commanded by the Constable Charles d'Albret	In 1415 Henry V invaded France, resuming the Hundred Years War. A French army of 20,000 men, mainly armoured knights and men-at-arms, met Henry's force of 6,000, two-thirds of whom were archers, on a battlefield between two forests. The English longbow, cumbersome French armour and mud won the day for Henry, opening the door for him to conquer Normandy.	The English

	The Battle of ...	When?	Where?	Who?	Why?	Who won?
5	Bosworth	22 August 1485	Bosworth, Leicestershire	Richard III, of the House of York V Henry Tudor, of the House of Lancaster	Bosworth was the last major battle of the Wars of the Roses. The Houses of Lancaster and York had been at war since 1455. Henry had made a secret deal with Lord Stanley, who was supposed to be on Richard's side. When Stanley revealed his true colours during the battle, the tide turned for Richard and the Yorkist army was defeated.	Henry Tudor, who became Henry VII.
6	Flodden	9 September 1513	Branxton, Northumberland	James IV's Scots V Earl of Surrey's English	Henry VII invaded France, forcing James IV to attack England in order to uphold Scotland's 'Auld Alliance' with France.	The English

The Battle of …	When?	Where?	Who?	Why?	Who won?
7 The Spanish Armada	29 July 1588	The North Sea off Gravelines, the coastal border area between France and the Spanish Netherlands	Admiral Lord Howard and the English fleet V The Spanish fleet under the Duke of Medina Sidonia	Wanting to conquer England and make it a Catholic country again, King Philip II of Spain ordered an invasion, sending a fleet of ships to lead the way. Drake's use of fire ships, and bad weather, helped him best the Spanish fleet.	The English
8 Edge Hill	23 October 1642	Edge Hill, Warwickshire	Charles I's Royalist army V Earl of Essex's Parliamentary troops	Edgehill was the first battle of the English Civil War. Charles marched from Shrewsbury towards London with his newly raised army, while Essex marched out to meet him. The two armies were roughly the same size (14,500 men). After only three hours of fighting neither side was able to make headway, and they broke off the fight as darkness descended.	The battle was a draw, but Charles I 'won' in that London was open to him. However, he didn't follow up on this opportunity.

	The Battle of ...	When?	Where?	Who?	Why?	Who won?
9	Naseby	14 June 1645	Naseby, Northamptonshire	Prince Rupert's Royalist army V Sir Thomas Fairfax's Parliamentary troops	At the height of the English Civil War, Cromwell's New Model Army brought King Charles's chances of winning the war to an end. The Parliamentary cavalry was initially pushed back by the Cavaliers, and the infantry soon followed. However, Cromwell's horse wheeled to attack the Royalist flank and the superior numbers of the Roundheads began a total rout of the Cavaliers.	Cromwell's Roundheads

	The Battle of ...	When?	Where?	Who?	Why?	Who won?
10	Blenheim	13 August 1704	Blenheim, Bavaria	The English under the Duke of Marlborough V French and Bavarian forces	Blenheim was a major battle in the War of the Spanish Succession (1701–14), which was fought in Europe and on the Mediterranean. It was the first in which Britain played a major military role in European military affairs. Marlborough marched 250 miles across Germany from the Netherlands to confront the French at Blenheim, destroying two-thirds of their army and capturing its commander, Marshal Tallard.	The English

The Battle of …	When?	Where?	Who?	Why?	Who won?
11 Culloden	16 April 1746	Culloden Moor, Inverness	Bonnie Prince Charlie's Jacobite Scots V British troops (Scots and English) under the Duke of Cumberland	Charles Stuart had invaded England, attempting to take the crown from George I, but was forced back into Scotland, as far as the Highlands. The Jacobites under Charles attempted a night march to surprise the British army but when it became obvious they could not come close enough in time for a dawn attack, the Jacobites were forced to retreat to their camp at Culloden Moor. The ill-fed and exhausted Jacobites were then poorly prepared when Cumberland ordered his men to march on them.	The British

The Battle of …	When?	Where?	Who?	Why?	Who won?
12 Trafalgar	21 October 1805	Off Cape Trafalgar, Cadiz, Spain	The Royal Navy under Admiral Lord Nelson V Combined French and Spanish fleet under the French Admiral, Pierre Villeneuve	The most significant naval battle of the Napoleonic Wars; a Royal Navy fleet of 27 ships of the line destroyed an allied French and Spanish fleet of 33 ships. The French and Spanish lost 22 ships, while the British lost none. Admiral Lord Nelson died late in the battle, having already ensured his place as Britain's greatest naval hero.	The British

	The Battle of …	When?	Where?	Who?	Why?	Who won?
13	Balaclava	25 October 1854	Balaclava, a town in the Crimea, Ukraine	The British army under Lord Raglan and the French army under General François Certain Canrobert V The Russian army under Prince Aleksandr Sergeyevich Menshikov	Britain entered the Crimean War (1854–6) between Russia and Turkey on the side of the Turks to protect her Mediterranean sea routes. The Battle of Balaclava was a key battle during the war, being the first of two attempts by the Russians to break the Siege of Sevastopol. It is famous for the disastrous cavalry charge led by Lord Cardigan. Thanks to Alfred, Lord Tennyson's poem, 'The Charge of the Light Brigade', it has become a symbol of warfare at its most courageous and, at the same time, tragic.	The battle ended in a draw, with both sides retaining their starting positions.

The Battle of ...	When?	Where?	Who?	Why?	Who won?
14 The Siege of Lucknow	July–November 1857	Lucknow, India	The British East India Company V The Indian rebels	The state of Oudh had been annexed by the British East India Company and the provincial governor, Wajid Ali Shah, exiled to Calcutta the year before the rebellion broke out. During the Indian Mutiny (1857) the city of Lucknow was besieged by Indian rebels, relieved by the forces of the British East India Company, besieged again, and relieved for a second time.	The British East India Company

	The Battle of …	When?	Where?	Who?	Why?	Who won?
15	The Defence of Rorke's Drift	22–23 January 1879	Rorke's Drift, a mission station in Natal, South Africa	The British garrison under John Chard and Gonville Bromhead V The Zulu warriors of Prince Dabulamanzi	The defence of Rorke's Drift immediately followed the British army's defeat at the Battle of Isandlwana earlier the same day, part of the Anglo-Zulu War of 1879. Against all odds, 139 British soldiers defended their garrison against an assault by 4,000–5,000 Zulu warriors. The successful defence of the outpost is one of the British armed forces' finest hours, and one of history's finest defences.	The British
16	The Siege of Mafeking	October 1899–May 1900	Mafeking, South Africa	The British army under Colonel (later Lord) Baden-Powell V General Piet Cronje Boers	One of the most famous British actions in the Second Boer War (1899–1902), the lifting of the Siege of Mafeking was a decisive victory for the British and a crushing defeat for the Boers.	The British

	The Battle of ...	When?	Where?	Who?	Why?	Who won?
17	Jutland	31 May 1916	The North Sea, off the coast of Jutland, Denmark	The Royal Navy's British Grand Fleet commanded by Admiral Sir John Jellicoe V The Imperial German Navy's High Seas Fleet commanded by Vice-Admiral Reinhard Scheer	The Battle of Jutland was the largest naval battle of the First World War and the only full-scale clash between battleships. The Germans wanted to trap and destroy part of the Grand Fleet so as to help break the British naval blockade of the North Sea. The Royal Navy wanted to engage and cripple the High Seas Fleet, thereby keeping the German force bottled up and away from their own shipping lanes.	The battle was inconclusive but both sides claimed victory; the British a strategic victory, the Germans a tactical victory

	The Battle of ...	When?	Where?	Who?	Why?	Who won?
18	The Somme	July– November 1916	Around the River Somme, France	The Allied forces of the French and English V The German army on the Western Front	French Field Marshal Joffre planned a grand offensive employing British and French troops. The aim was to win the war on the Western Front with a decisive breakthrough. On the first day of the battle, the British advanced, only to be caught in the German barbed wire and massacred by machine gun fire. The British lost 57,450 men and gained a mere 1,000 yards. The French did only slightly better.	A battle of attrition, it simply petered out by 19 November. The Allies had won a strip of land 30 miles long and seven miles wide.

	The Battle of …	When?	Where?	Who?	Why?	Who won?
19	Britain	10 July–31 October 1940	In the skies over Britain	The British Royal Air Force V The German Luftwaffe	The Battle of Britain was a strategic effort by the German Luftwaffe to gain air superiority over the Royal Air Force, at the height of the Second World War. It was the first major campaign to be fought entirely by air forces. If it had been successful, planned amphibious assault and airborne landings in Britain would have followed.	The British Royal Air Force
20	Normandy	June–August 1944	Normandy, France	The Allied forces of Britain, Australia, Canada, France and the United States V The occupying German army	Codenamed Operation Overlord, the Battle of Normandy was the long awaited Allied invasion of France and the opening of the Second Front during the Second World War. It remains the largest seaborne invasion in history with over 156,000 troops crossing the English Channel from the United Kingdom to Normandy	The British and their Allies

A Brief History of Britain
(from 1066–1945)

If your knowledge of British history is based on what you've picked up from television documentaries and what you can remember of the *Blackadder* TV series, then have no fear. *Match Wits With The Kids* is here to help.

1066 And All That:
From Conquest to Constitution (1066–1500)

1066 saw William, Duke of Normandy, wrest control of the English throne from the Saxon Earl Harold of Wessex (who had taken the throne after the death of Edward the Confessor, even though Edward had named William as his heir), following his victory at the **Battle of Hastings**. The time that followed is known as the Norman Conquest and the battle itself is recorded in the Bayeux Tapestry.

So that William I (the Conqueror) might assess his new kingdom, he commissioned a survey, known as the **Domesday Book**. William, and the Norman kings after him, imposed the feudal system which organised the way the land was managed.

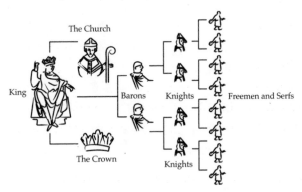

The Church

King

Barons   Knights   Freemen and Serfs

The Crown

Knights

The feudal system

William faced rebellion on a number of occasions and dealt swiftly and brutally with any uprisings, which helped establish Norman dominance. The Normans also built castles from which they could impose their iron rule of the surrounding lands. These began as motte and bailey constructions of earth and wood but as soon as was practicable they were replaced with stone castles.

In return for land 'lent' to them by the king in their position as tenants-in-chief, Norman barons and knights were expected to serve time in the king's army and to provide him with soldiers. A knight's son would prepare to become a knight himself from childhood. At age seven he would be sent to live in another nobleman's castle where he would serve as a page. At fifteen he would become squire to a knight and learn war-craft. The squire would become a knight at 21, if his lord or the king thought he was ready, after undergoing a vigil (a night of prayer).

Did you know...?
The tenets of knighthood, which included codes of conduct regarding how a knight should behave in the company of ladies, became idealised in the ideas of courtly love and chivalry. The word chivalry itself comes from the French for knight, *chevalier*.

A knight's lands were called his manor. The preferred methods of farming used a three-yearly cycle of crop rotation (whereby each of the three fields in turn would be left fallow for a year, allowing the soil to recover its nutrients), with the peasant villeins (the people who lived in villages) being given strips of land to work. A peasant's life was inextricably tied to the seasons and was very hard.

Things didn't improve for the average peasant until after the **Black Death**. By 1300 the population of England was three times what it had been at the time of the Norman Conquest, but then in **1348** the plague struck. Brought from Europe by rats infected with fleas (the actual plague-carriers), the Black Death swept through the populace, bringing chaos across the country. One-third of the population of Europe was wiped out (approximately 25 million people). For those who survived, however, conditions improved. With fewer workers around, wages rose and the feudal system began to go into decline.

Towns grew in importance during the medieval period and from the 12th to the 13th centuries, over 140 new settlements were built. They grew up around ports, trade centres, river crossings, castles and larger religious centres, such as cathedrals. Craftsmen living in the towns formed societies called guilds.

The Catholic Church also had great influence over people's lives, partly because the bishops were landowners equal to the barons (in terms of both how much land they owned and their social standing). Some men and women took vows of poverty, chastity, obedience and stability, joined a monastery (for the men) or a convent (for the women), and became monks and nuns, giving up the worldly for the spiritual.

As a result of religious discontentment and the introduction of the first poll tax, **1381** saw the uprising known as the **Peasants' Revolt**, led by Wat Tyler (who was ultimately beheaded for his troubles).

During his reign, Edward I (a.k.a. Longshanks) conquered Wales but was unable to do the same to Scotland. Led by such figures as William Wallace (a.k.a. Braveheart) and Robert the Bruce, the Scots resisted the English, with the **Battle of Bannockburn** in **1314** being a notable Scottish victory.

Things didn't go well for the monarchy in general during this time, as the medieval period also saw a reduction in the power wielded by the monarch, with Parliament growing in prominence. In **1215** the barons forced King John to sign the **Magna Carta** at Runnymede, a charter including 63 clauses which told the king what he could and couldn't do (including limiting how much tax he could charge).

Parliament was effectively co-founded by Simon de Montfort (who ruled as regent for seven years, until Henry III was sixteen) and Edward I. De Montfort made sure that two knights from each county and two rich men from each chartered town were elected to join a meeting at Westminster Abbey in 1258 to protest against high levels of taxation.

Edward understood that the monarch needed 'the consent of the realm' and so called the '**model Parliament**' in **1295** to discuss how the country should be run. He actually needed those attending to agree to pay taxes which would fund his battles against the Welsh, the Scots and the French.

Richard II did not agree with the sentiment of needing anyone's consent other than his own, which resulted in him being overthrown by his own barons and replaced with Henry Bolingbroke, who became Henry IV. Parliament continued to grow in importance during the Tudor period and by 1500 it was a vital instrument in helping to run the country.

⚘ ⚘ ⚘

Dynastic Discontent:
From Kingdom Come to a United Kingdom (1500–1750)

In 1509, Henry VIII became king, after the death of his father Henry VII, who had established the Tudor dynasty following his triumph over Richard III at the **Battle of Bosworth** in **1485**. However, the new dynasty was still in danger, and England would most likely face another civil war if the king could not produce a male heir. After the death of Prince Arthur, Henry married his elder brother's widow, Catherine of Aragon. They had six children but only one survived beyond infancy and that was a daughter, Mary.

When Henry fell for the charms of Anne Boleyn in 1527 he sent the Archbishop of Canterbury, Cardinal Thomas Wolsey, to see the Pope, that the pontiff might grant him a divorce from Catherine. His request was denied, as the Bible forbade remarriage. Henry's response was to remove Wolsey from office and replace him with Thomas Cranmer.

The new Archbishop of Canterbury declared that Henry's marriage to Catherine had been unlawful and so king and queen were divorced. Henry married Anne Boleyn in 1533 but the only heir she bore him was another girl, Elizabeth.

Henry's desire for a son led him to have Anne executed so that he might marry Jane Seymour, who at last gave him Edward, the male heir he so wanted. Jane died soon after as a result of complications arising during childbirth.

Henry went on to marry three more times, first Anne of Cleves (whom he divorced), then Catherine Howard (whom he also had executed) and lastly Catherine Parr (who had already been married twice herself and went on to outlive him).

Did you know...?

A popular rhyme exists to help the budding history scholar remember what happened to each of Henry VIII's six wives.

Divorced, beheaded, died; divorced, beheaded, survived.

However, if you are going to be pedantic, Henry VIII was actually married only twice. On becoming head of the new Church of England, Henry himself declared that his marriage to Catherine of Aragon had been illegal. He also annulled his marriages to Anne Boleyn, Anne of Cleves and Catherine Howard. So according to Henry, he was only ever married to Jane Seymour and Catherine Parr.

Because of Henry's scant regard for the Pope and the Catholic Church, Pope Clement VII had him excommunicated, but Parliament named him the **Supreme Head of the Church** instead in **1534**. Catholics who refused to accept Henry's new position were executed. The period **1537–9** saw the **dissolution of the monasteries**, during which Henry had these establishments closed, taking their lands for himself, a process that was overseen by Thomas Cromwell.

Did you know...?

The monarch bears the title *Fidei defensor*, meaning 'Defender of the Faith'. Ironically, this title was first awarded to Henry VIII (the man who did more damage to the Catholic Church in this country than any other) by Pope Leo X after Henry wrote a book attacking the Protestant ideas of the German monk, Martin Luther.

Henry VIII died in **1547** and the nine-year-old Prince Edward became Edward VI. During his reign, England became a truly Protestant nation and this period, known as the **Reformation**, saw the introduction of a new Protestant Prayer Book.

Edward died in 1553, aged only fifteen, and his 37-year-old sister Mary became queen. She is now known affectionately as 'Bloody Mary' since during her reign England saw a return to Catholicism (Mary's husband being the Catholic King Philip II of Spain), with the queen herself ordering that 284 Protestants be burned at the stake. Two of these martyrs were the bishops Nicholas Ridley and Hugh Latimer, who were burned in Oxford in 1555.

Mary died without an heir of her own in 1558 and so her younger half-sister ascended to the throne. After years of religious persecution running rife throughout England, Queen Elizabeth I wanted her realm to be united under one Anglican Church. She found a middle way, pleasing as many people as possible by allowing them to believe in a wide-ranging set of ideas, so long as they lived peacefully and obeyed the law.

She still had other problems to deal with, however, most notably Mary Stuart (a.k.a. Mary Queen of Scots), her Catholic cousin. Mary believed she had a claim to the English throne and so became the focus for those who wanted to see England as a Catholic country again. Realising the threat Mary posed, but not wishing to execute a family member, Elizabeth kept her under virtual house arrest for nearly twenty years. With plots continuing to form with Mary as their figurehead, she was executed in 1587 on Elizabeth's reluctant orders.

In **1588** England was threatened by the **Spanish Armada**, part of King Philip II of Spain's plan to conquer the country and make it Catholic again. Under the command of Francis Drake (and helped by bad weather) the attack was repelled.

Despite the difficulties that faced Elizabeth, during her reign England became a richer and more stable country. This was helped by increasing overseas trade and the settlement of colonies, particularly in the Americas. The slave trade in particular proved to be very profitable.

Did you know...?
The state of Virginia in America was named in honour of Elizabeth I, who was known as the Virgin Queen because of the fact that she never ... *ahem* ... married.

When Elizabeth died in 1603, having never married or produced an heir, she was succeeded, ironically, by the son of Mary Queen of Scots, James VI of Scotland, who then also became James I of England. James argued with Parliament over religion as well as his belief in the 'divine right of kings'.

James's heir, Charles I, also quarrelled with Parliament, as he seemed to believe that he could rule the country almost as a dictator, and without the 'consent of the realm'. He married a Catholic, which annoyed the Protestants of England, collected 'ship money' (a tax to fund a navy) without permission, and refused to obey Parliament and heed the advice of MP-appointed councillors.

These incidents, and others like them, ultimately led to Parliament taking control of the army and from there, in **1642**, the country descended into **civil war**.

The Cavaliers, the king's troops, were noblemen and their followers. The Roundheads were the parliamentary supporters: merchants, townspeople, farmers and the like. Their leader was Oliver Cromwell, backed up by his 'New Model Army'. In 1646 Charles was captured. The king threw out Cromwell's idea that the monarch should rule with Parliament's consent and, after bringing the Scots into the war, was put on trial for treason. He was found guilty and executed in 1649.

From **1649–60** England became a republic (a country without a monarch), sometimes called the **Commonwealth**, led by

Cromwell. Following Cromwell's death in 1658, his son Richard took over as Lord Protector but he was so unsuited to the position that in 1660, Parliament offered the throne to Charles I's son, who was living in exile on the Continent. He became Charles II and was dubbed 'The Merry Monarch' because his reign brought an end to the austerity of Puritan England. This period is called the **Restoration**.

During Henry VIII's reign, Wales had been joined with England as a result of the Acts of Union. English control of Ireland began with Elizabeth I taking land there to give to her Protestant supporters, a practice that continued under Cromwell. In 1691 William III (a.k.a. William of Orange) attacked Ireland, punishing the Irish people for opposing English rule, although the country wasn't officially joined to Britain until the **1801 Act of Union**.

Scotland became part of the United Kingdom in **1707**, but many Scots (especially the Highlanders) objected to English rule. In **1745** Bonnie Prince Charlie and his army invaded England but were defeated at the **Battle of Culloden**. And so, by **1750**, the **United Kingdom** (almost as we know it today) had been formed.

ᛉ ᛉ ᛉ

Rise of the Machines:
From Revolution to Reform (1750–1900)

At the beginning of the **18th century**, most people in England lived in the south, the south-west and East Anglia, but 200 years later the most densely populated parts of the country were those that surrounded important sites connected to the **Industrial Revolution**.

In 1801 the population of England was 11.5 million, and yet by 1901, only 100 years later, it was 42.1 million! This was due to a rising birth rate, coupled with a falling death rate as standards of public health improved.

This dramatic increase in population size resulted in an increased demand for food and industrially produced goods. This inspired both farmers, who knew money was to be made from improving food production, and industrialists, such as factory owners and inventors.

From 1750–1820 around 5 million acres of land were enclosed using fences and hedges. The **General Enclosure Act** of **1801** made enclosure compulsory, allowing wealthy landowners to create new farms. People who could not prove that they were legal tenants lost their land.

As farming was modernised, and the Norfolk four-course rotation system was introduced, fields were no longer left fallow. Heavier and healthier types of cattle and sheep were bred. Fertilisers were used to make the land more profitable. And thanks to advances made during the Industrial Revolution, farm machinery was now made from cheaply produced iron rather than wood.

However, the **mid-19th century** saw people start to move away from the country to work in the rapidly **growing towns**. Cheap food imported from places like Canada and Argentina saw a decline in the fortunes of some British farmers, forcing people to seek employment in urban, rather than rural, settings.

Before the Industrial Revolution, everything had to be produced at home or in cottage industries. However, the increasing need for goods from the rising population meant that this domestic system could no longer provide the necessary output. Thanks to the work of a number of lauded inventors, machines were designed that could keep up with the demand.

One such man was James Hargreaves, who invented the **'Spinning Jenny'**[86] in **1764**; this helped spinners produce more yarn, which was needed by the weavers to make into clothes. However, the development of such machines – which included **Arkwright's water frame** and **Crompton's 'mule'** – meant the home-employed spinners lost their jobs and were forced to go and work in the factories. The same thing then happened to the weavers, who had become rich making clothes for the growing populace, when weaving became mechanised in 1785.

Advances in the production of cast iron, and later wrought iron, meant that in the space of 60 years or so, people went from making cooking pots to building bridges from iron. The most important invention of the time, however, was the steam engine. In 1763, James Watt improved Newcomen's engine (invented in 1712) and by **1782** Watt, Matthew Boulton (a factory owner) and William Murdock were able to build an engine capable of driving all manner of machines, which in turn made **cheap mass production** a reality.

In **1825** George Stephenson took the idea a step further and built the **first passenger engine** in the world. It ran from Stockton to Darlington. The Manchester to Liverpool railway soon followed.

Not everyone welcomed the changes that came about because of the Industrial Revolution. In **1819**, people holding a political protest at St Peter's Field, Manchester, against a backdrop of mass unemployment caused by machines and rising food prices,

---

[86] Named after his wife!

were killed in what is now known as the **Peterloo Massacre**. Luddites (named after one Ned Ludd) were workers who feared that machines were stealing their jobs from them and so set about destroying them.

Another creation of the Industrial Age was a new industrial middle class, which emerged as the factory owners became richer and richer. At the same time, as a direct consequence of the industry-driven growth of the towns, the position of the poor became increasingly dire. Child labour was used in mills and mines as children could be paid less than adults.

The plight of such children, and adult workers as well, resulted in a number of factory and public health reforms. These were spearheaded by people like Lord Shaftesbury (Ashley Cooper), Robert Owen, Sir Robert Peel and Dr Thomas Barnardo. They resulted in laws safeguarding employees from having to work overly long hours and protecting them from the hazards of using dangerous machinery.

1833	**Factory Act**	Children under the age of nine may not be employed.
1842	**Coal Mines Act**	Children are banned from working underground.
1844	**Factory Act**	Children are allowed to work only for six-and-a-half hours a day.
1850	**Factory Act**	The workday is changed to correspond with the maximum number of hours that women and children can work.
1853	**Factory Act**	The working day for men and women in textile mills is fixed at ten hours.
1875	**Factory Act**	Children are banned from brickyard jobs, nail-making and the like. Workers have a half-day off on Saturdays.

Edwin Chadwick (1800–90) issued a report which starkly demonstrated the differences in death rates for people living in towns compared to those who lived in the countryside. In towns the poor suffered from terrible housing conditions, poor sanitation (as sewers were costly to install) and an inadequate diet.

In **1832** the **Great Reform Act** was passed, giving more people of the new industrial middle class the right to vote. However, the working classes were left out of the picture. Chartists (who supported a Charter of six points, which promoted votes for all) wanted to force Parliament to grant the Charter, and some were prepared to use violence to get their point across. Most MPs (who were from the middle or upper classes) did not believe that the poor had earned the right to vote.

However, the Great Reform Act did pave the way for true Parliamentary democracy in Britain. In 1867, skilled working class men (over the age of 21) were given the right to vote. By **1928**, all men and women over 21 could vote in secret ballots, with MPs being paid so that working-class people could now afford to become MPs. In **1900**, a joint venture by trade unionists and members of socialist societies established the **Labour Party**, hoping that one day Britain might be governed by a Labour government.

≀ ≀ ≀

A Century of War:
From the Western Front to East versus West (1900–1945)

On 28 June 1914, Archduke Franz Ferdinand, heir to the crown of Austria, was shot dead by a Serbian[87] in the capital of Bosnia,

---

[87] A student named Gavrilo Princip, a signed-up member of the Serbian nationalist Black Hand Gang.

Sarajevo. Thanks to a complicated spider's web of treaties held between nations, on **12 August 1914**, as a result of the assassination, Britain and France declared war on Austria; the **First World War** had begun.

At first people all over Europe were excited by the prospect of war, many young men seeing it as their patriotic duty to volunteer to join the army. Much of the initial fighting took place in Northern France and Belgium. **Britain**, **France** and **Russia** (the **Triple Entente**) faced off against **Germany**, **Austria** and **Italy** (the **Triple Alliance**). The war was not expected to last beyond Christmas.

However, the German Schlieffen Plan (designed to capture Paris as quickly as possible) failed, and so the troops on both sides dug in. What followed on the Western Front was nearly four years of trench warfare. The war became a war of attrition; the first side to run out of weapons and soldiers would lose.

The First World War wasn't fought only on land. There were notable battles at sea, with the Germans in particular employing U-boats (submarines). Planes and tanks were also used for the first time towards the end of the war. A horrendous 9 million soldiers died from 1914–18 as a result of the fighting.

The war came to end thanks in part to the United States joining the war on the side of the allies of the Triple Entente, and also the blockading of German ports, which resulted in severe food shortages. The German Kaiser Wilhelm II (1859–1941) escaped to Holland and a new government took over in Germany in place of the old regime. They asked for a ceasefire, and at 11 o'clock in the morning on **11 November 1918**,[88] the First World War ended.

The war had a long-lasting effect on Britain. It led to an improvement in the diet of the poorer working classes, women earned the right to vote, it saw the development of propaganda, and war memorials were raised in practically every village in the country.

The **Treaty of Versailles** severely punished the losers of the war, Germany in particular. This was one of the reasons why Hitler and his National Socialist Party (the Nazis) came to power (following the collapse of the German economy and the Weimar Republic) which, in turn, led to there being a Second World War.

Despite **Neville Chamberlain's** assurances of **'Peace in our time'**, in September 1938 Germany annexed the German-speaking Sudetenland from the rest of Czechoslovakia. On **3 September 1939** Britain and France declared war on Germany once again. Both Russia and America joined the war on the side of the Allies in 1941, after Germany attacked Russia and Japan bombed Pearl Harbour respectively.

After five years of battles – at sea, in the air and on the land – right across the globe, on **6 June 1944** (**D-Day**) allied troops from Britain, the United States and Canada landed on the beaches of Normandy as part of 'Operation Overlord'. By September they had liberated France and Belgium, and on **30 April 1945** Hitler committed suicide as the Allied forces advanced on Berlin. On **8 May 1945**, Germany surrendered.

---

[88] Now remembered every year on Armistice Day, with the poppy used as the symbol of the commemoration. The poppy was the first flower to appear on the battlefield of France and Belgium after the Great War ended, and its colour has come to signify the blood of the fallen.

Although this date saw victory in Europe, the war against Germany's ally Japan continued until August. Japan surrendered following the dropping of the first atomic bombs[89] on the cities of **Hiroshima** and **Nagasaki**.

1945 might have seen the end of one world war, but in a way another was about to begin. After the Second World War the victorious leaders Churchill (Britain), Roosevelt (USA) and Stalin (Russia) met to discuss the fate of Germany, agreeing to divide it between them. Europe was divided by what Churchill described as an **'iron curtain'**, with Stalin's army effectively seizing Poland, Bulgaria, Hungary, Romania, Czechoslovakia and Yugoslavia, and imposing communist rule upon them. These Eastern European countries all became part of the Union of Soviet Socialist Republics (or USSR), Stalin's new dictatorship. The resulting **Cold War** between the East and the West lasted for 45 years, from the end of the Second World War through to the collapse of the USSR in 1990.

In Britain, the years following the Second World War saw the introduction of the **Welfare State** and the **National Health Service**, a growth in immigration, the building of the motor-ways and high-rises and the growing affluence of all. The austerity of the war years was over and Britain, although it had lost its Empire, was a global power nonetheless, very different to the country that William I had conquered 900 years earlier.

---

[89] Called, rather incongruously, 'Little Boy' and 'Fat Man'.

❀ Spot Test! ❀

So many dates, so many names! That's why it's best to test when they're fresh; it helps to stamp history into your memory.

But how agile is your memory, parents? Have the kids turned it into a dusty relic that crumbles when touched? And kids, your memories are in great shape, no doubt about that – but is there space for important historical stuff in among all that encyclopaedic knowledge of computer games?

Sharpen your pencils, don't peek at each other's answers (it probably won't help anyway) and let's see what you know!

1) What does CE stand for in dates?
2) The year 1234 is in which century?
3) Which royal house did Alfred the Great (871–99) belong to?
4) Which three monarchs were children of Henry VIII?
5) Who was the first Labour prime minister?
6) When was the Defence of Rorke's Drift?
7) When did the Black Plague reach England?
8) Who or what were the Luddites?
9) Which flower is used to commemorate Armistice Day?
10) In what year did the USSR collapse?

1) *Common Era.* 2) *The 13th century.* 3) *The House of Wessex.* 4) *Edward VI (1547–53), Mary I (1553–8) and Elizabeth I (1558–1603).* 5) *Ramsay MacDonald (1924).* 6) *22–23 January 1879.* 7) *1348.* 8) *19th-century workers who destroyed machinery, believing it was stealing their jobs. They were named after their leader, Ned Ludd.* 9) *The poppy.* 10) *1990.*

Chapter Seven

GEOGRAPHY
Around the World in a Day

Geography (from the Greek *gaia* meaning 'Earth' and *graph-ein* 'to write') is the study of people and places (although the word literally means 'writing about the Earth').

There will be elements of geography that *Match Wits With The Kids* won't be able to help you with. For example, the truly devoted student of geography will be able to produce carefully drawn field sketches, accurately labelled maps and clear diagrams to help explain their work. You won't find any of that here.

However, what you will find, alongside familiar topics concerning physical geography, common Ordnance Survey map symbols and compass points, is information which children do not necessarily need to learn at school any more, but which you did – countries and their capitals, cities of the UK, the Beaufort Scale – updated as required for the 21st century.

So come on, what are you waiting for? You have the world at your feet.[90]

---

[90] Or, rather, in your hands.

❧ X Marks the Spot ❧

Probably the first thing that most people think of when you mention the word geography is spending a double lesson in a dusty classroom, in the company of a dusty old teacher with patches on the elbows of his jacket, poring over even dustier maps.

There are of course many different types of maps, from globes and atlases[91] to the London Tube map and the good old *A to Z*. Maps are all around us, in shopping centres, guiding us around tourist attractions, even on the back of takeaway menus showing you where to collect your Friday night curry.

Maps can be used for all sorts of purposes, and not just to find out how to get from A to B. They can provide us with historical information, inform us of political allegiances, tell us where national boundaries lie, impart information about population size and density, and even inform us of how land is used.

However, there are a few things that almost all maps have in common, and that is that they have a scale, they pass on information about distance, and they give us some idea of direction, usually in the form of a compass point.

Of course there are always going to be exceptions, such as Paul Garbutt's schematic diagram of the London Underground (little changed from when he designed it in 1964), which rejects any semblance of accurate distances and locations to create the most navigable and useful map possible.

---

[91] According to Greek myth, Atlas was the Titan who held up the sky (*not* the Earth). His image was reproduced on the covers of early collections of maps, with the world resting on his shoulders, hence the modern use of his name to describe a book of maps.

Direction, scale and distance

Direction helps us to describe where something is in relation to something else, and is given using the points of the compass. Usually the four points of the compass, **north**, **east**, **south** and **west**, will suffice (recalled using the mnemonic 'Naughty Elephants Squirt Water') but these can be sub-divided to give greater accuracy. However, sometimes that is still not enough and a sixteen-point compass is required, which looks like this:

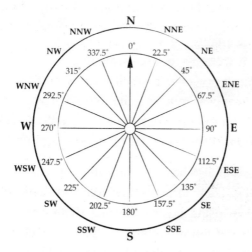

Handily, the varying directions shown on the compass are all composed from the four basic points (so don't forget those naughty elephants). NNW, for example, simply means 'north by northwest' and ESE likewise stands for 'east by southeast'. When faced with two points such as WSW and SSW, it can be hard to remember which one is indicating further south. The trick is to look at the first letter. This tells you which of the main points it is closest to. In this case, west by southwest is closer to west; south by southwest is nearer to south and therefore the more southerly of the two.

Unless it is clearly shown on the map to be otherwise, convention has it that north is at the top. On Ordnance Survey (or OS) maps, light blue grid lines run north to south and east to west.

Scale helps us understand how much smaller a map is when it is compared to what it actually represents in the real world. A map that has a scale of 1:100,000, for example, is 100,000 times smaller than what it represents. In this case, 1 cm on the map would be equal to 100,000 cm – or 1 km – on the ground.

As the scale of a map increases, so does the level of detail, although, inevitably, it will represent a smaller area on the ground, as it were. So, a large-scale map makes objects appear relatively large but over a small area. A small-scale map will make objects appear much smaller but will cover a significantly larger area. With OS maps, no matter what the scale, the light blue grid squares always equal 1 km^2 on the ground.

Some maps will also have an indication of what the land being represented is like in terms of its height and shape, or relief. This can be shown using layer colouring (with low land coloured green and very high mountains purple) or using contour lines. On an OS map, these are thin brown lines which join places that are at the same height above sea level. Contour lines usually go up in 10 m increments and have their height written on them. Exact heights can be marked using either spot heights (a dot with a number next to it) or triangulation points (a blue triangle with a dot inside, and the height in metres written next to it).

Grid references

The **Ordnance Survey** divides Britain into a national grid, with each grid square (identified by a two-letter grid reference) covering an area 100 km by 100 km. The grid is technically known as OSGB36 (Ordnance Survey Great Britain 1936).

Four-figure grid references pinpoint an area of 1 km^2 on an OS map. To find a grid reference, always follow the same rule: along the hall and up the stairs. In other words, start with the first two figures (the eastings) and move along the bottom of the map until you find them. Then move up the side until you find the second two numbers (the northings). Where these two lines meet, above and to the right of that point is the grid square you are after.

Six-figure gird references determine an area of only 100 m^2 on an OS map. You find a six-figure grid reference much as you would a four-figure grid reference. Follow the numbers along the bottom of the map until you find the first two numbers of the grid reference (the eastings). Imagine the next square along is divided into ten smaller increments. The third number refers to one of these increments. Then move to the side of the map and find the fourth and fifth numbers of the grid reference (the northings). The sixth number pinpoints a position related to one of the ten imaginary increments in the next square up. Where the two lines meet is the location you are seeking.

Using grid references in this way, any place in Britain can be accurately located.

Did you know...?

The Ordnance Survey is the national mapping agency for Great Britain but its name reflects its original military purpose – mapping Britain during the Napoleonic Wars. However, its origins go back to 1747, when King George II commissioned a military survey of the Scottish highlands in the aftermath of the Jacobite revolt of 1745. Then in 1790, the Board of Ordnance (one of the predecessors of the Ministry of Defence) began a national military survey, starting with the south coast of England, expecting an invasion from France.

Common OS map symbols

The **map symbols** commonly found on OS maps are either **tiny drawings** (that look like the thing they represent in real life), **lines** of different colours and thicknesses (to represent roads, railways, rivers and the like), and **colours** used to shade larger areas and relating to land use (showing things like forests, large bodies of water, farmland and open countryside).

There are also capital **letters** (usually describing a particular type of building or other object), **abbreviations** of words, used in order to save space (and not shown on the map key), and **tourist information** symbols, which are always blue (and show places of interest or recreational areas).

The following are some of the most commonly occurring symbols found on OS maps:

Abbreviations

P Post office

PH Public house

MS Milestone

MP Milepost

CH Clubhouse

PC Public convenience (in rural areas)

TH Town Hall, Guildhall or equivalent

CG Coastguard

Boundaries

+ — + — + National

◆—◆—◆—◆—◆ District

—·—·—·—· County, Unitary Authority, Metropolitan District or London Borough

Railways

———————— Track (multiple or single)

Station

LC Level crossing

Embankment

Cutting

Bridges, Footbridge

Tunnel

Public rights of way

·············· Footpath

— — — — Bridleway

— — — — — Road used as public path

+—+—+—+ Byway open to all traffic

Rock features

outcrop   650
cliff
600   scree

Tourist information

𝒊 Information centre

↘↗ Viewpoint

P Parking

▲ Youth hostel

✕ Picnic site

⋏ Camp site

🚐 Caravan site

✆ Public telephone

General features

ruin / Buildings   Quarry

Spoil heap, refuse tip or slag

Coniferous wood

Non-coniferous wood

Radio or TV mast

Places of worship
- with tower
- with spire, minaret or dome
- without such additions

△ Triangulation pillar

Windmill with or without sails

Windpump/Wind generator

Heights

═══50═══ Contours are at 10 metres vertical interval

•**144** Heights are to the nearest metre above mean sea level

☙ The World Map ☙

We are so used to seeing images of world maps nowadays that it is easy to forget that the accurate version we use today is only about 60 years old.[92]

However, when you look at a flat map of the world, you are actually looking at someone's attempt to map the surface of a sphere. The way that we are used to seeing the world isn't really how it appears in real life. Naturally, the most accurate map of the world would be depicted on the surface of another sphere, in other words, a **globe**.

But of course a globe is not the most convenient thing to carry around and you cannot see the entire surface of the world at the same time. So, cartographers transfer what is shown on a globe (a three-dimensional object) onto a flat map (a two-dimensional object). If you do this literally, you end up with something called an interrupted map, which looks like the map has been cut.

To represent the world as a horizontal rectangle, the cartographer has to deal with what is known as unavoidable distortion. Possibly one of the best-known projections of the Earth which suffers from such distortion is Mercator's Projection.[93] It is what is commonly known as a cylindrical projection and is usually shown in its equatorial aspect (in other words, the equator divides the map in half horizontally). Direction and shapes are accurate on a Mercator projection, but it distorts the actual size of landmasses to compensate for being a two-dimensional map of the world. However, as it is probably the one image that people are most familiar with, we are going to use it ourselves here.

---

[92] Much of the world was still relatively poorly known until the widespread use of aerial photography was used to create more accurate maps following the Second World War.

[93] Named after the Flemish geographer and cartographer Gerhard Kremer, better known with the Latinised name of Gerardus Mercator (1512–94), who presented it in 1569.

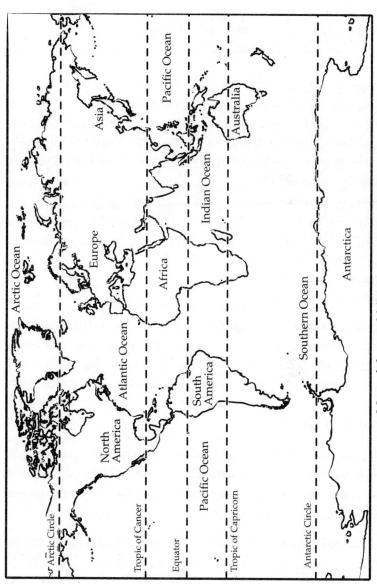

Map of the world (Mercator projection)

Continents

Our planet has seven continents. These are Africa, North America, South America, Antarctica, Asia, Europe and Australia (which used to be called Australasia).

Did you know...?

The driest place on Earth isn't in the Sahara Desert in Africa, or the Arizona Desert in North America. It is actually a place known as the Dry Valleys ... in Antarctica! Incredibly, the area is completely free of ice and snow, and it never rains there at all! In fact, parts of the Antarctic continent haven't seen any rain for about 2,000,000 years. But Antarctica is also the wettest place in the world, with 70 per cent of the Earth's water found there in the form of ice.

Oceans

The Earth is generally considered to have five major oceans, which are all connected to one another. They are the Arctic Ocean, the Atlantic (sometimes divided into the North Atlantic and South Atlantic) the Indian Ocean, the Pacific Ocean (also divided into the North Pacific and South Pacific) and the Southern Ocean.

Circles of latitude

The following are all imaginary lines or actual zones that encircle the world, following particular latitudes (the horizontal lines that run from east to west on maps), and which are characterised by weather patterns and climate.

The **Arctic Circle** is the parallel of latitude that runs 66° 33' 39" north of the Equator. The region north of this circle is the Arctic, and the zone to the south is called the Northern Temperate Zone.

The **Tropic of Cancer**, or Northern tropic, is the most northerly latitude at which the sun can appear directly overhead at noon (during the summer solstice). It lies 23° 26' 22" north of the Equator, and south of this latitude are the subtropics while to the north is the Northern Temperate Zone.

The **Equator** is the imaginary line, equidistant from the North Pole and the South Pole, which divides the Earth into a Northern Hemisphere and a Southern Hemisphere. It lies at a latitude of 0° and is approximately 40,075 km in length.

The **Tropic of Capricorn**, or Southern tropic, is the most southerly latitude at which the sun can appear directly overhead at noon (during the winter solstice). It lies 23° 26' 22" south of the Equator, and north of this latitude are the subtropics while to the south is the Southern Temperate Zone.

The **Antarctic Circle** lies at latitude 66° 33' 39" south of the Equator. The area south of the Antarctic Circle is known as the Antarctic, and the zone immediately to the north is called the Southern Temperate Zone.

The Prime Meridian and the International Date Line

The **Prime Meridian** is the meridian line of longitude which is defined as 0°. The modern Prime Meridian passes through Greenwich, London in the UK, and is also known as the **International Meridian**, or **Greenwich Meridian**.

The **International Date Line** is an imaginary line on the surface of the Earth, on the opposite side of the globe to the Prime Meridian at roughly 180° longitude, which offsets the date as one travels east or west across it. Crossing the International Date Line while travelling east results in one day being subtracted, and crossing it west results in one day being added. The Prime

Meridian and the opposite 180th meridian form a massive circle that divides the Earth into the Eastern Hemisphere and the Western Hemisphere.

The United Kingdom

By 1750, the **United Kingdom** (almost as we know it today) had been formed. The last official national census of the UK (carried out in 2001) recorded the populations of the country's cities and towns. The 60 largest settlements, with populations of over 100,000 each, were ranked as follows.

Rank	Where	Population size	City or town
1	London	7,172,091	City
2	Birmingham	970,892	City
3	Glasgow	629,501	City
4	Liverpool	469,017	City
5	Leeds	443,247	City
6	Sheffield	439,866	City
7	Edinburgh	430,082	City
8	Bristol	420,556	City
9	Manchester	394,269	City
10	Leicester	330,574	City
11	Coventry	303,475	City
12	Hull	301,416	City
13	Bradford	293,717	City
14	Cardiff	292,150	City
15	Belfast	276,459	City
16	Stoke	259,252	City
17	Wolverhampton	251,462	City
18	Nottingham	249,584	City
19	Plymouth	243,795	City
20	Southampton	234,224	City
21	Reading	232,662	Town

Rank	Where	Population size	City or town
22	Derby	229,407	City
23	Brighton and Hove	206,628	City
24	Dudley	194,919	Town
25	Newcastle-upon-Tyne	189,863	City
26	Northampton	189,474	Town
27	Portsmouth	187,056	City
28	Luton	185,543	Town
29	Preston	184,836	City
30	Aberdeen	184,788	City
31	Milton Keynes	184,506	Town
32	Westminster	181,766	City
33	Sunderland	177,739	City
34	Norwich	174,047	City
35	Walsall	170,994	Town
36	Swansea	169,880	City
37	Bournemouth	167,527	Town
38	Southend	160,257	Town
39	Swindon	155,432	Town
40	Dundee	154,674	City
41	Huddersfield	146,234	Town
42	Poole	144,800	Town
43	Oxford	143,016	City
44	Middlesbrough	142,691	Town
45	Blackpool	142,283	Town
46	Bolton	139,403	Town
47	Ipswich	138,718	Town
48	Telford	138,241	Town
49	York	137,505	City
50	West Bromwich	136,940	Town
51	Peterborough	136,292	City
52	Stockport	136,082	Town
53	Slough	126,276	Town
54	Gloucester	123,205	City
55	Watford	120,960	Town

Rank	Where	Population size	City or town
56	Rotherham	117,262	Town
57	Newport	116,143	City
58	Cambridge	113,442	City
59	Exeter	106,772	City
60	Eastbourne	106,562	Town

These top 60 towns and cities are marked on the map of the UK below:

Map of the 60 largest cities and towns in the UK

✈ ✈ ✈

Countries and Capitals

You would think that a straightforward question like 'How many countries are there in the world and what are the names of their capitals?' would have a straightforward answer. Unfortunately, that is not the case.

At the time of writing this at the start of 2008, the best answer to the question 'How many countries are there in the world?' is 194. The United Nations has 192 member nations, then there is the Vatican City (an independent and yet globally recognised country[94]) and Taiwan which, although it meets the requirements necessary to be considered an independent country or state, for political reasons is not recognised by the international community as such.

The world all around us is generally accepted to be a creation of evolution, and it is evolving still. Just as the continents have shifted and changed shape over the course of millions of years, so have the boundaries of countries expanded and constricted, with new countries being formed from old and even capital cities moving. And the process is still happening today.

While various groups (and sometimes nations) choose not to recognise certain countries, different factions within a nation dispute which city should be their country's capital.

For example, if this book had been written in 1990 the list presented below would have been shorter by a total of 32 countries! Fifteen new countries became independent with the dissolution of the USSR in 1991, and another five became independent

---

[94] And also the smallest state in the world, existing inside the city of Rome, with a total area of 0.2 square miles and a population of 770, none of whom are permanent residents.

following the dissolution of Yugoslavia.[95] That still leaves another twelve countries which have become independent for a variety of reasons.

You should bear in mind that the total of 194 countries does not include the dozens of territories and colonies which may seem to be countries but are, in fact, governed by another country. This includes Bermuda, Greenland, Palestine, Puerto Rico and Western Sahara, along with all the component parts of the UK (England, Scotland, Wales and Northern Ireland).

One last point, regarding capital cities: there are twelve countries around the world that have more than one capital city. This can be for a variety of reasons, but mostly because administrative, legislative, and judicial headquarters are split between two or more cities.

The following list is in alphabetical order of the names of the countries.

Country	Capital City
Afghanistan	Kabul
Albania	Tirana
Algeria	Algiers
Andorra	Andorra la Vella
Angola	Luanda
Antigua and Barbuda	Saint John's
Argentina	Buenos Aires
Armenia	Yerevan
Australia	Canberra
Austria	Vienna
Azerbaijan	Baku

---

[95] This change has probably been most noticeable if you are a fan of the Eurovision Song Contest!

Country	Capital City
The Bahamas	Nassau
Bahrain	Manama
Bangladesh	Dhaka
Barbados	Bridgetown
Belarus	Minsk
Belgium	Brussels
Belize	Belmopan
Benin	Porto-Novo (official capital); Cotonou (seat of government)
Bhutan	Thimphu
Bolivia	La Paz (administrative capital); Sucre (constitutional capital)
Bosnia and Herzegovina	Sarajevo
Botswana	Gaborone
Brazil	Brasília
Brunei	Bandar Seri Begawan
Bulgaria	Sofia
Burkina Faso	Ouagadougou
Burundi	Bujumbura
Cambodia	Phnom Penh
Cameroon	Yaoundé
Canada	Ottawa
Cape Verde	Praia
Central African Republic	Bangui
Chad	N'Djamena
Chile	Santiago
China	Beijing
Colombia	Bogotá
Comoros	Moroni
(Republic of the) Congo	Brazzaville
(Democratic Republic of the) Congo	Kinshasa
Costa Rica	San José

Country	Capital City
Cote d'Ivoire	Yamoussoukro (official capital); Abidjan (*de facto* capital)
Croatia	Zagreb
Cuba	Havana
Cyprus	Nicosia
Czech Republic	Prague
Denmark	Copenhagen
Djibouti	Djibouti
Dominica	Roseau
Dominican Republic	Santo Domingo
East Timor (Timor-Leste)	Dili
Ecuador	Quito
Egypt	Cairo
El Salvador	San Salvador
Equatorial Guinea	Malabo
Eritrea	Asmara
Estonia	Tallinn
Ethiopia	Addis Ababa
Fiji	Suva
Finland	Helsinki
France	Paris
Gabon	Libreville
The Gambia	Banjul
Georgia	Tbilisi
Germany	Berlin
Ghana	Accra
Greece	Athens
Grenada	Saint George's
Guatemala	Guatemala City
Guinea	Conakry
Guinea-Bissau	Bissau
Guyana	Georgetown
Haiti	Port-au-Prince

Country	Capital City
Honduras	Tegucigalpa
Hungary	Budapest
Iceland	Reykjavik
India	New Delhi
Indonesia	Jakarta
Iran	Tehran
Iraq	Baghdad
Ireland	Dublin
Israel	Jerusalem
Italy	Rome
Jamaica	Kingston
Japan	Tokyo
Jordan	Amman
Kazakhstan	Astana
Kenya	Nairobi
Kiribati	South Tarawa
(North) Korea	Pyongyang
(South) Korea	Seoul
Kuwait	Kuwait City
Kyrgyzstan	Bishkek
Laos	Vientiane
Latvia	Riga
Lebanon	Beirut
Lesotho	Maseru
Liberia	Monrovia
Libya	Tripoli
Liechtenstein	Vaduz
Lithuania	Vilnius
Luxembourg	Luxembourg
Macedonia	Skopje
Madagascar	Antananarivo
Malawi	Lilongwe
Malaysia	Kuala Lumpur

Country	Capital City
Maldives	Male'
Mali	Bamako
Malta	Valletta
Marshall Islands	Majuro
Mauritania	Nouakchott
Mauritius	Port Louis
Mexico	Mexico City
(Federated States of) Micronesia	Palikir
Moldova	Chisinau
Monaco	Monaco
Mongolia	Ulaanbaatar
Montenegro	Podgorica
Morocco	Rabat
Mozambique	Maputo
Myanmar (Burma)	Rangoon (Yangon); Nay Pyi Taw (administrative capital)
Namibia	Windhoek
Nauru	no official capital – government offices in Yaren District
Nepal	Kathmandu
Netherlands	Amsterdam (legal capital); The Hague (seat of government)
New Zealand	Wellington
Nicaragua	Managua
Niger	Niamey
Nigeria	Abuja
Norway	Oslo
Oman	Muscat
Pakistan	Islamabad
Palau	Melekeok
Panama	Panama City
Papua New Guinea	Port Moresby
Paraguay	Asunción
Peru	Lima

Country	Capital City
Philippines	Manila
Poland	Warsaw
Portugal	Lisbon
Qatar	Doha
Romania	Bucharest
Russia	Moscow
Rwanda	Kigali
Saint Kitts and Nevis	Basseterre
Saint Lucia	Castries
Saint Vincent and the Grenadines	Kingstown
Samoa	Apia
San Marino	San Marino
Sao Tome and Principe	Sao Tome
Saudi Arabia	Riyadh
Senegal	Dakar
Serbia	Belgrade
Seychelles	Victoria
Sierra Leone	Freetown
Singapore	Singapore
Slovakia	Bratislava
Slovenia	Ljubljana
Solomon Islands	Honiara
Somalia	Mogadishu
South Africa	Pretoria (administrative capital); Cape Town (legislative capital); Bloemfontein (judiciary capital)
Spain	Madrid
Sri Lanka	Colombo (official capital); Sri Jayewardenepura Kotte (legislative capital)
Sudan	Khartoum
Suriname	Paramaribo

Country	Capital City
Swaziland	Mbabane (administrative capital); Lobamba (royal and legislative capital)
Sweden	Stockholm
Switzerland	Bern
Syria	Damascus
Taiwan	Taipei
Tajikistan	Dushanbe
Tanzania	Dar es Salaam (*de facto* capital); Dodoma (legislative capital)
Thailand	Bangkok
Togo	Lome
Tonga	Nuku'alofa
Trinidad and Tobago	Port-of-Spain
Tunisia	Tunis
Turkey	Ankara
Turkmenistan	Ashgabat
Tuvalu	Vaiaku village, Funafuti province
Uganda	Kampala
Ukraine	Kyiv
United Arab Emirates	Abu Dhabi
United Kingdom	London
United States of America	Washington DC
Uruguay	Montevideo
Uzbekistan	Tashkent
Vanuatu	Port-Vila
Vatican City (Holy See)	Vatican City
Venezuela	Caracas
Vietnam	Hanoi
Yemen	Sanaa
Zambia	Lusaka
Zimbabwe	Harare

☂ The Restless Planet ☂

Although at times it may feel like the Earth can be rather a cold place, beneath the thin crust[96] of solid rock which forms its outer surface, the interior of our planet is a seething ball of unimaginable heat.

The **crust** itself is between 3 miles (5 km) and 56 miles (90 km) thick, the thickest areas being the continents and the thinnest points found at the bottom of the sea. Beneath the crust lies the **mantle**, a layer of semi-solid rock which, although hot enough to melt (existing at temperatures as high as 5,000°C), remains solid as a result of the incredible pressures exerted upon it by the rock above.

1,800 miles (2,900 km) below the mantle we reach the **outer core**, an expanse of liquid iron and nickel. 1,300 miles (2,100 km) thick, the outer core reaches temperatures exceeding 5,000°C. Right at the heart of the planet is the **inner core**, which is thought to be a solid ball of iron and nickel. Over 1,700 miles (2,800 km) across, the core is believed to be 5,500°C, making it as hot as the surface of the sun!

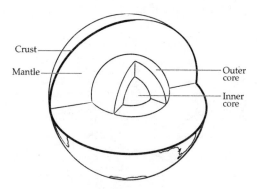

Crust

Mantle

Outer core

Inner core

The structure of the Earth

---

[96] To give you an accurate idea of just how thin the Earth's crust is, if our planet was an apple, the crust would be only as thick as the apple's skin!

The Earth's crust is broken into sections called **tectonic plates** which are constantly in motion, sliding over the semi-solid mantle, moving a few centimetres a year. There are seven major plates and twelve smaller ones, which are categorised as either continental plates (which cannot sink into the mantle, being less dense, and so form the landmasses) or oceanic plates (which are heavier and so can sink into the mantle, and form the sea bed).

It is the movement of the tectonic plates that has shaped the face of our world, changing it constantly over hundreds of millions of years. This movement is also responsible for such phenomena as earthquakes and volcanoes.

Earthquakes

Earthquakes mainly occur where two tectonic plates, which are moving at different speeds or in different directions, meet and then lock together due to friction (called a **conservative boundary**). The pressure builds until a plate breaks along a fault line (such as the San Andreas Fault in California, on the western coast of the USA). When this happens an earthquake occurs, and the effects can be truly devastating.

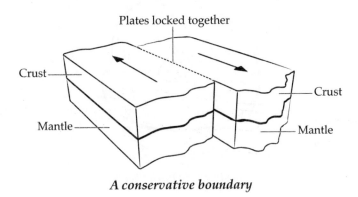

A conservative boundary

However, earthquakes can also occur where oceanic plates are moving apart (a **constructive boundary**), where oceanic and continental plates meet (a **destructive boundary**) and where continental plates collide and buckle to form mountains (a **collision boundary**).

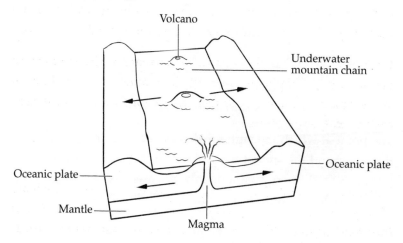

A constructive boundary

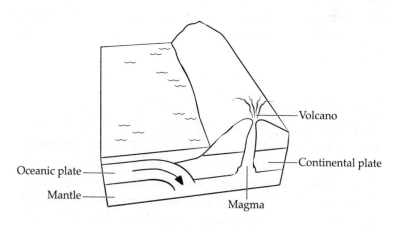

A destructive boundary

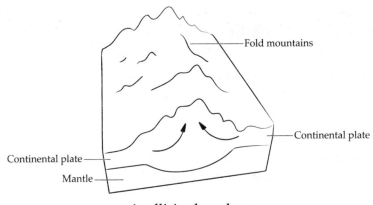

A collision boundary

The point at which the fault breaks beneath the ground is called the focus, and the spot at the surface directly above it is the epicentre. Stored energy is suddenly released as seismic waves, which ripple out from the epicentre in all directions.

If an earthquake occurs at a point on the sea bed,[97] the resulting shock waves can create a tsunami, a tidal wave up to 40 m in height. The speed at which tsunamis travel depends on the ocean depth, sometimes exceeding 500 mph in the deep ocean but slowing to 20 or 30 mph in the shallower waters near land. In less than 24 hours, a tsunami can cross the Pacific Ocean! When the giant wave hits land, entire coastal settlements can be wiped out.

Did you know...?

On Boxing Day, 26 December 2004, an earthquake off the coast of Indonesia triggered a massive tsunami which left nearly 230,000 people dead or missing, and another 2 million homeless. It was one of the worst natural disasters in history, inundating coastal communities with waves up to 30 m (100 feet) high, with Indonesia, Sri Lanka, India and Thailand being among the countries hardest hit. The undersea quake that

---

[97] Also known as a seaquake, funnily enough.

caused the tsunami had a magnitude of between 9.1 and 9.3, and was the second largest ever recorded on a seismograph.

Incredibly sensitive instruments called seismometers are used to measure earthquakes, recording the vibrations they pick up on a seismograph. The strength of an earthquake is also rated using the Richter Scale, which measures how much energy is released.[98] Earthquakes can also be assessed using the Mercalli Scale, which measures the amount of damage caused.

Did you know...?
An estimated 1.5 million earthquakes occur every year world-wide. There are approximately 6,000 with a magnitude of 4.0 or higher on the Richter Scale, but generally only one of these will be of magnitude 8.0. One of the better known casualties of the great San Francisco earthquake of 1906 (which was measured at magnitude 7.8), was a cow that fell into the San Andreas Fault when the quake occurred, trapping it in the ground.

The science of predicting earthquakes is still far from exact. Although scientists know where they are likely to occur, determining when is another matter entirely. Techniques used in the quest to accurately predict earthquakes include mapping the locations of previous quakes, looking out for series of small tremors called foreshocks, which could indicate that a bigger quake is coming, watching for changes in water levels which might be caused by the movement of the Earth's crust, and observing the behaviour of animals. It seems that some animals can tell when an earthquake is about to happen, even if we cannot. Pigs, rats and even fish have all been observed behaving strangely prior to a quake.

---

[98] Every level on the Richter Scale is, incredibly, ten times more powerful than the one that comes before it.

Did you know...?

The Greek god of the sea, Poseidon, was also called 'Earth-Shaker' because the Ancient Greeks believed that he was the one who caused earthquakes. In the past the Japanese believed that a great catfish, or *namazu*, lay curled up under the sea, with the islands of Japan resting on its back. A demigod, or *daimyojin*, held a heavy stone over its head to keep it still, but once in a while, when the *daimyojin* was distracted, the catfish was able to move, and the Earth trembled.

Volcanoes

Named after Vulcan, the Roman god of fire, **volcanoes** come in various shapes and sizes and are classified as being either **active** (having erupted only recently and expected to erupt again in the future), **dormant** (may erupt in the future but inactive for the time being) or **extinct** (having not erupted for several thousand years and not likely to at any time in the future).

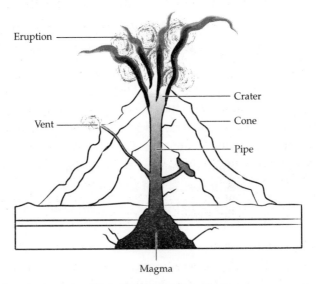

The structure of a volcano

All volcanoes are made up of the same parts: a vent, pipe, crater and cone. The vent is an opening at the Earth's surface, and a volcano may have more than one of these. The pipe is the passageway through which magma rises to the surface (from a magma chamber within the Earth's crust) during an eruption.

The crater is the bowl-shaped depression at the top of the volcano where ash, lava and other pyroclastic materials are released. Solidified lava, ashes, and cinder from earlier eruptions form the volcano's cone.

When a volcano erupts it produces various effects which cause devastation to the surrounding countryside. Clouds of superheated gas, ash and even pieces of lava can blast out from the volcano at speeds of over 120 mph (190 kph). This is called **pyroclastic flow**. Mudflows can also result, as ash mixes with rain (or even melted ice from the summit) and pours down the side of the volcano. Rivers of lava (as much as 1,200°C in temperature) steadily destroy everything in their path, while ash falls from the sky, enough to bury roads, crops and even whole buildings.

Did you know...?

When Mount Vesuvius erupted in AD 79, pumice and ash ejected from the volcano buried the town of Pompeii, while a mudslide poured down the volcano's western slope, engulfing the coastal town of Herculaneum. Of the two sites, Herculaneum was the better preserved for the archaeologists because it was buried in mud rather than much of it being burnt by scalding hot ash first, as happened at Pompeii. However, Pompeii is the better known because it is the more extensive site. Much of Herculaneum still lies buried under modern Naples.

Volcanoes usually occur at **constructive boundaries** (such as the Mid-Atlantic Ridge where underwater volcanoes in particular are found), and **destructive boundaries** (such as around the

Pacific Ring of Fire). There are a number of different types of volcano as well.

Type	Characteristics	Example
Ash volcano	These are cones with steep sides which are slightly concave, formed when ash from an eruption falls back to the ground, piling up in layers.	Paricutín (Mexico)
Composite volcano	Also called strato-volcanoes, these are high and conical, also with steep sides, formed by alternating layers of ash and lava.	Hekla (Iceland) Mt Fuji (Japan) Mt St Helens (USA) Stromboli (Italy) Vesuvius (Italy)
Dome volcano	These have steep convex sides and are formed by eruptions of thick, sticky lava which cools before it can flow far from the crater.	Lassen Peak (USA) Puy de Dome (France)
Shield volcano	These are wide, with gently sloping sides, formed by eruptions of thin, runny lava, which travels a long way from the crater before cooling.	Erta Ale (Ethiopia) Ferdinandia (Galapagos Islands) Masaya (Nicaragua) Mauna Loa (Hawaii) Tolbachik (Russia)

Nowadays, volcanoes are closely monitored for signs of an imminent eruption, by means of satellite images (which can even reveal changes in temperature inside a volcano), gas detectors which record levels of gases such as sulphur dioxide and carbon dioxide in the surrounding air, and seismometers, which detect earthquake tremors caused by the volcano filling with magma before an eruption. The trouble is that large numbers of people around the world live near or even on volcanoes, because volcanic soil is so rich in nutrients and excellent for growing crops, such as the grape vines found thriving in vineyards on the slopes of Vesuvius.

☔ **Water World** ☔

One thing has shaped the land on which we live more than any other, and that is water. Let's face it, without good old H$_2$O there wouldn't be any life at all on planet Earth. Water from rivers has altered the contours of the landscape around us, while in ages past, icy glaciers carved out great valleys and mountain passes on an even more impressive scale.

But to really understand the impact that water has had on our world, we need to start by looking at the **water cycle** (also known, rather grandly, as the **hydrological cycle**).

The water cycle

It is worth remembering that the water that emerges when we turn on a tap, that falls from the sky as rain or snow, that fills our baths, swimming pools, rivers and oceans, is the only water that has ever existed on planet Earth. That means that it is the same water that our parents drank, our grandparents washed with, our great grandparents sailed upon … that the dinosaurs drank, and that amphibians emerged from as the first land-dwelling creatures.

The water cycle describes the on-going process whereby water is transferred between the sea, the atmosphere and the land. Because it is a continuous cycle, we could start looking at it at any point. However, it makes sense to start with how the water leaves the oceans in readiness to fall back to the land as rain or snow.

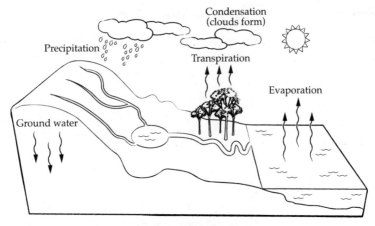

The water cycle

Water in the seas and other large bodies of water (such as lakes and rivers) is warmed by the sun and evaporation occurs. The water becomes water vapour, which then rises into the atmosphere. Water is also released as vapour from the leaves of trees and other plants, a process called transpiration, and this water vapour also ascends into the atmosphere.

Air cools as it rises and when it is cold enough, condensation occurs. As a result, the water vapour carried within the air forms clouds made up of tiny water droplets. These droplets bump into one another and combine to form raindrops. When they are heavy enough, these fall back to Earth as rain. This is called precipitation, which can also take the form of snow, hail or sleet.

Rain water soaks into the ground and starts to flow back to the sea either on the surface, in the form of streams and rivers, or through underground soil and rock. Ground water flows very slowly through porous rocks (carving out cave systems over millions of years) forming an aquifer (or water table) beneath the surface. In this way, under the influence of gravity, water eventually returns to the sea where the process begins all over again.

Rivers

As water emerges from springs at the tops of hills and mountains it flows across the land, first as streams and then in the form of rivers, as the streams join together. The river steadily shapes the land around it through both erosion (wearing away the rock and soil it passes over) and deposition (dropping the suspended load of silt it carries on its way to the sea).

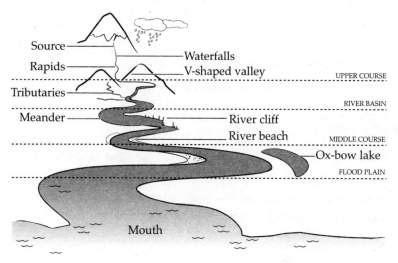

The stages of a river

In its upper course, a river flows from its source (the place where the river begins[99]) and then falls steeply over a stony bed. Waterfalls and rapids are common at this stage, cutting through river-worn gorges. In these upland areas, river valleys are both narrow and steep-sided and so are called V-shaped valleys.

The area of land that contains a river and its tributaries (those smaller rivers and streams which flow into the main water

---

[99] A river is likely to have more than one source.

course[100]) is a river basin. The watershed is the area of high land that separates one or more drainage basins.[101]

In its middle course the river valley widens, its floor becomes flatter, and the river adopts a winding course. Each meander has a steep bank on the outside bend, called a river cliff. On the inner side, where the current is slacker, deposited material forms a river beach.

In its lower course, close to where the river meets the sea, the river widens still further as it traces a winding path over the area of land known as the flood plain. At this stage ox-bow lakes can form when a meander becomes cut off from the main river during a flood. If there is much flat land in this area, there may be a large estuary.

The point where the river meets the sea is called its mouth. If the sea is shallow, and without strong tides, a delta may form as the river deposits its load. If this is the case, the river will split into many smaller distributaries.

Coast

As well as shaping the landscape by means of rivers, water is also constantly changing the topography of the land where it meets the sea. Coastal landscapes change in a considerably quicker and more dramatic way.

Headlands and bays are formed in areas with differing rock types. Softer rocks are eroded more swiftly by the action of the sea, forming the bays. The headlands are made of harder rock

---

[100] The point where streams or rivers merge is called the confluence.

[101] Rather than being that mysterious transitional time of 9:00 p.m. after which suddenly anything goes on TV.

which takes longer to wear away, and so are left projecting into the sea.

The rocks that form headlands, however, are also worn away over time and this erosion forms caves, arches, stacks and eventually stumps. All of these coastal features are created when faults (areas of weakness in the headland) are abraded by the endless action of the waves.

The first feature to form at a fault is a cave. When the cave eventually breaks through the headland it becomes an arch. When the arch itself collapses, what is left behind is a stack, and when this topples into the sea, its rocky base is called a stump.

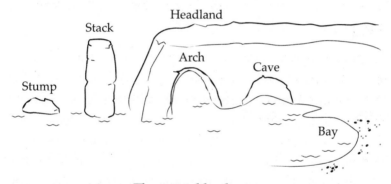

The coastal landscape

Beaches are formed when waves transport and deposit material. The sand and stones of a beach might come from eroded cliffs, offshore banks of shingle, or material carried from elsewhere along the coast (a process referred to as longshore drift) or even deposited by rivers on reaching the sea.

A spit is a coastal feature formed where a curved beach extends into the sea at a point where there is a break in the coastline or at the mouth of a river. Longshore drift helps to form the spit which, as it grows, can develop a hooked end. Sand dunes form in the middle of the spit, while mud is deposited in the sheltered area behind it, where a salt-marsh will then develop.

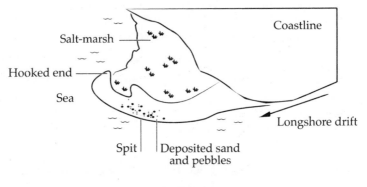

A spit

Glaciers

Glaciers are vast, slow-moving rivers of ice, found in frozen mountainous areas and at the poles. Glaciers have an even more devastating eroding effect on the landscape than rivers, although the process takes much longer. Water freezes around loose stones and boulders and the resulting ice then draws the rocks with it as it moves forwards under the force of gravity. This is an effect called plucking. Blocks of rock trapped beneath the glacier scrape away at the valley floor beneath, gouging out dramatic geographical features. U-shaped valleys are formed by the action of glaciers, as are ribbon lakes.

The last **Ice Age** in Britain lasted from about 1,000,000–20,000 years ago. During that time the northern and eastern parts of the British Isles were covered in ice.[102] Glaciers formed, which then moved down mountain valleys and beyond with great erosive power.

---

[102] At this time, glaciers covered 32 per cent of the total land area of the planet!

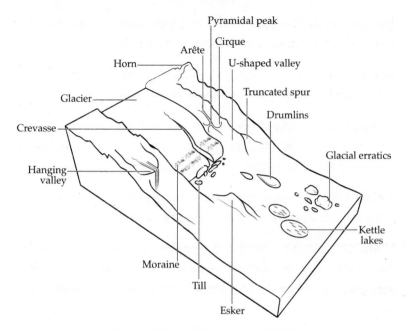

The structure and effects of a glacier

Arête – a narrow, knife-edge ridge separating two cirques.

Cirque – a feature where the side of a mountain has been scooped out (also called a corrie in the British Isles).

Crevasse – a giant crack in the surface of the glacier, formed at points where a glacier flows more rapidly.

Drumlins – teardrop- or egg-shaped hills, blunt at one end and tapered at the other, formed when ice is moving forward but melting at the same time. Boulder clay and till is deposited by the ice when it comes to a small obstacle (such as an outcrop of rock), with most of the material dropped at the 'upstream' end. The 'downstream' end is then shaped by the ice. Drumlins are found in swarms called a 'basket of eggs'.

Eskers – winding hills formed by streams on or under a glacier.

Hanging valleys – occur when a tributary valley joins a main valley where the latter has been more deeply eroded by a glacier.

Glacial erratics – are large rocks which have been carried by the glacier, and then dropped when the ice-river retreats.

Horns – the steeply carved sides of mountains into sheer surfaces and points, such as the Matterhorn, in the Alps. Arêtes are groups of horns in a row.

Kettle lakes – lakes formed by a melted chunk of ice left by a retreating glacier. They can be transient or permanent.

Moraine – a long, dark band of debris created when the glacier pushes or carries along rocks and soil as it moves. Medial moraines run down the middle of a glacier, lateral moraines run along the sides, and terminal moraines are found at the end, or snout. A retreating glacier will create a series of recessional moraines, which demarcate the points where its length stabilised for a period of time.

Pyramidal peak – formed when three or more cirques form in the side of one mountain.

Ribbon lakes – found at the bottom of U-shaped valleys, gouged out by glaciers during the last Ice Age.

Tarn – a lake found inside a cirque.

Till – material from a glacier deposited over an area.

Truncated spurs – hilly spurs between valleys which have been cut through by the action of ice.

U-shaped valley – a V-shaped valley later eroded by an advancing glacier. The valley sides are steeper and the valley floor flatter after the glacier retreats.

Did you know...?

Glaciers store approximately 75 per cent of the world's fresh-water and cover 10 per cent of all land area on the planet. During a surge (a period of rapid glacier movement) an alpine glacier can flow at the rate of 50–100 m a day. If all the glaciers and the rest of the ice covering the land melted, sea levels around the world would rise by approximately 70 m.

Lakes

The definition of a lake is a body of water[103] that is larger and deeper than a pond,[104] and surrounded by a body of land. If it is big enough, a large lake can also be called an inland sea. Most of the lakes on Earth are found within the Northern Hemisphere and at higher latitudes.

There are many names for lakes, depending on where you are in the world. Scotland has its lochs, Ireland its loughs, in the English Lake District there are the meres (lakes that are broad in relation to their depth), and then there are the tarns (mountain lakes, sometimes called corrie lochs).

Did you know...?

60 per cent of the world's lakes are found in Canada. It is estimated that there are more than 31,000 lakes with a surface area larger than 3 km², with many more that are smaller than that.

Most lakes have some sort of natural outflow by which they lose water. However, there are those which have no such outflow and instead lose water purely through evaporation and underground seepage.

---

[103] Usually fresh water, but not always, as in the case of the Dead Sea.

[104] In the UK, the widely accepted definition of a pond is 'a man-made or natural water body which is between 1 m² and 2 hectares in area, which holds water for four months of the year or more'.

Many lakes have been put to good use by Man, with just as many having been artificially created for various purposes, from generating hydro-electric power to creating reservoirs for domestic use and for recreation.

Did you know...?
Astronomers have found evidence of lakes on other planets within our solar system. For example, Titan, one of Saturn's moons, has lakes filled with liquid hydrocarbons, such as methane and ethane.

Lakes are formed as a result of a number of different natural processes, as well as by mankind's intervention. Below is a list of a few of the many different types of lake, with details of how they are formed, along with examples for each one.

Type of lake	How it is formed	Example
Artificial lake	A river is dammed so that the river valley behind the dam floods, creating an artificial lake. Artificial lakes are also formed by deliberate human excavation or by flooding a disused excavation site, such as a mine or quarry.	Lake Nasser, Egypt
Fjord lake	This type of lake occurs in a glacially-eroded valley that has been eroded below sea level.	Framvaren, Norway
Ox-bow lake	An ox-bow lake is formed when a bend in a river becomes isolated. As a result, ox-bow lakes are shallow and crescent-shaped.	Reelfoot Lake, Tennessee, USA
Ribbon lake	The advance and retreat of glaciers can scrape depressions in the ground. After the glacier has gone, these depressions fill with water and become ribbon (or finger) lakes.	Lake Windermere, UK

Type of lake	How it is formed	Example
Salt lake	A salt lake forms where there is no natural outlet for the water or where the water evaporates rapidly and the drainage surface of the water table has a higher-than-normal salt content.	The Dead Sea, Israel and Jordan
Underground lake	This type of lake forms under the surface of the Earth's crust, and may be associated with caves, aquifers, or springs.	Darfur Lake, Sudan

☔ Weather ☔

It's Britain's favourite topic of conversation, it can make a difference to your whole day and, love it or loathe it, if there's one thing you can't escape in this country, it's the weather. But what is 'weather'?

To put it simply, weather is the condition of the atmosphere at a particular place and a particular time. On the other hand, climate is the average weather conditions for a place.[105]

Changes in what the weather is like are recorded in terms of temperature, precipitation,[106] air pressure, wind and cloud cover. It is no wonder that people spend so much time talking about the weather, as it has a big impact on their everyday lives; it affects transport, work, farming, energy usage, tourism and even sport.

When you were at school, you probably had to learn tables that helped determine wind speeds and strengths, as well as types of cloud. Just in case you've forgotten what those were, we're going to look at them again here.

Did you know...?

The Earth's atmosphere is a thin layer of gases that surrounds the Earth. It is composed of 78 per cent nitrogen, 21 per cent oxygen, 0.9 per cent argon, 0.04 per cent carbon dioxide, and includes trace amounts of other gases. It was formed when gases like carbon dioxide, water vapour, sulphur dioxide and nitrogen were released from the interior of the Earth, via volcanoes and other processes, while the planet was still young. Life forms on Earth have since modified the composition of the atmosphere as they have evolved over countless millennia.

---

[105] Based on data collected over the last 40 years!
[106] Rain, snowfall, sleet and hail are all forms of precipitation.

Wind

The **Beaufort Scale** (of wind force) is used to measure wind speeds and their effects. It was developed by Admiral Sir Francis Beaufort (1774–1857) in 1805 to help sailors at sea estimate wind speeds through simple observations. The modern Beaufort Scale (with winds ranked from 0 to 12) is as follows:

Beaufort number	Wind speed kph (mph)	Description
0	0 (0)	**Calm** – smoke rises vertically; sea is flat.
1	1–6 (1–3)	**Light air** – the wind is visible in smoke; sea has ripples but without crests.
2	7–11 (4–7)	**Light breeze** – wind is felt on exposed skin and leaves rustle; sea has small wavelets with crests, but not breaking.
3	12–19 (8–12)	**Gentle breeze** – leaves and twigs on trees are in constant motion; there are large wavelets at sea, with crests beginning to break.
4	20–29 (13–18)	**Moderate breeze** – wind raises dust and loose paper; small branches begin to move; small waves at sea.
5	30–39 (19–24)	**Fresh breeze** – smaller trees start to sway; sea has longer waves with some foam and spray.
6	40–50 (25–31)	**Strong breeze** – large branches are now in motion and whistling is heard in overhead wires; umbrellas become difficult to use; large waves at sea with foamy crests and spray.
7	51–62 (32–38)	**Moderate gale** – whole trees are in motion; effort is needed to walk against the wind; sea heaps up and foam begins to streak.
8	63–75 (39–46)	**Fresh gale** – twigs are broken from trees; cars veer on road; moderately high waves with breaking crests at sea and streaks of foam.

Beaufort number	Wind speed kph (mph)	Description
9	76–87 (47–54)	**Strong gale** – light structural damage on land; high waves at sea with dense foam; considerable spray as wave crests start to roll over.
10	88–102 (55–63)	**Storm** – trees are uprooted and there is considerable structural damage; very high waves, and the sea surface is white; visibility is reduced at sea.
11	103–119 (64–73)	**Violent storm** – widespread structural damage; exceptionally high waves.
12	120+ (74+)	**Hurricane** – considerable and widespread structural damage; huge waves at sea with the air filled with foam and spray; sea white with driving spray and visibility is greatly reduced.

The wind, and the kind of weather it carries with it, is determined by the movements of air masses. An **air mass** is a large body of air with similar temperature and humidity. There are five air masses that affect the weather in Europe.

Air mass classification	Origin	Characteristics
Tropical Maritime	From the south-west, over the Azores or the Caribbean.	Mild and moist; the weather it brings is characterised by low cloud, drizzle and hill fog.
Tropical Continental	From the south over North Africa.	Warm and dry; can affect the UK from March to October, although is most common in June, July and August.
Polar Maritime	From the north-west, over the North Atlantic.	Cool and moist; the most familiar air mass in the UK, bringing showers, hail and thunder, according to the season.

Air mass classification	Origin	Characteristics
Polar Continental	From the east over Scandinavia and Russia.	Cool and dry; the UK's lowest temperatures occur under this air mass.
Arctic Maritime	North from the Arctic Ocean.	Cold and moist; a more direct form of Polar Maritime (making the air colder and giving it a lower humidity), between October and May it can bring snow.

Clouds

Quite simply, clouds are accumulations of water droplets or solid ice crystals that are visible floating in the lowest part of Earth's atmosphere[107] and are moved by the wind. Clouds are formed when water vapour in the air condenses around microscopic dust particles and the like, which happens when bodies of warm and cold air meet.

Clouds are classified in terms of what they look like as well as how high they are in the atmosphere. **Cirro** (from the Latin *cirrus* meaning 'curl of hair') is used to describe clouds at altitudes above 20,000 feet (6,100 m). **Alto** (from *altus* meaning 'high') describes mid-altitude clouds, between 6,000 and 20,000 feet (1,800–6,100 m). Low-altitude clouds do not have a special term applied to them. Very low altitude clouds, ones that hug the ground, have a very technical name: **fog**.

The prefix **nimbo** or the suffix **nimbus** (both meaning 'rain'), strangely enough indicate that the cloud can produce precipitation

---

[107] Called the troposphere, from the Greek *tropos* meaning 'turning' or 'mixing'. Most of the phenomena we associate with day-to-day weather, which involves a great deal of turbulent mixing, occur in the troposphere.

of some kind. **Cumulo** ('heap') refers to clouds that appear to be piled up. **Strato** ('layer') refers to wide, flat, layered clouds.

Did you know...?

The idea of classifying clouds according to their base height, rather than the cloud top, was proposed by Luke Howard (1772–1864), a British manufacturing chemist and an amateur meteorologist, in 1802, as part of a presentation to the Askesian Society – a debating club for scientific thinkers, established in 1796 in London.

Type of cloud	Altitude	Characteristics
Cumulo-nimbus	Near ground up to 75,000 feet (Vertical clouds)	Also called thunderheads, they can cause lightning, thunder, hail, heavy rains, strong winds, and tornadoes.
Cirro-stratus	Above 18,000 feet (High-altitude clouds)	Appearing in sheets, they are thin and wispy, often located above thunderheads.
Cirrus	Above 18,000 feet (High-altitude clouds)	Mostly composed of ice crystals, they are thin, wispy and thread-like in appearance.
Cirro-cumulus	Above 18,000 feet (High-altitude clouds)	Small, puffy, patchy clouds, sometimes with a wave-like appearance.
Alto-cumulus	6,500–20,000 feet (Middle-altitude clouds)	Scattered, medium-sized puffy and patchy clouds. They often occur in linear bands.
Alto-stratus	6,500–20,000 feet (Middle-altitude clouds)	Thin and uniform in shape.

Type of cloud	Altitude	Characteristics
Strato-cumulus	Below 6,500 feet (Low-altitude clouds)	Broad and flat on the bottom but puffy on the top.
Cumulus	Below 6,500 feet (Vertical clouds)	Puffy and piled up.
Stratus	Below 6,500 feet (Low-altitude clouds)	Thick- to thin-layered, flat, uniform clouds but with poorly defined edges. They are mostly made up of liquid droplets.
Nimbo-stratus	Below 6,500 feet (Low-altitude clouds)	Uniform, dark, flat and low, featureless clouds that produce precipitation. Again, mostly made up of liquid droplets.
Fog	In contact with the ground (Ground-hugging clouds)	Very low stratus clouds which are also mainly made of liquid droplets.

Did you know...?

An aeroplane's contrail (which is short for condensation trail) is the cloud-like vapour trail left behind when the aircraft flies in cold, clear but also humid air. The contrail is formed from the water vapour contained in the jet's engine exhaust.

Did you know...?

Some clouds form due to interactions with particular geographical features. One of the strangest of these is the geographically specific cloud Morning Glory (I kid you not!). It is a rolling, cylindrical cloud which appears unpredictably over the Gulf of Carpentaria in Northern Australia. Due to a powerful 'ripple' in the atmosphere, it is possible to 'surf' the cloud in an unpowered glider.

➤ Spot Test! ➤

That's how the world works, eh? Who would've thought it. And all this time you thought ox-bow lakes just existed because your geography teacher at school said they did. A living, breathing, moving, changing planet indeed!

Kids, do you ever feel that talking to your parents is like a collision boundary? Or parents, maybe you see your little darlings as more akin to a destructive boundary? Either way, if you've learnt your geography properly, you'll now be able to talk at much greater (and more interesting) length about the weather …

So, to show off what you know, here are ten questions to answer as quickly as possible.

1) What did Paul Garbutt design in 1964?
2) Which type of map shows buildings in more detail – a large-scale or a small-scale map?
3) Where is the driest place on Earth?
4) In which hemisphere would you find the Tropic of Capricorn?
5) Of which country is Tripoli the capital city?
6) What type of boundary is the San Andreas Fault, California?
7) From who or what do we get the word 'volcano'?
8) What is the name of the process that helps to form a spit?
9) What type of lake is Lake Windermere, and what formed it?
10) What does the number 10 on the Beaufort Scale signify?

Chapter Eight

MODERN FOREIGN LANGUAGES
Mind Your Language!

French has always been a mainstay of the British school curriculum, due to France being one of the UK's nearest neighbours and possibly, in part, because of a mutually shared history of conflict (either fighting with each other or against each other), and maybe because at one time the English ruling classes were descended from French forebears.

Possibly again due to a shared history of conflict, or maybe because again, once upon a time, the royal family of the British Isles were of German extraction, the German language has also been taught in British schools for decades.

And with Spanish now the third most spoken language across the globe[108] (with 333 million speakers worldwide), more and more children are learning it in British schools as well.

There is no way that we can cover everything that a student of any one of these modern foreign languages needs to know in a book like this. However, what we *can* do is provide you with enough basic knowledge to remind you of some of the French you learnt at school or help you brush up on your holiday Spanish.

You will find that each of the sections about the three languages has been broken down in the same way, providing you with a basic vocabulary as well as a brief factfile about each of the countries.

So, what are you waiting for? *Allons-y, schnell schnell, date prisa* and away we go.

---

[108] After Mandarin Chinese and English.

❧ French ❧

French (*français*) is what is known as a Romance language (one which evolved from Latin around the 9th and 10th centuries). Although it originated in **France** (from the Latin *Francia*, meaning 'land of the Franks'), it is also spoken in many other countries around the world, from Luxembourg, southern Belgium and western Switzerland in Europe, to Quebec, New Brunswick, Ontario (and other parts of Canada), as well as parts of Louisiana in North America. It is also still spoken in the former French colonies of North and West Africa; Haiti, Martinique and Guadeloupe in the Caribbean; in French Guiana in South America; and in Tahiti as well as many other islands found in Oceania.

It is worth remembering that French was once the language of the English court and the educated classes. And of course it is also known internationally as the language of love, perhaps because it has a certain *je ne sais quoi* about it.

Although French uses the same 26 letters of the alphabet as English, they are pronounced differently, as follows:

A	–	*ah*	N	–	*en*
B	–	*bay*	O	–	*oh*
C	–	*say*	P	–	*pay*
D	–	*day*	Q	–	*koo*
E	–	*euh*	R	–	*ehr*
F	–	*ef*	S	–	*ess*
G	–	*jhay*	T	–	*tay*
H	–	*ahsh*	U	–	*oo*
I	–	*ee*	V	–	*vay*
J	–	*jhee*	W	–	*doo-bluh-vay*
K	–	*kah*	X	–	*eeks*
L	–	*el*	Y	–	*ee grek*
M	–	*em*	Z	–	*zed*

What follows is a modern French phrasebook which includes much of the basic vocabulary you would need if you were to visit our Gallic cousins for your holidays this year.

Getting by ...
The basics

Hello!	*Bonjour!*
Hi!	*Salut!*
How are you?	*Comment ça va?*
Fine, thank you	*Bien, merci*
May I introduce myself to you?	*Est-ce que je peux me présenter à vous?*
I am ...	*Je suis ...*
I am called ...	*Je m'appelle ...*
I come from England	*Je viens de l'Angleterre*
I come from Wales	*Je viens du Pays de Galles*
I come from Scotland	*Je viens de l'Écosse*
I come from Northern Ireland	*Je viens de l'Irlande du Nord*
I come from Eire	*Je viens de la République d'Irlande*
I come from Great Britain	*Je viens de la Grande-Bretagne*
What is your name?	*Comment vous appelez-vous?* (formal)
	Comment t'appeles-tu? (informal)
Where do you come from?	*D'où venez-vous?*
Please	*S'il vous plaît*
Thank you	*Merci*
You're welcome	*De rien*
Yes	*Oui*
No	*Non*
Pardon?	*Comment?*
Excuse me	*Excusez-moi*
I'm sorry	*(Je suis) Désolé(e)*
What's the time?	*Quelle heure est-il?*
Goodbye	*Au revoir*
Bye!	*Salut!*
Good evening	*Bonsoir*
Good night	*Bonne nuit*
I can't speak French (well)	*Je ne parle pas (bien) français*
Do you speak English?	*Parlez-vous anglais?*
I don't understand	*Je ne comprends pas*
I am lost	*Je suis perdu(e)*

I am ill	*Je suis malade*
May I use your phone?	*Puis-je utiliser votre téléphone?*

Getting around ...

Travel, transport and directions

How much is a ticket to ...?	*Combien coûte le billet pour ...?*
One ticket to ... please	*Un billet pour ... s'il vous plaît*
Where does this train/bus go to?	*Où va ce train/bus?*
Where is the train/bus to ...?	*Où est le train/bus pour ...?*
Does this train/bus stop in ...?	*Ce train/bus s'arrête-t-il à ...?*
When does the train/bus for ... leave?	*Quand part le train/bus pour ...?*
When will this train/bus arrive in ...?	*Quand ce train/bus arrivera-t-il à ...?*
A one-way ticket	*Un aller simple*
A round trip ticket	*Un aller-retour*
Where is ...	*Où se trouve ...*
the train station?	*la gare?*
the bus station?	*la gare routière?*
the airport?	*l'aéroport?*
town centre?	*le centre-ville?*
the suburbs?	*la banlieue?*
the youth hostel?	*l'auberge de jeunesse?*
the hotel?	*l'hôtel?*
Is it far?	*C'est loin?*
Can you show me on the map?	*Pouvez-vous me montrer sur la carte?*
Turn left	*Tournez à gauche*
Turn right	*Tournez à droite*
Straight ahead	*Tout droit*
That way	*Par là*
Towards the...	*Vers le/la ...*
Past the...	*Après le/la ...*
Before the...	*Avant le/la ...*
North	*Nord*
South	*Sud*
East	*Est*
West	*Ouest*
Take me to ... please	*Déposez-moi à ... je vous prie*
How much does it cost to get to ...?	*Combien cela coûte-t-il d'aller à ...?*
Take me there, please	*Amenez-moi là, s'il vous plaît*

Getting a room ...
Board and lodging

Do you have any rooms available?	*Avez-vous des chambres libres?*
How much is a room for one person?	*Combien coûte une chambre pour une personne?*
How much is a room for two people?	*Combien coûte une chambre pour deux personnes?*
Does the room come with ...	*Est-ce que dans la chambre il y a ...*
a bathroom?	*une salle de bain?*
a telephone?	*un téléphone?*
a TV?	*une télé?*
Do you have anything bigger?	*Vous n'avez pas de chambre plus grande?*
Do you have anything cheaper?	*Vous n'avez pas de chambre moins chère?*
I will stay for ... night(s)	*Je compte rester ... nuit(s)*
Can you suggest another hotel?	*Pouvez-vous me suggérer un autre hôtel?*
Is breakfast included?	*Le petit déjeuner est-il inclus?*
What time is breakfast?	*À quelle heure est le petit-déjeuner?*
Is dinner included?	*Le dîner est-il inclus?*
What time is dinner?	*À quelle heure est le dîner?*
Can you wake me at ...?	*Pouvez-vous me réveiller à ...?*
I want to check out	*Je veux vous signaler mon départ*

Getting out ...
Food, drink and shopping

A table for one person, please	*Une table pour une personne, s'il vous plaît*
A table for two people, please	*Une table pour deux personnes, s'il vous plaît*
Can I see the menu, please?	*Puis-je voir la carte?*
Breakfast	*Le petit-déjeuner*
Lunch	*Le déjeuner*
Dinner	*Le dîner*
Are you ready to order?	*Vous avez choisi?*
I would like ...	*Je voudrais ...*
chicken	*du poulet*

beef	*du boeuf*
fish	*du poisson*
seafood	*des fruits de mer*
ham	*du jambon*
sausage	*des saucisses*
snails	*des escargots*
frogs' legs	*des cuisses de grenouilles*
cheese	*du fromage*
eggs	*des oeufs*
salad	*une salade*
(fresh) vegetables	*des légumes (frais)*
(fresh) fruit	*des fruits (frais)*
bread	*du pain*
the day's special	*le plat du jour*
May I have a cup of …?	*Puis-je avoir une tasse de …?*
May I have a glass of …?	*Puis-je avoir un verre de …?*
May I have a bottle of …?	*Puis-je avoir une bouteille de …?*
coffee	*café*
tea (the drink)	*thé*
with milk	*au lait*
orange juice	*jus d'orange*
Coke	*Coca*
(sparkling) water	*eau (gazeuse)*
beer	*bière*
red wine	*vin rouge*
white wine	*vin blanc*
May I have some …?	*Puis-je avoir du …?*
salt	*sel*
black pepper	*poivre*
butter	*beurre*
Excuse me, waiter?	*S'il vous plaît, monsieur/madame?*[109]
Where is the toilet?	*Où sont les toilettes?*
I'm finished	*J'ai fini*
It was delicious	*C'était délicieux*
The bill, please	*L'addition, s'il vous plait*
Do you serve alcohol?	*Servez-vous des boissons alcoolisées?*
A beer, please	*Une bière, s'il vous plait*
Two beers, please	*Deux bières, s'il vous plait*

---

[109] It's worth noting that if you are trying to get the attention of a waiter, shouting 'Garçon!' is considered offensive and should be avoided!

A pint, please	*Un demi-litre, s'il vous plait*
One more, please	*Encore un/une autre, s'il vous plait*
Another round, please	*Un autre pour la table, s'il vous plait*
When is closing time?	*À quelle heure fermez-vous?*
Is there …	*Est-ce qu'il y a …*
a bakery	*une boulangerie*
a grocer's	*une épicerie*
a chemist's	*une pharmacie*
Near here	*Près d'ici*
How much is this?	*Combien ça coûte?*
OK, I'll take it	*D'accord, je le/la prends*
I need …	*J'ai besoin …*
a postcard	*d'une carte postale*
postage stamps	*des timbres*
a pen	*d'un stylo*
an English-language newspaper	*d'un journal en anglais*
an English–French dictionary	*d'un dictionnaire anglais–français*
That's all	*C'est tout*

Other useful words and phrases

Numbers

1	*un*		19	*dix-neuf*
2	*deux*		20	*vingt*
3	*trois*		21	*vingt-et-un*
4	*quatre*		22	*vingt-deux*
5	*cinq*		23	*vingt-trois*
6	*six*		30	*trente*
7	*sept*		40	*quarante*
8	*huit*		50	*cinquante*
9	*neuf*		60	*soixante*
10	*dix*		70	*soixante-dix*
11	*onze*		80	*quatre-vingts*
12	*douze*		90	*quatre-vingt-dix*
13	*treize*		100	*cent*
14	*quatorze*		200	*deux cent*
15	*quinze*		300	*trois cent*
16	*seize*		1,000	*mille*
17	*dix-sept*		2,000	*deux mille*
18	*dix-huit*		1,000,000	*un million*

All the colours of the rainbow

black	*noir/noire*	orange	*orange*
white	*blanc/blanche*	pink	*rose*
grey	*gris/grise*	purple	*violet/violette*
red	*rouge*	brown	*brun/brune*
blue	*bleu/bleue*	silver	*argent*
yellow	*jaune*	gold	*or*
green	*vert/verte*		

The passage of time

Monday	*lundi*	yesterday	*hier*
Tuesday	*mardi*	tomorrow	*demain*
Wednesday	*mercredi*	now	*maintenant*
Thursday	*jeudi*	later	*plus tard*
Friday	*vendredi*	before	*avant*
Saturday	*samedi*	after	*après*
Sunday	*dimanche*	morning	*le matin*
January	*janvier*	afternoon	*l'après-midi*
February	*février*	evening	*le soir*
March	*mars*	night	*la nuit*
April	*avril*	weekend	*le week-end*
May	*mai*	holiday	*les vacances*
June	*juin*	spring	*le printemps*
July	*juillet*	summer	*l'été*
August	*août*	autumn	*l'automne*
September	*septembre*	winter	*l'hiver*
October	*octobre*	Merry Christmas!	*Joyeux Noël!*
November	*novembre*	Happy Birthday!	*Bon anniversaire!*
December	*décembre*		
today	*aujourd'hui*		

Our favourite topic of conversation … the weather!

It's nice weather	*Il fait beau*
It's raining	*Il pleut*
It's cloudy	*Il est nuageux*
It's windy	*Il est venteux*
It's snowing	*Il neige*

Friends and relations

the family	*la famille*
father	*le père*
mother	*la mère*
brother	*le frère*
sister	*la soeur*
son	*le fils*
daughter	*la fille*
grandfather	*le grand-père*
grandmother	*la grand-mère*
grandson	*le petit-fils*
granddaughter	*la petite-fille*
cousin (male)	*le cousin*
cousin (female)	*la cousine*
uncle	*l'oncle*
aunt	*la tante*
nephew	*le neveu*
niece	*la nièce*
husband	*le mari*
wife	*la femme*
boyfriend	*le copain*
girlfriend	*la copine*
friend	*l'ami(e)*
my friends	*mes amis*

Factfile: France

Location	Western Europe, bordering the Bay of Biscay and the English Channel, between Belgium and Spain, southeast of the UK; bordering the Mediterranean Sea, between Italy and Spain. Geographic coordinates: 46' 00" N, 2' 00" E.
Area	547,030 km²
Land boundaries	2,889 km
Coastline	3,427 km
Climate	Cool winters and mild summers, but mild winters and hot summers along the Mediterranean. Occasional strong, cold, dry, north-to-north-westerly wind known as the *mistral*.
Terrain	Mostly flat plains or gently rolling hills in the north and west. The rest is mountainous, especially the Pyrenees in the south and the Alps in the east.
Population	60,876,136 (July 2006 estimate) Life expectancy at birth: 79.73 years
Capital	Paris

Type of government	Republic
Head of state	The President of the French Republic (Nicolas Sarkozy, since May 2007)
National holiday	Bastille Day, 14 July (1789)
National flag	*Le drapeau tricolore* (French Tricolor), three equal vertical bands of blue (on the flagpole side), white and red. The origin of the French flag dates to 1790 and the French Revolution.
National anthem	*La Marseillaise* (*The Song of Marseille*)
Currency	Euro
Famous French people from history	William the Conqueror (c.1028–87) – monarch Joan of Arc (1412–c.1431) – soldier and saint The Montgolfier brothers (1745–99) – inventors Napoleon Bonaparte (1769–1821) – statesman Alexandre Dumas (1799–1850) – writer Victor Hugo (1802–85) – writer Ferdinand de Lesseps (1805–94) – developer of the Suez Canal Louis Braille (1809–52) – inventor Louis Pasteur (1822–95) – chemist Gustave Eiffel (1832–1923) – structural engineer and architect Camille Saint-Saëns (1835–1921) – composer Claude Monet (1840–1926) – impressionist painter Claude Debussy (1862–1918) – composer Marie Curie (1867–1934) – physicist and chemist Antoine de Saint-Exupéry (1900–44) – writer and aviator

Did you know...?

At the start of the 20th century, frogs' legs were considered unpalatable by the British. However, the French chef, Escoffier, while working at the Carlton Hotel in London, had them accepted by none other than the Prince of Wales, by having them listed on the menu as *cuisses de nymphes aurore*, or 'legs of the dawn nymphs'.

❧ German ❧

German (*Deutsch*) is a West Germanic language and, funnily enough, it is the main language of Germany, Austria, and Liechtenstein. It is widely spoken in Switzerland as well as parts of Namibia. It is also a regional language in Alsace (German: *Elsass*) and Lorraine in France, in the Italian province of South Tyrol (German: *Südtirol*, Italian: *Alto Adige* or *Sudtirolo*), in a small part of eastern Belgium, and in Luxembourg, alongside French and Luxembourgian.

Standard German (*Hochdeutsch*) is spoken by many people in much of Eastern Europe as a second language, where small groups of German minorities live in Poland, Hungary and Romania. This is as a result of the historical influence of the former Austrian Empire and Germany over the region, and also thanks to the radical border changes that were made after the Second World War. There are yet more small isolated communities of German speakers in Russia, the Central Asian Republics and Australia, as well as in both North and South America.

German uses the 26 letters of the English alphabet (but with the addition of a letter unique to German called *esszet*, which has a double-ess sound.) When pronounced in German, the name of almost every letter contains the sound which it usually represents.

A	–	*ah*	O	–	*oh*
B	–	*beh*	P	–	*peh*
C	–	*tseh*	Q	–	*kuh*
D	–	*deh*	R	–	*err*
E	–	*eh*	S	–	*ess*
F	–	*eff*	T	–	*teh*
G	–	*geh*	U	–	*uh*
H	–	*hah*	V	–	*fau*
I	–	*eeh*	W	–	*weh*
J	–	*vot*	X	–	*iks*
K	–	*kah*	Y	–	*üppsilon*
L	–	*ell*	Z	–	*tsett*
M	–	*emm*	ß	–	*ess-tsett*
N	–	*enn*			

What follows is a modern German phrasebook which includes much of the basic vocabulary you would need if you were to visit our Germanic cousins for your holidays this year.[110]

Getting by ...

The basics

Good day	*Guten tag*
Hello!	*Hallo!*
How are you?	*Wie geht es?*
Fine, thank you	*Danke, gut*
May I introduce myself to you?	*Darf ich mich Ihnen vorstellen?*
I am ...	*Ich bin ...*
I am called ...	*Ich heiße ...*
I come from England	*Ich komme aus England*
I come from Wales	*Ich komme aus Wales*
I come from Scotland	*Ich komme aus Schottland*
I come from Northern Ireland	*Ich komme aus Nordirland*
I come from Eire	*Ich komme aus Irland*
I come from Great Britain	*Ich komme aus Großbritannien*
What is your name?	*Wie heißen Sie?* (formal)
	Wie heißt du? (informal)

---

[110] But, as Basil Fawlty would say, 'Just don't mention the war!'

Where do you come from?	*Woher Kommen Sie?*
Please	*Bitte*
Thank you	*Danke sehr*
You're welcome	*Bitte sehr*
Yes	*Ja*
No	*Nein*
Pardon?	*Wie bitte?*
Excuse me	*Entschuldigen Sie*
I'm sorry	*Es tut mir leid*
What's the time?	*Wie spät ist es?*
Goodbye	*Auf Wiedersehen*
Bye!	*Tschüß!*
Good evening	*Guten Abend*
Good night	*Gute Nacht*
I can't speak German (well)	*Ich kann nicht (so gut) Deutsch sprechen*
Do you speak English?	*Sprechen Sie Englisch?*
I don't understand	*Ich verstehe das nicht*
I am lost	*Ich habe mich verirrt*
I am ill	*Ich bin krank*
May I use your phone?	*Kann ich dein/Ihr Telefon benutzen?*

Getting around …

Travel, transport and directions

How much is a ticket to …?	*Was kostet eine Fahrkarte nach …?*
One ticket to … please	*Eine Fahrkarte nach … bitte*
Where does this train/bus go to?	*Wohin fährt dieser Zug/Bus?*
Where is the train/bus to…?	*Wo ist der Zug/Bus nach…?*
Does this train/bus stop in …?	*Hält dieser Zug/Bus in …?*
When does the train/bus for … leave?	*Wann fährt der Zug/Bus nach … ab?*
When will this train/bus arrive in …?	*Wann kommt dieser Zug/Bus in … an?*
A one-way ticket	*Eine Einfache Fahrt*
A round trip ticket	*Eine Rückfahrkarte*
Where is …	*Wo ist …*
the train station?	*der Bahnhof?*
the bus station?	*der Bushaltestelle?*
the airport?	*der Flughafen?*
town centre?	*das Stadtmitte?*
the youth hostel?	*die Jugendherberge?*
the hotel?	*das Hotel?*

Can you show me on the map?	*Kannst du/Können Sie mir das auf der Karte zeigen?*
Turn left	*Links abbiegen*
Turn right	*Rechts abbiegen*
Straight ahead	*Geradeaus*
That way	*Dorthin*
Towards the …	*Richtung …*
Past the …	*Nach dem/der/dem …*
Before the …	*Vor dem/der/dem …*
North	*Norden*
South	*Süden*
East	*Osten*
West	*Westen*
Take me to … please	*Bitte bringen Sie mich zum/zur/nach …*
How much does it cost to get to …?	*Wieviel kostet es bis zum/zur/nach …?*
Take me there, please	*Bringen Sie mich bitte dahin*

Getting a room …
Board and lodging

Do you have any rooms available?	*Haben Sie ein Zimmer frei?*
How much is a room for one person?	*Was kostet ein Einzelzimmer?*
How much is a room for two people?	*Was kostet ein Doppelzimmer?*
Does the room come with …	*Ist das Zimmer mit …*
a bathroom?	*Bad?*
a telephone?	*Telefon?*
a TV?	*Fernseher?*
Do you have anything bigger?	*Haben Sie etwas größeres?*
Do you have anything cheaper?	*Haben Sie etwas billigeres?*
I will stay for … night(s)	*Ich bleibe eine Nacht/ … Nächte*
Can you suggest another hotel?	*Können Sie mir ein anderes Hotel empfehlen?*
Is breakfast included?	*Ist Frühstück inklusive?*
What time is breakfast?	*Wann gibt es Frühstück?*
Is supper included?	*Ist Abendessen inklusive?*
What time is supper?	*Wann gibt es Abendessen?*
Can you wake me at …?	*Können Sie mich um … Uhr wecken lassen?*
I want to check out	*Ich möchte abreisen*

Getting out …
Food, drink and shopping

A table for one person, please	*Ein Tisch für eine Person, bitte*
A table for two people, please	*Ein Tisch für zwei Personen, bitte*
Can I see the menu, please?	*Ich hätte gerne die Speisekarte?*
Breakfast	*Das Frühstück*
Lunch	*Das Mittagessen*
Tea (the meal)	*Die Kaffee und Kuchen*
Dinner	*Das Abendessen*
What are you having?	*Was nehmen Sie?*
I would like …	*Ich möchte …*
chicken	*Huhn*
beef	*Rindfleisch*
fish	*Fisch*
seafood	*Meeresfrucht*
ham	*Schinken*
sausage	*Wurst*
cheese	*Käse*
eggs	*Eier*
salad	*Salat*
(fresh) vegetables	*(frisches) Gemüse*
(fresh) fruit	*(frisches) Obst*
bread	*Brot*
May I have a cup of …?	*Ich hätte gern eine Tasse …?*
May I have a glass of …?	*Ich hätte gern ein Glas …?*
May I have a bottle of …?	*Ich hätte gern eine Flasche …?*
coffee	*Kaffee*
tea (the drink)	*Tee*
with milk	*mit Milch*
orange juice	*Orangensaft*
Coke	*Cola*
sparkling water	*Mineralwasser*
tap water	*Leitungswasser*
beer	*Bier*
red wine	*Rotwein*
white wine	*Weißwein*
May I have some …?	*Kann ich etwas … haben?*
salt	*Salz*
black pepper	*Pfeffer*
butter	*Butter*
Excuse me, waiter?	*Entschuldigung?*

Where is the toilet?	*Wo ist die Toilette, bitte?*
I'm finished	*Ich bin fertig*
It was delicious	*Es hat gut geschmeckt*
The bill, please	*Zahlen, bitte*
Do you serve alcohol?	*Haben Sie alkoholische Getränke?*
A beer, please	*Ein Bier, bitte*
Two beers, please	*Zwei Bier, bitte*
One more, please	*Noch einen/eine/eins, bitte*
Another round, please	*Noch eine Runde, bitte*
When is closing time?	*Wann schließen Sie?*
Is there ...	*Gibt es ...*
a bakery	* eine Bäckerei geschäft*
a grocer's	* ein Lebensmittelgeschäft*
a chemist's	* eine Apotheke*
Nearby	*In der Nähe*
How much is this?	*Was kostet das?*
OK, I'll take it	*OK, ich nehme es*
I need ...	*Ich brauche ...*
a postcard	* eine Postkarte*
postage stamps	* Briefmarken*
a pen	* einen Stift*
an English-language newspaper	* eine englischsprachige Zeitung*
an English–German dictionary	* ein Englisch–Deutsch Wörterbuch*
Anything else?	*Sonst noch etwas?*

Other useful words and phrases

Numbers

1	*eins*	13	*dreizehn*	40	*vierzig*
2	*zwei*	14	*vierzehn*	50	*fünfzig*
3	*drei*	15	*fünfzehn*	60	*sechzig*
4	*vier*	16	*sechzehn*	70	*siebzig*
5	*fünf*	17	*siebzehn*	80	*achtzig*
6	*sechs*	18	*achtzehn*	90	*neunzig*
7	*sieben*	19	*neunzehn*	100	*einhundert*
8	*acht*	20	*zwanzig*	200	*zweihundert*
9	*neun*	21	*einundzwanzig*	300	*dreihundert*
10	*zehn*	22	*zweiundzwanzig*	1,000	*eintausend*
11	*elf*	23	*dreiundzwanzig*	2,000	*zweitausend*
12	*zwölf*	30	*dreißig*	1,000,000	*eine Million*

All the colours of the rainbow

black	*schwarz*	orange	*orange*
white	*weiß*	pink	*rosa*
grey	*grau*	purple	*violett*
red	*rot*	brown	*braun*
blue	*blau*	silver	*silber*
yellow	*gelb*	gold	*gold*
green	*grün*		

The passage of time

Monday	*Montag*	yesterday	*gestern*
Tuesday	*Dienstag*	tomorrow	*morgen*
Wednesday	*Mittwoch*	now	*jetzt*
Thursday	*Donnerstag*	later	*später*
Friday	*Freitag*	before	*vor*
Saturday	*Samstag*	after	*nach*
Sunday	*Sonntag*	morning	*der Morgen*
January	*Januar*	afternoon	*der Nachmittag*
February	*Februar*	evening	*der Abend*
March	*März*	night	*die Nacht*
April	*April*	weekend	*das Wochenende*
May	*Mai*	holiday	*die Ferien*
June	*Juni*	spring	*der Frühling*
July	*Juli*	summer	*der Sommer*
August	*August*	autumn	*der Herbst*
September	*September*	winter	*der Winter*
October	*Oktober*	Merry Christmas!	*Fröhliche*
November	*November*		*Weihnachten!*
December	*Dezember*	Happy Birthday!	*Alles Gute zum*
today	*heute*		*Geburtstag!*

Our favourite topic of conversation ... the weather!

It's nice weather	*Das Wetter ist schön*
It's raining	*Es regnet*
It's cloudy	*Es ist wolkig*
It's windy	*Es ist windig*
It's snowing	*Es schneit*

Friends and relations

the family	*die Familie*
father	*der Vater*
mother	*die Mutter*
brother	*der Bruder*
sister	*die Schwester*
son	*der Sohn*
daughter	*die Tochter*
grandfather	*der Grossvater*
grandmother	*die Grossmutter*
grandson	*der Enkelsohn*
granddaughter	*die Enkeltochter*
cousin (male)	*der Cousin*
cousin (female)	*die Cousine*
uncle	*der Onkel*
aunt	*die Tante*
nephew	*der Neffe*
niece	*die Nichte*
husband	*der Ehemann/der Mann*
wife	*die Gattin/die Frau*
boyfriend	*mein Freund*
girlfriend	*meine Freundin*
friend	*der Freund/die Freundin*
my friends	*meine Freunde*

Factfile: *Germany*

Location	Central Europe, bordering the Baltic Sea and the North Sea, between the Netherlands and Poland, south of Denmark. Geographic coordinates: 51' 00" N, 9' 00" E.
Area	357,021 km^2
Land boundaries	3,621 km
Coastline	2,389 km
Climate	Temperate and marine; cool, cloudy, wet winters and warm summers; occasional warm mountain wind, known as the *foehn*.
Terrain	Lowlands in the north, uplands in centre, and Bavarian Alps in south.
Population	82,422,299 (July 2006 estimate) Life expectancy at birth: 78.8 years
Capital	Berlin

Type of government	Federal republic
Head of state	The President of Germany (Horst Koehler, since 1 July 2004)
National holiday	Unity Day, 3 October (1990)
National flag	The *Dienstflagge der Bundesbehörden* (the state flag of the federal authorities), or *Bundesdienstflagge* for short, is a tricolour with three equal horizontal bands of black (top), red, and gold. The German flag dates back to the Weimar Republic of Germany (1919–33).
National anthem	*Das Lied der Deutschen* (The Song of the Germans), also known as *Das Deutschlandlied* (The Germany song)
Currency	Euro
Famous German people from history	Albrecht Dürer (1471–1528) – painter Martin Luther (1483–1546) – theologian Georg Friedrich Händel (1685–1759) – composer The Brothers Grimm (Jakob 1785–1863 & Wilhelm 1786–1859) – collectors of fairy tales Richard Wagner (1813–83) – composer Karl Marx (1818–83) – philosopher and sociologist Johannes Brahms (1833–97) – composer Friedrich Nietzsche (1844–1900) – existentialist philosopher Max Planck (1858–1947) – physicist Richard Strauss (1864–1949) – composer Albert Einstein (1879–1955) – physicist Walter Gropius (1883–1969) – architect F.W. Murnau (1888–1931) – film director Max Ernst (1891–1976) – surrealist painter Manfred von Richthofen, the Red Baron (1892–1918) – fighter pilot and air ace

Did you know...?

In Germany the short interjection '*shhh*' means 'hurry up'.

♟ Spanish ♟

Spanish (*castellano* or *español*) is the third most spoken language in the world. A Western Romance language by origin, Spanish is closely related to Portuguese, Catalan, French, Italian and Romanian. Although it originated in Spain, where it is also known as Castilian, it is also spoken in Mexico and all of Central and South America (except for Brazil, Guyana, French Guiana and Suriname). Spanish is also spoken in Cuba, Puerto Rico, the Philippines, the Dominican Republic and other Caribbean islands. For many people in the United States of America, especially in California, Texas, south Florida and elsewhere in the Southwest, it is a first language.

The Spanish alphabet has 30 letters in total, pronounced as follows:

A	–	*ah*	N	–	*eh nay*
B	–	*bay*	Ñ	–	*en yay*
C	–	*th-ay*	O	–	*oh*
CH	–	*cheh*	P	–	*pay*
D	–	*deh*	Q	–	*koo*
E	–	*eh*	R	–	*eh ray*
F	–	*eh fay*	RR	–	*eh rray*
G	–	*hay*[111]	S	–	*eh say*
H	–	*ah chay*	T	–	*tay*
I	–	*ee*	U	–	*ooh*
J	–	*ho tah*[112]	V	–	*oobeh*
K	–	*kah*	W	–	*oobeh-doble*
L	–	*el lay*	X	–	*eh kees*
LL	–	*eh yay*	Y	–	*ee gree yay gah*
M	–	*eh may*	Z	–	*seh ta* or *theh-ta*

---

[111] The *h* here is like the *ch* in *loch*.
[112] The *ho* is a guttural sound in the back of the throat.

What follows is a modern Spanish phrasebook which includes much of the basic vocabulary you would need if you were to visit our Hispanic cousins for your holidays this year.

Getting by ...
The basics

Hello!/Hi!	*Hola!*
How are you?	*¿Cómo estás?*
Fine, thank you	*Muy bien, gracias*
May I introduce myself to you?	*¿Me permite presentarme?*
I am ...	*Yo soy ...*
I am called ...	*Me llamo ...*
I come from England	*Soy de Inglaterra*
I come from Wales	*Soy de Gales*
I come from Scotland	*Soy de Escocia*
I come from Northern Ireland	*Soy de Irlanda del Norte*
I come from Eire	*Soy de la República de Irlanda*
I come from Great Britain	*Soy de Gran Bretaña*
What is your name?	*¿Cómo se llama usted?* (formal)
	¿Cómo te llamas? (informal)
Where do you come from?	*¿De dónde viene usted?*
Please	*Por favor*
Thank you	*Gracias*
You're welcome	*De nada*
Yes	*Sí*
No	*No*
What did you say?	*¿Qué has dicho?*
Excuse me (mild apology)	*Perdón*
Excuse me (may I get past)	*Con su permiso*
I'm sorry	*Lo siento*
What's the time?	*¿Qué hora es?*
Goodbye	*Hasta luego*
Bye!	*Adiós!*
Good evening	*Buenas tardes*
Good night	*Buenas noches*
I can't speak Spanish (well)	*No hablo (bien) español*
Do you speak English?	*¿Hablas inglés?*
I don't understand	*No entiendo*
I am lost	*Estoy perdido/a*

| I am ill | *Estoy enfermo/a* |
| May I use your phone? | *¿Puedo usar su teléfono?* |

Getting around ...
Travel, transport and directions

How much is a ticket to ...?	*¿Cuánto cuesta un billete a ... ?*
One ticket to ... please	*Un billete a ... por favor*
Where does this train/bus go to?	*¿A donde va este tren/autobús?*
Where is the train/bus to ...?	*¿Donde está el tren/autobús hacia ...?*
Does this train/bus stop in ...?	*¿Para este tren/autobús en ...?*
When does the train/bus for ... leave?	*¿Cuándo sale el tren/autobús hacia ...?*
When will this train/bus arrive in ...?	*¿Cuándo llegará este tren/autobús a ...?*
A one-way ticket	*Un billete sencillo*
A round trip ticket	*Un billete de ida y vuelta*
Where is ...	*¿Dónde está ...?*
the train station?	*la estación de tren?*
the bus station?	*la estación de autobuses?*
the airport?	*el aeropuerto?*
town centre?	*el centro?*
the suburbs?	*las afueras*
the youth hostel?	*el hostal?*
the hotel?	*el hotel?*
Can you show me on the map?	*¿Puede enseñarme/mostrarme en el plano?*
Turn left	*Gire/doble/da vuelta a la izquierda*
Turn right	*Gire/doble/da vuelta a la derecha*
Straight ahead	*Recto adelante*
That way	*Aquel camino*
Towards the ...	*Hacia el/la ...*
Past the ...	*Pasado el/la ...*
Before the ...	*Antes de ...*
North	*Norte*
South	*Sur*
East	*Este*
West	*Oeste*
Take me to ... please	*Lléveme a ... por favor*
How much does it cost to get to ...?	*¿Cuánto cuesta ir hasta/a ...?*
Take me there, please	*Déjeme ahí, por favor*

Getting a room …
Board and lodging

Do you have any rooms available?	*¿Hay habitaciones libres?*
How much is a room for one person?	*¿Cuánto cuesta una habitación para una persona?*
How much is a room for two people?	*¿Cuánto cuesta una habitación para dos personas?*
Does the room come with …	*¿Tiene la habitación …*
a bathroom?	*baño?*
a telephone?	*teléfono?*
a TV?	*televisión?*
Do you have anything bigger?	*¿Tiene algo un poco más grande?*
Do you have anything cheaper?	*¿Tiene algo un poco más barato?*
I will stay for … night(s)	*Me quedaré … noche(s)*
Can you suggest another hotel?	*¿Puede recomendarme otros hoteles?*
Is breakfast included?	*¿El desayuno va incluido?*
What time is breakfast?	*¿A qué hora es el desayuno?*
Is supper included?	*¿La cena va incluida?*
What time is supper?	*¿A qué hora es la cena?*
Can you wake me at …?	*¿Puede despertarme a las …?*
I want to check out	*Quiero dejar el hotel*

Getting out …
Food, drink and shopping

A table for one person, please	*Una mesa para una persona, por favor*
A table for two people, please	*Una mesa para dos personas, por favor*
Can I see the menu, please?	*¿Puedo ver el menú, por favor?*
Breakfast	*El desayuno*
Lunch	*La comida*
Dinner	*La cena*
Are you ready to order?	*¿Está listo para ordenar?*
I would like …	*Quiero …*
chicken	*el pollo*
veal	*la ternera*
fish	*el pescado*
seafood	*los mariscos*
ham	*el jamón*
sausage	*la salchicha*
cheese	*el queso*
eggs	*los huevos*

salad	*la ensalada*
(fresh) vegetables	*las verdura (frescas)*
(fresh) fruit	*la fruta (fresca)*
bread	*el pan*
May I have a cup of …?	*¿Me puede poner/traer una taza de …?*
May I have a glass of …?	*¿Me puede poner/traer un vaso de …?*
May I have a bottle of …?	*¿Me puede poner/traer una botella de …?*
coffee	*café*
tea (the drink)	*té*
with milk	*con leche*
orange juice	*zumo/jugo de naranja*
Coke	*Coca-Cola*
(sparkling) water	*agua (con gas)*
beer	*cerveza*
red wine	*vino tinto*
white wine	*vino blanco*
May I have some …?	*¿Me puede dar un poco de …?*
salt	*sal*
black pepper	*pimienta*
butter	*mantequilla*
Excuse me, waiter?	*¡Camarero!*
Where is the toilet?	*¿Dónde está el baño?*
I'm finished	*He acabado/terminé*
It was delicious	*Estaba delicioso/muy bueno*
The bill, please	*La cuenta, por favor*
Do you serve alcohol?	*¿Hay alcohol?*
A beer, please	*Una cerveza, por favor*
Two beers, please	*Dos cervezas, por favor*
A pint, please	*Una jarra de cerveza, por favor*
One more, please	*Otro/a … por favor*
Another round, please	*Otra ronda, por favor*
When is closing time?	*¿Cuándo cierra(n)?*
How much is this?	*¿Cuánto cuesta?*
OK, I'll take it	*De acuerdo, me lo llevaré*
I need …	*Necesito …*
a postcard	*una postal*
postage stamps	*sellos*
a pen	*un bolígrafo*
an English-language newspaper	*un periódico/diario en inglés*
an English–Spanish dictionary	*un diccionario ingles–español*
Anything else?	*¿Algo más?*

Other useful words and phrases
Numbers

1	*uno*	19	*diecinueve*
2	*dos*	20	*veinte*
3	*tres*	21	*veintiuno*
4	*cuatro*	22	*veintidós*
5	*cinco*	23	*veintitrés*
6	*seis*	30	*treinta*
7	*siete*	40	*cuarenta*
8	*ocho*	50	*cincuenta*
9	*nueve*	60	*sesenta*
10	*diez*	70	*setenta*
11	*once*	80	*ochenta*
12	*doce*	90	*noventa*
13	*trece*	100	*cien*
14	*catorce*	200	*doscientos*
15	*quince*	300	*trescientos*
16	*dieciséis*	1,000	*mil*
17	*diecisiete*	2,000	*dos mil*
18	*dieciocho*	1,000,000	*un millón*

All the colours of the rainbow

black	*negro*	orange	*naranja*
white	*blanco*	pink	*rosa*
grey	*gris*	purple	*púrpura*
red	*rojo*	brown	*marrón*
blue	*azul*	silver	*plata*
yellow	*amarillo*	gold	*oro*
green	*verde*		

Match Wits With The Kids

The passage of time

Monday	lunes	today	hoy
Tuesday	martes	yesterday	ayer
Wednesday	miércoles	tomorrow	mañana
Thursday	jueves	now	ahora
Friday	viernes	later	después
Saturday	sábado	before	antes
Sunday	domingo	after	después de
January	enero	morning	la mañana
February	febrero	afternoon/evening	la tarde
March	marzo	night	la noche
April	abril	weekend	el fin de semana
May	mayo	holiday	las vacaciones
June	junio	spring	la primavera
July	julio	summer	el verano
August	agosto	autumn	el otoño
September	septiembre	winter	el invierno
October	octubre	Merry Christmas!	¡Feliz Navidad!
November	noviembre	Happy Birthday!	¡Feliz cumpleaños!
December	diciembre		

Our favourite topic of conversation ... the weather!

It's nice weather	Hace bueno
It's raining	Está lloviendo
It's cloudy	Está nublado
It's windy	Está ventoso
It's snowing	Está nevando

Friends and relations

the family	la familia	cousin (female)	la prima
father	el padre	uncle	el tío
mother	la madre	aunt	la tía
brother	el hermano	nephew	el sobrino
sister	la hermana	niece	la sobrina
son	el hijo	husband	el esposo/marido
daughter	la hija	wife	la esposa/mujer
grandfather	el abuelo	boyfriend	el novio
grandmother	la abuela	girlfriend	la novia
grandson	el nieto	friend (male)	el amigo
granddaughter	la nieta	friend (female)	la amiga
cousin (male)	el primo	my friends	mis amigos

Factfile: Spain

Location	Southwestern Europe, bordering the Bay of Biscay, Mediterranean Sea, North Atlantic Ocean, and Pyrenees Mountains, southwest of France. Geographic coordinates: 40' 00" N, 4' 00" W.
Area	504,782 km^2
Land boundaries	1,917.8 km
Coastline	4,964 km
Climate	Temperate, with clear, hot summers in the interior, but more moderate and cloudy along the coast. Cloudy, cold winters in the interior, but partly cloudy and cool along the coast.
Terrain	Large, flat to dissected plateau surrounded by rugged hills. Pyrenees in the north.
Population	40,397,842 (July 2006 estimate) Life expectancy at birth: 79.65 years

Capital	Madrid
Type of government	Parliamentary monarchy
Head of state	King of Spain (Juan Carlos I, since 22 November 1975)
National holiday	National Day, 12 October (1492)
National flag	Three horizontal bands of red (top), yellow (double width), and red with the national coat of arms on the flagpole side of the yellow band. The coat of arms includes the royal seal framed by the Pillars of Hercules, which are the two promontories (Gibraltar and Ceuta) on either side of the eastern end of the Strait of Gibraltar.
National anthem	*La Marcha Real* (The Royal March)
Currency	Euro
Famous Spanish people from history	Trajan (53–117) – Roman Emperor Hadrian (76–138) – Roman Emperor El Cid (c.1044–99) – soldier Tomás de Torquemada (1420–98) – Grand Inquisitor Francisco Pizarro (1471–1541) – conqueror of Inca Empire Hernán Cortés (1485–1547) – explorer and conquistador Miguel de Cervantes (1547–1616) – author Diego Velázquez (1599–1660) – painter Gaspar Sanz (1640–1710) – composer Francisco Goya (1746–1828) – painter Antoni Gaudí (1852–1926) – architect Pablo Picasso (1881–1973) – artist Joan Miró (1893–1983) – painter and sculptor Salvador Dalí (1904–89) – surrealist artist

Did you know...?

The name of one of the world's most infamous prisons, the legendary Alcatraz Island located in San Francisco Bay, means 'pelican' in Spanish.

❦ Spot Test ❦

You've made it through the languages! By now you should be a multilinguist *par excellence*. Or at least, you should be happy booking yourself into a nice comfy hotel and buying a bottle of reasonably priced wine when abroad.

So parents, will you be the ones to choose the next family holiday? Or kids, do your language abilities put your parents to shame? Maybe we'll see you *sur la plage* in the near future … if you can wade your way successfully through this teasing vocab test first.

Dictionaries closed, pens at the ready and begin!

1) What is the French for 'a one-way ticket'?
2) How do you say, 'I need some stamps' in French?
3) Who was Ferdinand de Lesseps?
4) Name three countries, other than Germany, in which German is spoken.
5) How do you say, 'How are you?' in German?
6) What is the German for 'Happy Birthday!'?
7) What would you say if you wanted to tell a Spanish friend you came from Wales?
8) What is the Spanish for 'thirty'?
9) What were the occupations of the famous Spaniards, Trajan and Hadrian?
10) What does the name of the infamous prison on Alcatraz Island mean in Spanish?

---

1) *Un aller simple.* **2)** *J'ai besoin des timbres.* **3)** *The developer of the Suez Canal.* **4)** *Austria, Liechtenstein, Switzerland, Namibia, France, Italy, Belgium and Luxembourg.* **5)** *Wie geht es?* **6)** *Alles Gute zum Geburtstag!* **7)** *Soy de Gales.* **8)** *Treinta.* **9)** *They were both Roman Emperors.* **10)** *Pelican.*

Chapter Nine

CLASSICS

Latin is a language as dead as dead can be ...

When people talk about learning Classics, they are of course referring to the learning of Latin, with possibly a little Ancient Greek thrown in, and a smidgeon of culture from the ancient world on top of that. The word Classics originates, appropriately enough, from the Latin word *classicus* which means 'of the highest class'. So, in other words, if you want to appear clever and well-educated, carelessly adding a little throw-away Latin into the conversation at dinner parties can do wonders for your reputation and social standing. In fact it will make you look like a right *teneo-is-totus*.[113]

You may already be aware of the following short rhyme:

Latin is a language
As dead as dead can be.
First it killed the Romans
And now it's killing me.

However, as is evidenced by many examples in everyday life and the modern world around us, Latin is anything but dead. It is used in legal jargon, it appears at the end of television programmes, footballers and film stars have it tattooed all over their bodies, and people still speak it, on occasion, although without necessarily realising they're doing so. It even appears in the magical world of Harry Potter.

---

[113] Latin for 'know-it-all'.

Latin (or *lingua Latina*) is the most commonly taught ancient language in schools, and one which is currently enjoying something of a resurgence, so that is what we are going to focus on in this chapter.

The Latin Alphabet

Surely one of the greatest legacies of the Romans is their alphabet, which has been almost universally adopted by the modern languages of Europe and America. When it was being used by writers such as Caesar, Horace, Livy and Pliny in what is now called the Classical period, it had only 23 letters. These were identical to those we use now but there was no 'j', 'v' or 'w'. The capital letter 'V' appeared only as the capital form of 'u' but in time came to represent the same letter in the lower case as well.

Did you know...?
The two letters 'y' and 'z' appear in the Latin language only in words that are of Greek origin!

ΩΩΩ

A common Latin vocabulary

What is a common Latin vocabulary and, in a book like this, where do you start? So many of the words we use every day are descended from Latin. The vocabulary that is taught in schools, therefore, is mainly taken from the works of the Roman authors, such as Tacitus, Virgil, Cicero, Ovid and Catullus, who were writing between 180 BC and AD 120.

Amazing as it may sound, Latin is a language with a relatively small vocabulary, and one of the challenges facing anyone trying to learn it is that many words have many different – and even widely varying – meanings.

So, what we have done here is to provide you with a list that is made up of Latin words which are still used today. Frequently they are used in an everyday context, even if those doing so do not realise that they are speaking Latin or, more often than not, abbreviations of it. Hopefully the following will go some way towards helping you sound suitably intelligent when quizzed by those less knowledgeable than yourself about how to complete their Latin homework.

A Modern Latin Phrasebook

Ad hoc – 'for this purpose' – commonly used to mean temporarily useful.

Ad infinitum – 'without end' – going on and on and on and on …

Ad nauseam – 'endlessly' – used to refer to things that go on and on to the point of making you sick.

Agenda – 'things to be done' – now used to mean a list of items, or things to be done, that might be discussed at, say, a meeting.

Alias – 'also known as' – although *alias* originally meant 'at another time'.

Alma mater – 'nourishing mother' – normally used to refer to one's old school or university.

Alter ego – 'other self' – a favourite of super spies and comic book superheroes.

Anno Domini – 'in the year of our Lord' – usually abbreviated to AD (which does *not* mean 'after death').

Annus horribilis – 'a terrible year'.

Annus mirabilis – 'a wonderful year'.

Ante meridiem – 'before midday' – but normally you will see it written as a.m. after a time: e.g. 10:30 a.m.

Aqua pura – 'pure water'.

Aqua vitae – 'water of life' – variously whisky, brandy and vodka.

Ave Maria – 'hail Mary' – how often you find yourself saying this, depends on whether you're Catholic or not, and, if you are, how badly behaved you have been.

Bona fide – 'in good faith' – although this expression is more commonly used to mean that something is genuine, e.g. it was a bona fide mistake on my part.

Carpe diem – 'seize the day' – or, make the most of now.

Caveat – 'warning' – which literally means 'let him beware'. From this we get *caveat emptor* which means 'buyer beware' and similarly *cave canem*, famously seen on a mosaic in the Roman city of Pompeii, accompanied by the picture of a canine, and which means 'beware of the dog'.

Circa – 'about' – often abbreviated to c. and followed by a date in history textbooks.

Codex – 'a book' or 'a manuscript'.

Compos mentis – 'of sound mind' – in other words, sane.

Cornucopia – 'horn of plenty' – seen as much as read or spoken, particularly in paintings and architectural details.

Cum laude – 'with praise' – sometimes encountered in the phrase *magna cum laude*, meaning 'with great praise', and used in relation to academic awards.

Curriculum vitae – 'CV' – although the phrase actually means 'the course of your life'. If you're in any doubt, your CV lists all your academic achievements and, in later life, your career history, along with a few personal interests thrown in there too.

De facto – 'in reality' – meaning that this is what is actually happening and not what should be happening or what is allegedly happening, e.g. 'because the owner never turned up, I was the *de facto* manager of the chippie'.

Dei gratia – 'by the grace of God' – most commonly seen on British coins as part of the phrase *dei gratia regina fidei defensor*, meaning 'By the grace of God the Queen, Defender of the Faith'.

Deus ex machina – 'god from the machine' – a contrived event that resolves a problem at the last moment, a common device used by lazy authors of second-rate science fiction.

Dramatis personae – 'the persons of the drama' – the list of characters in a play.

Ecce homo – 'behold the man'.

Ego – 'I' – but used in English to mean the consciousness of one's own identity. 'I think, therefore I am' (which translated into Latin is *cogito, ergo sum*).

Exempli gratia – 'for example' – often abbreviated to e.g.

Ergo – 'therefore'.

Erratum – 'mistake' – sometimes you will open a book to find an errata slip, listing all the mistakes that were discovered after the book went to print. I hope that you didn't find such a slip in the front of this book.

Et alii – 'and the other people' – normally just written as *et al.*

Et cetera – 'and the rest' – literally meaning 'and the other things' but usually written *etc.*

Exeat – 'holiday' – usually used nowadays only by boarding schools to describe a long weekend off from school for the boarders.

Exit – 'way out'.

Ex libris – 'from the library of' – normally found only on bookplates these days.

Folio – 'edition' – well known thanks to its connection with Shakespeare's First Folio. It comes from the Latin word *folium* meaning 'leaf' or 'page'.

In absentia – 'while absent' – it is one of those facts of life that you are usually *in absentia* when the really important decisions are made.

In extremis – 'in the furthest reaches' – as in, being close to death.

In flagrante delicto – 'caught red-handed' – although it should actually be translated as 'in the middle of a burning crime' and so should surely be used in reference to arsonists rather than illicit lovers caught in the act.

In loco parentis – 'in the place of a parent' – anyone looking after a child who isn't actually theirs. Teachers and grandparents regularly act *in loco parentis*.

In memoriam – 'in memory of'.

In situ – 'in the place' – or meaning that something is in its original situation.

In vino veritas – 'in wine, the truth' – in other words, people have a nasty habit of telling the truth when they're drunk.

In vitro – 'artificial' – as in '*in vitro* fertilisation', i.e. test-tube babies.

Ipso facto – 'by that very fact' – usually used in the context of a statement that contradicts itself and so proves the opposite, e.g., 'If you have to ask yourself if you like my cooking, then *ipso facto*, you don't.'

Magister Artium – 'Master of Arts' – usually abbreviated to MA after somebody's name.

Magna Carta – 'Great Charter' (literally 'Great Paper') – specifically referring to the one issued by King John in 1215, granting various liberties.

Magnum opus – 'great work' – or somebody's masterpiece, whether it be a book, a symphony, or the garden shed you took three weeks to put up by yourself.

Mea culpa – 'my fault' – or, to put it simply, 'Whoops!'

Medicinae Doctor – 'Doctor of Medicine' – more often used as the abbreviation MD by American medical practitioners.

Memorandum – 'a thing to be remembered' – which has become a note of something to be remembered or a memo.

Memento mori – 'remember to die' – a timely warning reminding you that you're not going to live forever, and used to refer to anything that reminds you or your own mortality, such as a skull, a ticking clock, an hourglass, daytime television …

Modus operandi – 'a way of working' – popular now in relation to tracking down serial killers by means of their *modus operandi*. Lovely.

Nil desperandum – 'do not despair'.

Non sequitur – 'it doesn't follow' – something which doesn't make sense because it doesn't have any apparent connection to what came before it.

Nota bene – 'note well' – better known by its abbreviation NB.

Odi et amo – 'I hate and I love' – the very definition of the intensity of passion.

Pater noster – 'Our Father' – and, by extension, the Lord's Prayer.

Per annum – 'per year' – normally used in relation to your pay and then the amount of tax you've paid.

Per capita – 'individually' – usually used in relation to statistics to indicate the average *per person* for any particular thing, whether it be income, illness or crime rate.

Per se – 'in and of itself' – or, taken alone. As in, 'Reading this chapter will not make you an expert in the field of Classics, *per se*. You would need to study for years to achieve such a goal.'

Persona non grata – 'an unacceptable person' – in other words, one who is not welcome in the company of others.

Post meridiem – 'after midday' – as with a.m., although, in this case, p.m.

Post mortem – 'after death' – now refers to an autopsy, in other words, what happens to the body after death to determine what the cause of death was.

Pro forma – 'for form's sake' – now normally an invoice or a standard form that has to be filled in.

Pro rata – 'in proportion to' – or according to the rate.

Quasi – 'as if' – often used these days in conjunction with another word to mean something made-up or bearing only a resemblance to the real thing, as in 'quasi-religious'.

Quod est demonstrandum – 'the thing that is to be proved' – but usually encountered only as the three letters QED.

Quid pro quo – 'something for something' – in other words, 'there's no such thing as a free lunch'. How true.

Quo vadis? – 'Where are you going?'

Re – 'concerning' – as in 're: your planning application', literally 'in the matter of'.

Requiescat in pace – 'rest in peace' – often reduced to the letters RIP, particularly on tombstones.

Rigor mortis – 'the stiffness of death' – one of the recognisable signs of death is the stiffening of a corpse's muscles.

Sic – 'thus' or 'as follows' – usually used in brackets after a word to denote that although the spelling of that word may appear wrong, that is how it is intended to be spelt.

Status quo – ' the state of things' – meaning the current, existing state of affairs. If you maintain the status quo you keep things just as they are currently.

Tabula rasa – 'clean slate' – in other words, one that is blank, used now to refer to an empty mind.[114]

Tempus fugit – 'time flies'.

Terra firma – 'firm land' – but used to mean 'dry land', as in 'back on terra firma' once safely ashore again, or after the plane touches down safely.

Urbi et orbi – 'to the city and the world' – nowadays normally encountered only in relation to speeches made by the Pope.

Verbatim – 'exactly as said' – as in to quote someone word-for-word.

Versus – 'against' – and can be shortened to *v*.

Via – 'by way of'.

Vice versa – 'the change being turned' – or rather, on the other hand.

Vox populi – 'voice of the people' – the term is often used in broadcasting when referring to interviews with members of the public, and is shortened to the rather catchy 'vox pop'.

---

[114] Not something that anybody reading this book need worry about.

🎭 **Latin Grammar** 🎭

Before we go any further there's an awkward little word I'd like to get out of the way. Sex. There it is, I've said it.[115] And why exactly is it awkward? Well, simply because every Latin noun has a **gender**: **masculine** (he), **feminine** (she) or **neuter** (it).

This is a strange concept to students of English … except that it shouldn't be because all English nouns have a gender as well, it's just that unless something is specifically male or female (like boys and girls), it is considered to be neuter. We refer to a table as 'it', to an idea as 'it', to Saturday as 'it', and the same goes for carrots, colours, cats and cars. Of course, as language teachers always tell us, English is a particularly difficult language to learn[116] because it has so many curious exceptions. In the case of noun genders, two notable anomalies are ships and countries, which are always feminine, as in 'And bless all who sail in her', or 'Mother Russia'.

However, there are some helpful pointers in Latin which tell you which gender a noun belongs to. Most masculine words end –us, most feminine words end –a, and the neuter nouns end –um, although there are of course the odd exceptions. Things proceed logically from there, with an adjective which describes the noun taking the same gender form.

In case you're wondering, it is important to know the gender of a noun so that you know how it declines and can then recognise it when it appears in different **cases**.[117]

---

[115] Or rather written it, if you're pedantic about these sorts of things.

[116] But if that's true, why do so many millions of non-English-speaking people across the globe learn English as a second language?

[117] Don't worry if none of this makes sense to you yet – it will. Just keep reading.

The other thing that you bear in mind with Latin is that the Romans had funny ideas about the order that words go in within a sentence, at least it looks that way now. In English, verbs generally go in the middle of a sentence. In a Valentine's card to your sweetheart you might scribble the message,[118] 'I love you'. However, a lovelorn Roman would write, 'I you love'.

In Latin, the verb goes at the end of the sentence, following the subject (the person or thing the sentence is about) and the object. But as with all rules, this one was made to be broken (or at least bent a little) and so it doesn't always apply. As a rule of thumb, though, it's a pretty good one to start with.

ΩΩΩ

Unpacking the Cases

In Latin, according to how they are being used (in context), words are put into different cases which, more often than not, change the end of/spelling of the word. There are six cases altogether.[119]

Nominative

This is the case taken by the **subject** of a sentence, the subject being the main person or thing that the sentence is about. Consider the following:

Tom sang of his love for Angela from the rooftops.

The subject of this sentence is *Tom* and in Latin would be in the nominative.

---

[118] In an effort to disguise your handwriting.

[119] Although there is actually a seventh – the Locative case, used to indicate a location (which we do in English with the words 'in' or 'at'), e.g. in Rome – but it is so rare that scholars really talk only about six.

Vocative

This is the case taken by whatever it is (be it person or object) that is being addressed (in other words, spoken to) in the sentence.

Julie, can you let Dad know I'll be home late tonight?

Here *Julie* is the one being addressed, and so in Latin her name would appear in the vocative.

Accusative

This is the case that identifies the **object** of a sentence. In the example given with the nominative, Tom's *love* is the object of that particular sentence.

Genitive

This case is all about possession. It lets you know who it is (in the sentence, of course) that a particular thing belongs to, whether it be a mosaic, a villa or a slave girl. In the phrase:

the first and last voyage of the *Titanic*

Titanic is in the genitive as, here, 'the first and last voyage' belongs to the ship.

Dative

When something is done 'for' someone or 'to' something (else), whoever or whatever it is done to or for takes the dative. Considering Tom's song of love once more, *Angela* would be in the dative here.

Ablative

Similar to the dative, when something is done 'by', 'with' or 'from' something or someone, the relevant object or person is put in the ablative. Looking at our initial example one more time, the *rooftops* would be in the ablative here.

ΩΩΩ

Defining Declension

Declension is a suitably scholarly word meaning that Latin nouns, pronouns and adjectives have fixed stems to which different ent endings are added to express their gender, number and case. There are five declensions altogether, although the third declension is subdivided again into four groups. Any nouns belonging to a particular declension will break down in the same way.

First declension

First declension nouns are usually feminine and always end in –a. Take, for example, *villa* (a country house).

	Singular	**Plural**
Nominative	*villa*	*villae*
Vocative	*villa*	*villae*
Accusative	*villam*	*villas*
Genitive	*villae*	*villarum*
Dative	*villae*	*villis*
Ablative	*villa*	*villis*

Second declension

Second declension nouns are mainly masculine or neuter. If they are masculine, they end in –us, or –er, and decline as follows:

	Singular	Plural
Nominative	stilus	stili
Vocative	stile	stili
Accusative	stilum	stilos
Genitive	stili	stilorum
Dative	stilo	stilis
Ablative	stilo	stilis

	Singular	Plural
Nominative	liber	libri
Vocative	liber	libri
Accusative	librum	libros
Genitive	libri	librorum
Dative	libro	libris
Ablative	libro	libris

If you are wondering, *stilus* means 'pen', whereas the usual translation of *liber* is 'book' (although it can also mean 'the inner bark of a tree').

Neuter second declension nouns end in –um and decline like this:

	Singular	Plural
Nominative	bellum	bella
Vocative	bellum	bella
Accusative	bellum	bella
Genitive	belli	bellorum
Dative	bello	bellis
Ablative	bello	bellis

Bellum is the Latin for 'war'.[120]

---

[120] And they ask 'What is it good for?' Well, helping to explain second declension neuter nouns for a start!

Third declension

Third declension nouns are tricky customers. Generally they are short nouns, the stem of which can extend to a longer form from the accusative onwards. There are many irregular third declension nouns and, on top of that, they can be masculine, feminine or neuter. Take a look at *rex* (meaning 'king') declined below.

	Singular	Plural
Nominative	*rex*	*reges*
Vocative	*rex*	*reges*
Accusative	*regem*	*reges*
Genitive	*regis*	*regium*
Dative	*regi*	*regibus*
Ablative	*rege*	*regibus*

Third declension nouns are subdivided into different groups depending on whether they have vowel or consonant stems and what happens to them in the genitive plural. We won't be going into all the different forms here but, for the sake of this book, it is worth pointing out that the fourth group of third declension nouns are ones which were originally Greek nouns (such as the names of their heroes). Here is an example using *Pericles* (as in Shakespeare's *Prince of Tyre*).

	Singular
Nominative	*Pericles*
Vocative	*Pericle*
Accusative	*Periclem*
Genitive	*Periclis*
Dative	*Pericli*
Ablative	*Pericle*

There is no plural form of Pericles because there was only one of him, after all.

Fourth declension

Fourth declension nouns can be either masculine or neuter. The masculine form can catch you out because it ends in –us, like second declension masculine nouns, but declines in an entirely different way. Here is an example of a fourth declension masculine noun.

	Singular	Plural
Nominative	*manus*	*manus*
Vocative	*manus*	*manus*
Accusative	*manum*	*manus*
Genitive	*manus*	*manuum*
Dative	*manui*	*manibus*
Ablative	*manu*	*manibus*

Manus is a 'hand', from which we get such words as 'manual' and 'manipulate'. *Genu* on the other hand is a 'knee', from where we get the word 'genuflect' (meaning 'to bend the knee, especially in worship or as a sign of respect'). It is an example of a fourth declension neuter noun.

	Singular	Plural
Nominative	*genu*	*genua*
Vocative	*genu*	*genua*
Accusative	*genu*	*genua*
Genitive	*genus*	*genuum*
Dative	*genu*	*genibus*
Ablative	*genu*	*genibus*

Fifth declension

There are not very many fifth declension nouns, but the ones that do exist are everyday kind of words that get used frequently. They are mainly feminine and decline like this:

	Singular	**Plural**
Nominative	*dies*	*dies*
Vocative	*dies*	*dies*
Accusative	*diem*	*dies*
Genitive	*diei*	*dierum*
Dative	*diei*	*diebus*
Ablative	*die*	*diebus*

Dies is indeed an everyday word, as it is the Latin for 'day'.

ΩΩΩ

Clarifying Conjugation

Rather like declension with nouns, the word **conjugation** describes how Latin verbs have fixed stems to which are added different endings to denote person, number and tense (as well as voice, mood and aspect).

First, the good news. Whereas there are five declensions of Latin nouns, there are only four conjugations of Latin verbs. But it gets better: in general, all verbs in the present tense (meaning something is being done right now) closely follow the endings of the first conjugation verb *amare*, meaning 'to love'.

First conjugation

	Singular	Plural
First person	amo	amamus
Second person	amas	amatis
Third person	amat	amant

The verb *amare* lives on today in the Spanish *amor* and in French, the language of love itself, as *l'amour*.

The present tenses of the other three conjugations are as follows:

Second conjugation

	Singular	Plural
First person	deleo	delemus
Second person	deles	deletis
Third person	delet	delent

Delere means 'to destroy', from where we get the English word 'delete'.

Third conjugation

	Singular	Plural
First person	intellego	intellegimus
Second person	intellegis	intellegitis
Third person	intellegit	intellegunt

The Latin verb *intellegere* means 'to understand'; hence our own word 'intelligence'.

Fourth conjugation

	Singular	Plural
First person	*dormio*	*dormimus*
Second person	*dormis*	*dormitis*
Third person	*dormit*	*dormiunt*

Dormire, meaning 'to sleep', is the root of our words 'dormitory' and 'dormant'.

And now for the bad news … apart from there being another three conjugations for the wannabe Latin scholar to learn, future and past tenses come with their own endings and even changes to the root word as well. On top of that, because of the nature of the language, if you really want to master Latin you need to learn verb forms for at least six tenses, and then there are the different moods they can be in.

So, before we open that can of worms, here would seem to be as good a place as any to end our little discussion of the diversity of Latin grammar. Just remember, as in life, when it comes to learning Latin, *noli nothis permittere te terere.*[121]

---

[121] Literally, 'Don't let the b******s wear you down'.

🎭 Classical Civilisation 🎭

Of course the true classical scholar doesn't just study Latin (or even Ancient Greek, if they have the opportunity). No, anyone who would claim to be an expert in the field of Classics also needs to have an in-depth knowledge of the classical civilisations.

However, if you don't possess such an in-depth knowledge yourself, we present here a smattering which should at least get you out of any close scrapes at dinner parties, unless, of course, you happen to find yourself dining with a gaggle of Oxford dons who just happen to have a knowledge of the ancient world to rival that of Herodotus.[122]

ΩΩΩ

The Roman Empire

When people talk about the Roman Empire (*Res publica Romana* or *Imperium Romanum*) they are generally referring to a period of some 500 years, lasting from halfway through the 1st century BC through to nearly the end of the 4th century AD (although the Empire actually lasted in one form or another for 1,000 years after that). It was ruled and administered from its capital city, Rome (once a lowly city-state), hence the Roman Empire.

At its greatest extent in AD 117, the Roman Empire covered much of the known world at that time. It stretched from Hadrian's Wall, on the border of present-day Scotland, in the north, to Spain and Portugal in the west; as far as the Black Sea in the east, and including the whole of North Africa, including Egypt, at its southernmost limit. That is a total area of nearly 6 million km^2

---

[122] The Ancient Greek scholar now known as 'the father of History'. So, Chapter Six is his fault really.

(or 2,300,000 square miles) with a population of around 88 million people. So confident were the Romans of their absolute right to rule the known world as they saw it, that they knew the Mediterranean Sea as the *mare nostrum*, meaning 'our sea'.

The first Emperor

The Roman Empire is a fine example of autocratic government; one which is ruled over by one person, and one person alone, who has absolute power over the populace. In other words, whatever the Emperor said, went.

The Empire followed on from the Roman Republic, which had itself lasted for 500 years. There are three possible dates given as the time when the more democratic Republic turned into the dictatorship of the Empire. The first is 44 BC, when the legendary **Julius Caesar** (100–44 BC) was appointed perpetual dictator (*Dictator Perpetuus*). Like so many dictators before and since, Caesar's tenure didn't last for long and he came to an untimely end when a group of senators assassinated him, on the Ides of March (i.e. 15 March), the same year.

The second date, that of 2 September 31 BC, commemorates the victory of Caesar's heir, **Octavian**, over the forces of Mark Antony at the Battle of Actium. And the last suggested date is 16 January 27 BC, when the Roman Senate granted Octavian the honorary titles of *Augustus* (meaning 'elevated one') and *Princeps* ('First Citizen of the Roman Republic'). So Octavian became Caesar Augustus (27 BC–AD 14), the first Roman Emperor.

Did you know...?

142 different individuals were, or claimed to be, Emperor of either all or part of the Roman Empire, from the time of the first Emperor Augustus through to the death of the last Latin-speaking Emperor, Justinian, in AD 565.

The end of the Empire

The end of the Roman Empire is sometimes placed at 4 September AD 476, when the last Emperor of the Western Roman Empire, **Romulus Augustus**, was deposed without being replaced. However, **Diocletian**, who retired in AD 305, was the last sole Emperor of an undivided Empire whose capital was the city of Rome.

The Roman state lasted in one form or another from the founding of Rome[123] (classically considered to have occurred in 753 BC) to the fall of the Empire of Trebizond, a remnant of the Byzantine Empire, which had itself once been part of the Eastern Roman Empire (in AD 1461). By our reckoning, that's a total of 2,214 years!

ΩΩΩ

The Legacy of Rome

The impact that the Roman Empire had on the world can still be seen, quite clearly, in the world around us today. In time, many of the Romans' achievements were duplicated by other civilisations which came after them, but there is still much that we owe directly to Ancient Rome.

---

[123] Named after Romulus, who slew his twin brother, Remus, after the two of them founded the city on the slopes of the Palatine Hill overlooking the River Tiber.

The modern calendar, Christianity as we know it today, and many aspects of modern architecture are a direct legacy of the Roman Empire. We also have the Romans to thank for the roads that their armies constructed over the centuries, connecting all corners of the Empire. Its form of government has influenced all manner of constitutions including those of most European countries and many former European colonies, such as the United States. Our legal system grew out of that of Roman law, as does our civil service and modern methods of tax collection.[124]

Latin: the official language of an empire

The expansion of the Roman Empire spread Latin throughout Europe. Eventually it evolved into a number of distinctly different languages – including French, Italian, Spanish and Portuguese – and as a result influenced the development of many languages spoken in other parts of the world, such as those of Central and South America, as well as English.

At the height of Imperial Rome, however, Latin had developed into what were effectively two languages. First there was the formal written **Classical Latin**, which had evolved from an early stage of the spoken language and cannot be considered the same as the spoken Latin of any period. It remained barely unchanged right through the Middle Ages, by which time it was the official language of the Catholic Church.

Secondly there was the spoken **Vulgar Latin**, which, like any spoken language, changed depending on which region of the Empire you were in and transmuted over time. In fact, Vulgar

---

[124] Or, as Monty Python once put it, 'but apart from better sanitation and medicine and education and irrigation and public health and roads and a freshwater system and baths and public order … what *have* the Romans done for *us*?'

Latin changed so much that in the western provinces of the Empire it became the *lingua franca* which, in turn, was the source of modern languages such as Italian, Spanish and, of course, French.

Roman numerals

As well as providing us with some of the foundations of our own language, the Romans have also left us with their numbering system. **Roman numerals** are all written using only seven letters – I, V, X, L, C, D and M – which are then given numerical values. They can be seen all around us, on such disparate objects as clock faces and the facades of buildings and the end credits of television programmes.

The values assigned to the different letters (along with their Latin names) are as follows:

Symbol	Value	Latin name
I	1 (one)	*unus*
V	5 (five)	*quinque*
X	10 (ten)	*decem*
L	50 (fifty)	*quinquaginta*
C	100 (hundred)	*centum*
D	500 (five hundred)	*quingenti*
M	1,000 (thousand)	*mille*

Individual numbers between these values are made from multiple combinations of the seven basic letters. So we end up with:

Roman	Arabic[125]	Roman	Arabic	Roman	Arabic
I	1	XVI	16	C	100
II	2	XVII	17	CC	200
III	3	XVIII	18	CCC	300
IV	4	XIX	19	CD	400
V	5	XX	20	D	500
VI	6	XXV	25	DC	600
VII	7	XXX	30	DCC	700
VIII	8	XL	40	DCCC	800
IX	9	L	50	CM	900
X	10	LX	60	M	1000
XI	11	LXIX	69	MDCLXVI	1666[126]
XII	12	LXX	70	MCMXCIX	1999
XIII	13	LXXX	80	MM	2000
XIV	14	XC	90	MMVIII	2008
XV	15	XCIX	99	MMXII	2012

To help you remember the value of the Roman numeral symbols above ten, from smallest to largest, try this mnemonic:

Lazy **C**ows **D**on't **M**oo

Roman religion

The Romans were a highly religious, not to say superstitious, people who worshipped a whole pantheon of gods alongside the spirits of the household and their ancestors (the *lares* and *penates*). The names of many of the Roman gods live on today as the names of the planets of our solar system, and even as the names of people.

---

[125] The symbols which we normally use to represent numbers are actually known as Arabic numerals.

[126] 1666 is interesting because as a Roman numeral it is the largest number to use every symbol exactly once.

The best-known gods of the Romans are listed below, grouped into male first and female second.

Roman gods

Jupiter – king of the gods and god of the sky
Neptune – god of the sea, brother to Jupiter and Pluto
Pluto – god of the underworld, brother to Neptune and Jupiter
Mars – god of war
Apollo – god of the sun
Mercury – fleet-footed messenger of the gods
Vulcan – god of fire and smith of the gods
Saturn – god of farming and agriculture
Uranus – god of the sky, father of Jupiter
Cupid – god of love, son of Venus and Ares
Bacchus – god of wine
Aesculapius – god of medicine

Roman goddesses

Juno – god of women and childbirth, both wife and sister of Jupiter
Minerva – goddess of war and wisdom, daughter of Jupiter
Venus – goddess of love
Vesta – goddess of the hearth and home
Diana – goddess of hunting and the Moon
Terra – goddess of the Earth
Ceres – goddess of crops and the harvest
Proserpina – goddess of the springtime and queen of the underworld[127]
Victoria – goddess of victory[128]

ΩΩΩ

---

[127] Proserpina (better known by her Greek name, Persephone) was the daughter of Ceres. When Proserpina was stolen away by Pluto to be his queen, in her grief Ceres stopped the growth of all fruit and vegetables, causing winter to come to the world for the first time.

[128] The Greeks called Victoria, Nike. Now, where have you seen that name before?

Roman Britain

Every schoolchild knows (or at least should know) that the Romans invaded Britain (or Britannia, as they called it) in AD 43, during the reign of the Emperor Claudius (AD 41–54). However, this was not the first time such an invasion had been attempted. Julius Caesar made two expeditions to Britain in 55 and 54 BC, intending to punish the tribes living there for supporting the Gauls (the people who lived in modern-day France) in their fight against the Roman conquest of their lands.

The successful invasion was led by Aulus Plautius and the Second Legion.[129] (It is likely that it also involved the Ninth, Fourteenth and Twentieth Legions at various stages, as they are mentioned as being present during Boudicca's revolt.) The Romans were keen to plunder the British Isles for their natural resources. For a good 400 years before the invasion in AD 43, the Classical world had traded with the British for their tin.[130]

Boudicca: warrior queen of the Iceni

Although some of the Celtic tribes who were already living in Britain decided it was best to accept the Romans as their new masters and ally with them, not all of the native peoples gave in quite so easily. From AD 60–61, the southeast of Britain rose up against the Romans, under the leadership of the now legendary **Queen Boudicca**.[131]

---

[129] A legion was a section of the Roman army that comprised up to 5,200 soldiers under the command of a legate (*legatus legionis*).
[130] Although this didn't stop some early writers from refusing to believe that the British Isles even existed!
[131] For a time she was known as Boadicea (or Boudicea), after the Roman historian Tacitus spelt her name that way.

Boudicca's husband, King Prasutagus, ruler of the Iceni tribe which controlled much of East Anglia, had made a deal with the Romans, whereby on his death half his lands would go to the Emperor at the time, Nero (AD 54–68), in the hope that the rest would remain untouched. However, after Prasutagus's death, all his lands were seized by the Romans and, to add injury to insult, Boudicca and her daughters were assaulted.

Boudicca's campaign of vengeance began when the Iceni, joined by the Trinovantes tribe, destroyed the Roman colony at *Camulodunum* (modern-day Colchester). The Celts then managed to repel the units of the Ninth Legion that was sent to aid the colony.

Gaius Suetonius Paulinus, the Roman governor of Britain at that time, rode to *Londinium* (London), which was the next city in the path of the Celts' rampage, but turned tail again, declaring that it could not be defended. So, *Londinium* was destroyed, as was *Verulamium* (St Albans) after it. Roman historians writing at the time recorded that 70–80,000 people were killed in the three cities; men, women and children.

Having fled at first, Suetonius now regrouped with two of the three legions still available to him. Despite being heavily outnumbered by the Celts, the much better-equipped and more disciplined Roman soldiers defeated the rebels during the Battle of Watling Street. Rather than be taken by the Romans, Boudicca took poison and died. Although defeated in the end, Boudicca's revolt had been so devastating that the Emperor Nero was almost persuaded to withdraw from Britain altogether.

The end of Roman rule in Britain

In the 4th century AD, with Rome facing increased attacks from barbarian tribes on its borders, the officials and elements of the Roman army based in Britannia were withdrawn, leaving the native Romano-British people (as many of them now were) to face the increasing attacks of the Saxons (from northern Germany) alone.

Roman towns

During the 350 years of Roman occupation, many important settlements were founded which have lasted to this day. The following towns and cities were either established by the Romans themselves, or were extensively developed by them:

Alcester[132] – *Aluana*
Bath – *Aquae Sulis*
Binchester – *Vinovia*
Caerleon – *Isca Augusta*
Caerwent – *Venta Silurum*
Canterbury – *Durovernum Cantiacorum*
Carmarthen – *Moridunum*
Chelmsford – *Caeseromagus*
Chester – *Deva*
Chichester – *Noviomagus Regnorum*
Cirencester – *Corinium*
Colchester – *Camulodunum*
Corbridge – *Coria*
Dover – *Portus Dubris*

---

[132] If a place name has 'cester', 'chester' or 'caster' within it, it's a dead giveaway that it was once a Roman settlement, as all of these words are corruptions of the Latin *castra*, meaning a 'camp', such as the ones built by the Roman army.

Doncaster – *Danum*

Dorchester – *Durnovaria*

Exeter – *Isca Dumnoniorum*

Gloucester – *Glevum*

Leicester – *Ratae Corieltauvorum*

London – *Londinium*

Lincoln – *Lindum Colonia*

Manchester – *Mancunium*[133]

Northwich – *Condate*

St Albans – *Verulamium*

Salisbury – *Sorviodunum*

Silchester – *Calleva Atrebatum*

Towcester – *Lactodorum*

Whitchurch – *Mediolanum*

Winchester – *Venta Belgarum*

Wroxeter – *Viroconium Cornoviorum*

York – *Eboracum*

---

[133] Another Roman name for Manchester is *Mamucium,* although there is some disagreement over which should be the preferred term.

❧ **Famous Classical Faces** ❧

	Name	Dates	Greek or Roman?	Legacy
1	Homer	c. 8th century BC	Greek	A legendary poet, famous for being the creator of the epic poems the *Iliad* (which tells the story of the Trojan War) and the *Odyssey* (which relates the hero Odysseus' efforts to return home afterwards). However, like many legends, the truth might be somewhat different, as some scholars do not believe that Homer actually existed!
2	Sophocles	496 BC– c. 406 BC	Greek	A playwright, one of three whose tragedies have lasted to the modern age (the other two being Aeschylus and Euripides). It is believed he wrote as many as 120 plays during his lifetime, if not more, but only seven have survived intact to the present day. Of these, the best-known are *Antigone* and *Oedipus the King*.
3	Iktinos and Kallikrates	Unknown, lived during 5th century BC	Greek	The architects of the Parthenon in Athens, the temple dedicated to Athena, the goddess of wisdom. The Parthenon is one of the most famous Classical buildings still in existence.

	Name	Dates	Greek or Roman?	Legacy
4	Hippocrates	c. 460 BC– c. 370 BC	Greek	A physician, now often referred to as the 'father of medicine'. He rejected the idea that supernatural or divine forces caused illness, and his legacy to medical practice is just as relevant in the 21st century. Doctors today still swear a Hippocratic oath by which they promise to practise medicine ethically.
5	Plato	424/3 BC– 348/7 BC	Greek	Despite also being a mathematician and the founder of the first institution of higher learning in the Western world, the Academy in Athens, he is best known for his contributions as a philosopher. Along with the work of his teacher, Socrates, and his own student, Aristotle, Plato helped to lay the philosophical foundations of Western culture.

	Name	Dates	Greek or Roman?	Legacy
6	Decimus Junius Brutus Albinus	c. 85 BC–43 BC	Roman	A consul of the Republican era, he staged the first gladiatorial games in Rome in 264 BC in honour of his dead father, Junius Brutus Pera. Later, grisly spectacles were held in the famous Coliseum in the heart of Rome. This structure, along with the gladiators themselves, is one of our most enduring images of the Romans.
7	Virgil	70 BC–19 BC	Roman	A classical poet. He is most famous for writing the *Aeneid*, which tells the legendary story of Aeneas, the ancestor the Romans, and which (unsurprisingly) became the Roman Empire's national epic poem.
8	Ovid	43 BC–AD 17	Roman	A poet well known for his *Metamorphoses*, poems about incredible transformations found in Classical myth. Alongside Virgil and Horace he is regarded as one of the three canonical poets of Latin literature. We still come across his stories today, as some of Shakespeare's best-known plays, including *Romeo and Juliet*, have their roots in Ovid.

	Name	Dates	Greek or Roman?	Legacy
9	Pliny the Elder	23–79	Roman	He was an author and naturalist, as well as being a renowned naval and military commander. He is particularly well known for writing the *Naturalis Historia*, an early encyclopaedia which includes an eyewitness account of the eruption of Vesuvius at Pompeii.
10	Plutarch	46–120	Roman	A philosopher and author, he is best known for his biographies and his moral treatises, which have found a larger audience than that of any other ancient philosopher.
11	Tacitus	c. 56–c.117	Roman	A senator in his own time, he is now most famous as a historian of the Roman Empire. He wrote about the Emperors and their abuse of their position, and the invasion of Britain, and was one of the first secular writers to make reference to Jesus Christ.
12	Constantine	c. 272–337	Roman	Emperor from 306 to 337, he is best known for being the first Christian Roman Emperor. His reign saw an end to the institutionalised persecution of Christians in the Empire.

🎭 Spot Test! 🎭

The big exams may be just around the corner, but that's no reason not to have a final spot test to see how well you're picking things up as we go along. In fact, think of this as the final warm-up – the last chance to get in the best shape possible to match wits with the kids.

Kids, how have you done so far? Do you reckon you could run through your third declension verbs while your parents pant slowly along behind you? Or are your chances of showing grown-ups exactly what kids are made of as dead as Caesar himself?

Time to find out with the following questions:

1) What does the Latin phrase *annus mirabilis* mean?
2) Can you name four of the seven cases?
3) What is the Latin root for the English words 'dormitory' and 'dormant'?
4) Romulus and Remus were the twin brothers who founded Rome, but what was the name of the hill it was built upon?
5) What name did Octavian take when he became Roman Emperor in 27 BC?
6) Which of these Roman numerals has the higher value? For a bonus point, what is the sum of these numerals? M, D, L, C.
7) Diana was the goddess of which two things?
8) How many soldiers were in a legion?
9) Of whom was King Prasutagus the ruler?
10) What are the modern names of the following Roman towns or cities: *Durovernum Cantiacorum, Deva, Portus Dubris, Mancunium* and *Eboracum*?

---

1) *'A wonderful year.'* 2) Nominative, vocative, accusative, genitive, dative, ablative and the very rare locative. 3) *Dormire*, meaning 'to sleep'. 4) The Palatine Hill. 5) Caesar Augustus. 6) M = 1,000 and therefore has the highest value. D = 500, L = 50 and C = 100. Added together, they give a total of 1,650. 7) Hunting and the Moon. 8) 5,200. 9) The Iceni tribe. 10) These are now known as Canterbury, Chester, Dover, Manchester and York.

Chapter Ten

MATCH WITS WITH THE KIDS

Congratulations! You've made it to the end of the book and have refreshed your memory of what you learnt at school along the way. You might even have learnt something new.

But now the time has come and, as they say, the proof of the pudding is in the eating. How thoroughly did you read up on physics? Are you fully up to speed with British History again? Have you refreshed your holiday Spanish? Are you confident with the Classics?

There's no escaping it! You have reminded yourself of all those things you thought you had forgotten long ago, recalled from the dusty classrooms of your memory, and now you're ready – finally – to take on the know-it-all next generation and challenge your children.

It's time to match wits with the kids!

❧ Practice Test One ❧

1) What is the total number of degrees of the internal angles of a triangle?

2) On a directional compass, which point is the more southerly: southeast or south by southwest?

3) What is the Latin equivalent of the phrase 'seize the day'?

4) What part of speech is the word 'during'?

5) What does a probability of zero mean?

6) Who was the first *de facto* Prime Minister of Great Britain?

7) What is the French for holiday?

8) Where should the apostrophes go in the following sentence? *Jacks LPs were sold at last weeks jumble sale, held at All Saints church.*

9) What is the sum of the first four prime numbers?

10) What is the pH value of rain water?

11) Who was the first Tudor king?

12) What is a glacial erratic?

13) Who wrote *Howards End*?

14) Mr Singh bought his house for £270,000 three years ago. Since then it has risen in value by 25%. How much is it worth now?

15) Express the process of respiration as a word equation.

16) Who is Spain's current head of state?

17) What two things do plant cells have that animal cells do not?

18) What is the basic formula for Pythagoras' Theorem?

19) Who invented the 'Spinning Jenny'?

20) What is the name given to a poem made up of fourteen rhyming lines of the same length?

21) What travels at 300 million metres per second in air?

22) On an Ordnance Survey map, what do the thin brown lines indicate?

23) Translate the following sentence from German to English: *Ich komme aus Großbritannien.*

24) Which year would be represented by the Roman numerals MCMLXXI?

25) What is the chemical symbol for gold?

❦ Practice Test Two ❦

1) What is the French for 'Happy Birthday'?

2) What is the more correct term for the Queen's English?

3) If a map has a scale of 1:250,000, what distance on the ground would be represented by 4 cm on the map?

4) Where did the Peterloo Massacre of 1819 take place?

5) Which mineral is vital for root growth in plants?

6) What is the square root of 196?

7) What gives the planet Uranus its greeny-blue colour?

8) Who wrote *Le Morte D'Arthur*?

9) What is *'Das Wetter ist schön'* in English?

10) Who led the Scots to victory against the English at the Battle of Bannockburn?

11) How many degrees does a reflex angle have?

12) What is unusual about the capital city of South Africa?

13) What is the median of the following set of numbers? 7, 108, 56, 129, 49, 18, 24, 2, 32, 12, 74.

14) What example of imagery is 'She was as strict as a headteacher'?

15) What does the Latin phrase *'Anno Domini'* mean?

16) Mary works five 8-hour shifts a week as a waitress. She earns £5.00 an hour. She earns another £80.00 in tips. What is this amount as a percentage of her weekly wage?

17) What was Richard Owen's legacy to the world?

18) Which common chemical compound has the chemical formula $C_{17}H_{35}COONa$?

19) Who was Francisco Pizarro?

20) What is the area of a triangle with a base measuring 7 cm and a height of 2 cm?

21) What kind of historical source is the chapter on history in this book?

22) What is the present participle of 'to sleep'?

23) What did the Romans call the Mediterranean Sea?

24) What is another name for a cumulo-nimbus cloud?

25) Who was the last king of the House of Wessex?

🍃 Practice Test Three 🍃

1) What is 13 × 11?

2) When the nuclei of a sperm cell and an ovum fuse, what is the new cell that is produced called?

3) What happened to King Charles I in 1649?

4) What does the Mercalli Scale measure?

5) Which case is the Latin word *libros*?

6) What is *un diccionario ingles–español* in English?

7) Put 'I dance like Ginger Rogers' into the future perfect tense.

8) Jake has four pairs of black socks in his sock drawer and four red pairs. When he gets dressed in the dark, how many socks does he have to take out to guarantee he has a matching pair?

9) Which metal has the chemical symbol Hg and is liquid at a temperature of 20°C?

10) What sort of sentence is an interrogative?

11) Who was Queen for Nine Days?

12) What is the German for a grocer's?

13) Who devised the Law of Accelerated Motion?

14) What passes through Greenwich, London at 0° longitude?

15) Simplify the following equation: $(x + y)(x - 2) + 6y - 5x$

16) What part of speech is the word 'envy'?

17) How do you work out the average speed of a train in motion?

18) Mrs Jones is tiling her bathroom. She needs to tile an area of 2 m × 1.5 m on one wall, and an area of 4 m × 1.5 m on another wall. The tiles she has bought measure 10 cm². How many tiles will she need to complete the job?

19) On a map which uses layer colouring, what is indicated by the colour purple?

20) What is a queer fish?

21) When did the First World War end?

22) What is *la primavera* in English?

23) What are the primary colours of light?

24) On which date was Julius Caesar assassinated?

25) With which work of English literature is Geoffrey Chaucer most commonly associated?

❧ Practice Test Four ❧

1) Which type of rock is formed when magma cools and crystallises?

2) What does a colon indicate?

3) What is the Spanish for 'Good evening'?

4) What is a homophone?

5) What is 7^5?

6) In 2001, what was the third most populous city in the UK?

7) What is the plural of 'fish'?

8) For how long did the Wars of the Roses last?

9) How many lines of symmetry does an equilateral triangle have?

10) Which coastal feature is left behind when an arch collapses?

11) Which type of micro-organism can reproduce only inside living cells?

12) By what date was the United Kingdom formed?

13) Which modern English city was called *Aquae Sulis* by the Romans?

14) What is $(6 + 11) \times (8 - 4) - 4^3$?

15) Of what is a 'deafening silence' an example?

16) Which battle saw the infamous Charge of the Light Brigade?

17) How many member states make up the United Nations?

18) What is $1\frac{2}{3} \div \frac{5}{9}$?

19) What does the Latin word *intellegimus* mean?

20) To which phylum of the animal kingdom do earthworms belong?

21) What name is given to a volcano that is formed by alternating eruptions of ash and lava?

22) Which adjective has the meaning 'twisting, winding or convoluted'?

23) What is the national anthem of Germany called?

24) Who was the mother of Edward VI and, as a consequence, Henry VIII's favourite wife?

25) Why is there no sound in the vacuum of space?

❧ Practice Test Five ❧

1) Who was the first Prime Minister of Great Britain to officially be given that title?

2) What is the Latin for 'and the rest'?

3) What is the comparative adjective of 'much'?

4) How much energy is required to lift 1 kg a height of 1 m?

5) What circles the Earth at a latitude of 66° 33' 39" south?

6) Of what is the nucleus of an atom made?

7) Who led the Peasants' Revolt of 1381?

8) If $\dfrac{-3(x+4)}{-6} = 4$, find the value of x.

9) Who was the first Roman Emperor?

10) What is the German for 'A beer, please'?

11) Which part of speech is 'washed'?

12) Which city is the capital of Australia?

13) What is the sum of the interior angles of an octagon?

14) What did the Great Reform Act of 1832 do?

15) What is the approximate surface area of an adult human being's lungs?

16) What is the correct meaning of 'biennial'?

17) What is 564 − 465?

18) If someone closely resembles one of their parents, what could they be described as?

19) What is a watershed?

20) Which is the most abundant element in the human body?

21) What one event precipitated the First World War?

22) What is France's national holiday?

23) What is it that keeps the Moon orbiting the Earth, and the planets circling the sun?

24) Who led the British uprising against the Romans in AD 60–61?

25) Mr Singh is laying a circular concrete patio. If the radius of the circle is 1 m and the concrete needs to fill a hole 1 m deep, what volume of concrete does he need?

☙ **Answers** ☙

Practice Test One

1) 180°

2) South by southwest.

3) *Carpe diem.*

4) A preposition.

5) A probability of zero means that a particular outcome will never occur.

6) Robert Walpole, 1st Earl of Orford, was the first *de facto* PM. He served from 1721–42.

7) *Les vacances.*

8) Jack's LPs were sold at last week's jumble sale, held at All Saints' church.

9) 2 + 3 + 5 + 7 = 17 (which is also a prime number).

10) 5.5

11) Following the Battle of Bosworth in 1475, Henry Tudor became Henry VII, the first Tudor king.

12) A large rock dropped by a glacier as it retreats.

13) E.M. Forster.

14) 270,000 × 25% = 67,500. 270,000 + 67,500 = 337,500. So the house is now worth £337,500.

15) glucose + oxygen → carbon dioxide + water

16) King Juan Carlos I.

17) Plant cells have both a cell wall and chloroplasts (which contain the green chlorophyll necessary for photosynthesis to take place).

18) $a^2 + b^2 = c^2$

19) James Hargreaves invented the 'Spinning Jenny' in 1764. He named it after his wife.

20) A sonnet, as popularised by William Shakespeare.

21) Light.

22) The thin brown lines are contour lines which join places on a map that are at the same height above sea level.

23) I come from Great Britain.

24) 1971.

25) Au.

*/ */ */

Practice Test Two

1) *Bon anniversaire!*

2) Received pronunciation (or RP).

3) 10 km. 1:250,000 means 1 cm on the map is the same as 250,000 cm (or 2.5 km) on the ground, so 4 cm would be equivalent to 10 km (4 × 2.5 km).

4) St Peter's Field, Manchester.

5) Phosphorous.

6) 14.

7) Clouds of methane in its atmosphere.

8) Thomas Malory, in 1485.

9) It's nice weather.

10) Robert the Bruce. The battle took place on 23–24 June 1314.

11) A reflex angle has between 180° and 360°.

12) South Africa actually has three capital cities: Pretoria, the administrative capital, Cape Town, the legislative capital, and Bloemfontein, the judiciary capital.

13) The median value is 32.

14) A simile.

15) In the year of our Lord.

16) £80.00 is 40% of her weekly wage of £200.00.

17) The term 'dinosaur' (as well as the British Natural History Museum in London).

18) Sodium stearate, or in other words, soap!

19) He was the Spaniard who conquered the Incan Empire.

20) The area of the triangle is 7 cm².

21) A secondary written source.

22) Sleeping.

23) The *mare nostrum*, meaning 'our sea'.

24) A thunderhead.

25) Harold II. He was killed at the Battle of Hastings in 1066.

Practice Test Three

1) 143.

2) A zygote.

3) He was put on trial for treason, found guilty and, as a result, was executed.

4) The Mercalli Scale measures the amount of damage caused by an earthquake.

5) *Libros* is the accusative form of *liber*, Latin for 'book'.

6) An English–Spanish dictionary.

7) I *will have danced* like Ginger Rogers.

8) Three socks.

9) Mercury.

10) A question.

11) Lady Jane Grey, 10–19 July 1553.

12) *Ein Lebensmittelgeschäft.*

13) Galileo Galilei.

14) The Prime Meridian.

15) $x^2 - 7x + xy + 4y$.

16) An abstract noun.

17) Divide the distance travelled by the time taken to cover that distance.

18) Mrs Jones will need 900 tiles to cover 9 m² of wall.

19) High mountains.

20) 'Queer fish' is an English idiom meaning 'a strange person'.

21) The ceasefire came on the 11th hour of the 11th day of the 11th month, 1918.

22) Spring.

23) The primary colours of light are red, green and blue.

24) 15 March 44 BC, the Ides of March.

25) *The Canterbury Tales.*

✐ ✐ ✐

Practice Test Four

1) Igneous rock.

2) A colon indicates that something else is to follow, like a list.

3) *Buenas tardes.*

4) A homophone is a word that sounds the same as another but which has a different spelling or meaning.

5) 16,807.

6) Glasgow.

7) The plural of 'fish' is 'fish'. There is no change.

8) On and off, the Wars of the Roses lasted for 32 years.

9) An equilateral triangle has three lines of symmetry.

10) A stack.

11) A virus.

12) 1750.

13) Bath, in Somerset.

14) 4.

15) An oxymoron; an expression in which two contradictory words are used together.

16) The Battle of Balaclava, on 25 October 1854, during the Crimean War.

17) There are 194 member states of the UN.

18) 3.

19) We understand.

20) *Annelida*.

21) A composite volcano, or strato-volcano, like Mount Vesuvius in Italy.

22) Tortuous. (Not torturous!)

23) The national anthem of Germany is *Das Lied der Deutschen* ('The Song of the Germans'), otherwise known as *Das Deutschlandlied* ('The Germany Song').

24) Jane Seymour.

25) Sound is transmitted by vibrating particles. If there are no particles present, as in the empty void of outer space, then there is nothing to vibrate and so there cannot be any sound.

🖉 🖉 🖉

Practice Test Five

1) Sir Henry Campbell-Bannerman, in 1905.

2) *Et cetera.*

3) More.

4) 1 joule.

5) The Antarctic Circle.

6) Protons and neutrons.

7) Wat Tyler, who was later beheaded for his troubles.

8) $x = 4$.

9) Caesar Augustus (the Emperor formerly known as Octavian) who ruled from 27 BC–AD 14.

10) *Ein Bier, bitte.*

11) 'Washed' is the past participle of 'to wash'.

12) Canberra.

13) The sum of the interior angles of an octagon = $(8 - 2) \times 180° = 1080°$.

14) The 1832 Great Reform Act granted more people from the new industrial middle class the right to vote.

15) 140 m².

16) 'Biennial' means happening every two years.

17) 99.

18) A chip off the old block.

19) A watershed is an area of high land that separates one or more drainage basins.

20) Oxygen.

21) The assassination of Archduke Franz Ferdinand on 28 June 1914.

22) Bastille Day, 14 July. It commemorates the storming of the Bastille prison in 1789, at the start of the French Revolution.

23) Gravitational force.

24) Queen Boudicca of the Iceni tribe.

25) Mr Singh needs 3.14 m^3 of concrete.

❦ How Did You Do? ❦

So, time to own up. How did you fare when it came to matching wits with the kids? Have you graduated from the University of Life with a first-class degree, or has having children turned your brain to mush?

And kids, were your parents right when they moaned that 'Young people today – they don't know anything'? Or did you give the old fogeys a run for their money and prove that education wasn't necessarily better in their day?

To find out, turn your score out of 25 into a percentage[134] and consult the appropriate table below.

♛ PARENTS

100%	'Eureka!' You are a certified genius! Einstein and Aristotle have nothing on you. You are a veritable modern-day Da Vinci. Quick, sign up for MENSA right away!
80–99%	Got that gloating, self-satisfied smile ready? Good. Now walk up to the nearest ignorant teenager and smugly tell them that 'It wasn't all vocational qualifications and citizenship lessons in my day. In my day you received a proper, classical education.'
60–79%	Well done. You've matched wits with the kids and not come off too badly. But admit it; there are still some areas you need to polish up on, especially if you're going to help your own teenager complete that latest piece of crucial coursework!
40–59%	Ah, so you do remember some of what those dusty schoolmasters were trying to indoctrinate you with. You see, rote learning's not so bad really, is it? But what happens when you have to start thinking for yourself? (Not that it's ever stopped you so far.)

---

[134] Can't remember how? Then what are you doing here? You'd better go back and revise Chapter Two again!

20–39%	Okay, you've tried to bluff the younger generation by making out you knew it all already, but now you've been found out. Go back and actually try reading the book this time, rather than just scanning the amusing footnotes.
1–19%	Time to don the cardie and slippers and start flicking through those brochures for that retirement home down the road. The future definitely belongs to the kids.
0%	In less PC times you would have been stuck in the corner of the class with a paper cone on your head marked with a large letter 'D'. But as we are living in a more enlightened age we'll settle for 'educationally challenged'.

🏆 KIDS

100%	Well done, hotshot! You'll be graduating from University with a double-first before your 18th birthday at this rate. Go for it – the world is your oyster, and knowledge is the pearl!
80–99%	Excellent effort! Now you can hold your head up high and announce to the world that exams haven't got easier, it's just that kids today are more savvy and know what an internet search engine is for.
60–79%	Now we're talking. You see, all those nights burning the midnight oil to cram for that test or get that assignment finished were worth it. Keep up the good effort and before long those A stars are going to be coming your way.
40–59%	Not bad, but not great either. A score like this would get a 'could try harder' on your end-of-year report. Go back and gen up on all the bits you got wrong this time round.
20–39%	'Education? Am I bovvered?' Obviously not. Time to wake up, though – you're on your way to a future in which you're the parent who can't match wits with their kids …
1–19%	Youth really is wasted on the young, isn't it? When you should be cramming your head with knowledge you're mastering the intricate finger movements in an effort to become king of the consoles. If only that same effort was shown in your studies.
0%	I know it doesn't run off a battery and go *bleep* every now and again, but you do know what a book is, don't you? Perhaps you should wait until you can download the e-book version to your mobile/blackberry/MP3 player. Go on; get back to your iPod shuffle.

INDEX

acids and alkalis *see also* chemical reactions 153

Acts of Parliament 243
  Act of Union (1801) 240
  Coal Mines Act (1842) 243
  Factory Acts (1833–75) 243
  General Enclosure Act (1801) 241
  Great Reform Act (1832) 244

air mass classification 292–3

alcohol 37, 116, 140, 302, 313, 322

algebra 72–5

Amazon rainforest 123

amino acids 117

amphibians *see* animal kingdom

animal kingdom 126–7

Antarctic 257–9

angles, properties of 76

antibiotics 119

antibodies 120

Arctic 257–9

Arkwright's Water Frame 193, 242

atomic bomb 199, 247

atoms 117, 136–40, 143

averages (mean, median and mode) 98–9

bacteria 119–120, 125

bar charts 95–6

battles
  Actium 351
  Bannockburn 234
  Bosworth 202, 236
  Culloden 240
  D-Day 246
  famous battles 216–231
  Hastings 207, 232
  Watling Street 358

Beaufort Scale (of wind force) 249, 291

biological weathering 147

Black Death 233–4

blood
  capillaries 111
  cells 106, 120, 198
  group 129
  platelets 120
  supply 111

bones, muscles, ligaments and tendons 112

boundaries, collision 274

boundaries, constructive 273, 277

boundaries, destructive, 277

Byzantine Empire 352

capacity *see* measurement, units of

capital cities 263–70

capital letters *see also* punctuation marks 254, 331

carbohydrates 116

carbon dioxide 110–11, 122, 131, 140–1, 147, 150, 180, 278, 290

chemical compounds 135–42, 146–8, 150–1

chemical elements *see also* Periodic Table 136–42, 145, 150–1, 193

chemical reactions 118, 122, 147, 150–3

chemical weathering 147

child labour 243

chlorophyll 106, 122–3

chloroplasts 106, 123

chromosomes *see also* DNA 129–30

circles, properties of 85–7

clauses *see also* grammar, English 8–11, 14–15, 17

cloud, types of 293–5

Cold War 247

colours, spectrum of 154, 174–5

Commonwealth 210, 239

coordinates 91

Crompton's 'mule' 242

cube numbers 58
cytoplasm 106, 119

decimal point 56, 66–7
diameter 75, 86–7, 107
digits 56, 69
directed numbers *see also* integers 56, 61–2
direction, scale and distance 251
disease 117, 120, 196
DNA 124, 129, 200
Domesday Book 232

earthquakes 272–5
electric circuits 161–3
electromagnets 160, 194
elliptical orbits 179, 189
energy, renewable sources of 161
energy resources 161
energy, types of 161
energy transfer 164–6
enzymes 118, 120
epidermis 123
equations 72–5, 82, 142, 168–9
Equator 256, 258–9
fats, saturated and unsaturated 117
fertilisation 115, 336
Fibonacci sequence, the 69–71
First World War 229, 245–6
fish *see* animal kingdom
food chains and food webs 132
fractions 56, 59, 64–7
fungi 106, 119, 125, 128, 154

gases 137, 141–4, 150–2, 161, 177, 183, 192, 278, 290
genes 115, 119, 129
geothermal energy 161
glaciers, structure of 285–6
glucose 111, 122, 131–2, 139–40
golden ratio 70
grammar, English 8–24

grammar, Latin 342–9
gravity 157, 165, 167, 187, 192, 200, 280, 284
Greenwich Meridian 259

Hiroshima *see* atomic bomb
Hitler, Adolf 246
hormones 113
hydrochloric acid 118, 150, 153
hydroelectric power 161

Ice Age *see also* glaciers 284–6
immune system 120
indices 57, 62–4, 75
industrial pollution 148
Industrial Revolution 240–4
inheritance, genetic *see* DNA
integers *see also* directed numbers 56, 64, 82
International Date Line 259
International Meridian *see* Greenwich Meridian
invertebrates *see also* animal kingdom 113, 126

Kings & Queens
    Boudicca, Queen of the Iceni 357–8
    Juan Carlos I, King of Spain 326
    Mary, Queen of Scots 238
    of England 206–11
    Philip II, King of Spain 221
    Prasutagus, King of the Iceni 358
    Wilhelm II, Kaiser of Germany 245

lake, types of 286–9
Latin *see* grammar, Latin
latitude 258–9
length *see* measurement, units of
light, speed of 171
line graphs 96
liquids 142, 145, 166, 177
literary terms 45–50

Magna Carta 235
magnetic field 158–60
mammals *see* animal kingdom
maps 249–57
measurement, units of 91–2
mechanical weathering 147
menstrual cycle 114
metric system *see* measurement,
    units of
microbes 120
micro-organisms 119
minerals 116–17, 123, 146
mixtures 106, 136, 141–4
multiplication tables 57–9
muscles 107, 111–12, 338
mutation 129–30

Nagasaki *see* atomic bomb
National Health Service 247
National Socialist Party (Nazis)
    246
Natural Selection 130, 195
nicotine 116
Norman Conquest 206, 232–3
North Pole 259
Northern Hemisphere 259, 287
nouns *see also* speech, parts of
    English *see also* grammar 10–15,
        19–20, 34–6
    Latin *see also* grammar 340–7
number, rules of 59–60
numbers, prime 56–8

oceans 39, 119, 258, 274, 293, 325
oestrogen 113
one-dimensional shapes, properties
    of 78
operations, order of 63
Ordnance Survey *see also* maps 249,
    252–4
oxygen 110–11, 115, 122–3, 134,
    139–41, 151, 290

Peasants' Revolt 234
percentages 59, 68, 100
Periodic Table *see also* chemical
    elements 137–8
Peterloo Massacre 243
photosynthesis 107, 122–3, 132
pi 75, 87
pictograms 95
pie charts 96
Plague *see* Black Death
plants 105–7, 113, 120–31, 134, 147,
    161, 195, 280
points of the compass 251
political parties
    Conservative 213–15
    Labour 214–15, 244
    Liberal 213–15
    Tories 215
    Whigs 215
polygons, regular 84
pregnancy 115
Prime Meridian *see* Greenwich
    Meridian
prime ministers 212–15
prime numbers *see* numbers, prime
prisms 88–9, 174–5
probability 100–3
proportion 68, 70, 140–1, 184, 192, 338
proteins 116–19
puberty 113
punctuation marks 17–21
pyroclastic flow 277
Pythagoras' Theorem 82

quadrilaterals, properties of 83

radius *see also* circles 81, 86–9
rainbows 175
ratios 68–70, 80, 82, 87
reactivity 15112
Received Pronunciation 6–7
refraction 173–4

regular polygons, properties of 84
religions
    Christian 205
    Protestant 237
    Roman 276, 355–6
    Roman Catholic 234, 237, 353
reptiles *see* animal kingdom
respiration 110–11
Restoration 210, 240
Richter Scale 275
river, stages of 281–3
rock, types of 145–8, 271
Roman Britain 357
Roman Empire 350–3, 364
Roman gods *see* religions, Roman
Roman numerals 355
romance languages 298, 318
Rules of Attraction 158

scatter graph 97
Schlieffen Plan 245
Second World War 231, 246–7, 256, 308
sentences, compound and complex
    8–9, 44
sexual intercourse 114
skin 119, 127
slow uplift 148
solar system 136, 158, 179, 181–4,
    187, 288, 355
solids 142–3
sound waves 177
South Pole 259
Southern Hemisphere 259
Spanish Armada 221, 238
speech, parts of 11–16
spelling, rules of 27, 29–35
Spinning Jenny 242
square root 58
Standard English 5–7
statistics 93–5, 337
stomata 122

tangent 87
taxonomy 125, 193
tenses 22–3, 348–9
tessellation 79
testosterone 113–15, 140
three-dimensional solids, properties
    of 88
times tables 59, 103
tissue 107, 114, 120
toxins 119
triangles, properties of 80
Triple Alliance 245
Triple Entente 245
Tropic of Cancer 259
Tropic of Capricorn 259
turning forces 169
two-dimensional shapes, properties
    of 78

United Kingdom 206, 231, 235, 240,
    260, 270

verbs 12–14
Versailles, Treaty of 246
vertebrates *see also* animal kingdom
    113, 116, 126
viruses 119
vitamins 116–17, 198
vocabulary 297, 299, 309, 319, 331
volcano, types of 277–8
volume *see* measurement, units of

water cycle 279–80
weathering 145–8
weight *see* measurement, units of
Weimar Republic 246, 316
Welfare State 247
wind 145, 161, 290–3, 306, 316

zygote 115